Instructor's Manual and Test Bank to Accompany

— FOURTH EDITION —

TEN STEPS *to* ADVANCING COLLEGE READING SKILLS

John Langan

ATLANTIC CAPE COMMUNITY COLLEGE

Books in the Townsend Press Reading Series:

Groundwork for College Reading
Ten Steps to Building College Reading Skills
Ten Steps to Improving College Reading Skills
Ten Steps to Advancing College Reading Skills

Books in the Townsend Press Vocabulary Series:

Vocabulary Basics
Groundwork for a Better Vocabulary
Building Vocabulary Skills
Building Vocabulary Skills, Short Version
Improving Vocabulary Skills
Improving Vocabulary Skills, Short Version
Advancing Vocabulary Skills
Advancing Vocabulary Skills, Short Version
Advanced Word Power

Other Reading and Writing Books:

Everyday Heroes
English at Hand
A Basic Reader for College Writers
The Townsend Thematic Reader
Voices and Values: A Reader for Writers

Supplements Available for Most Books:

Instructor's Edition
Instructor's Manual and Test Bank
Computer Software (Windows or Macintosh)

Send book orders and requests for desk copies or supplements to:
Townsend Press Book Center
1038 Industrial Drive
West Berlin, New Jersey 08091

For even faster service, contact us in any of the following ways:
By telephone: 1-800-772-6410
By fax: 1-800-225-8894
By e-mail: townsendcs@aol.com
Through our website: www.townsendpress.com

Instructor's Manual and Test Bank to Accompany
Ten Steps to Advancing College Reading Skills, Fourth Edition
ISBN 1-59194-024-9
9 8 7 6 5 4 3 2 1

CONTENTS

MODEL NOTES AND ACTIVITIES FOR "FIVE ADDITIONAL READINGS"   42

TEST BANKS   54

First Test Bank (Mastery Tests A–D)   55

Note: There are four mastery tests for each skill, supplementing the six mastery tests in the book itself. These tests can be used at a variety of points along the student's path of working through the chapter and the mastery tests in the book.

Second Test Bank   147

Note: These tests—two for each skill— are identical to those on the computer software available with the book. They are here mostly for reference purposes for teachers using the software tests, but they can also be copied for use in class.

NOTES FOR INSTRUCTORS

On the first three pages of the Instructor's Edition of *Ten Steps to Advancing College Reading Skills*, Fourth Edition, I list some hints for teaching a reading course and for using the book. I add here some other comments.

Using a Class Contract

In the first class of the semester, I explain to students that I regard the course as a serious, professional relationship between them and me. I say that I want them to sign a professional contract for taking the course. I then pass out a contract for them to read and sign.

In my experience, the contract helps motivate younger students in particular to come to class and to assume responsibility for their own learning. Some of the older students don't need such a contract, but they welcome a clear presentation of basic ground rules regarding attendance and grading in the course.

A copy of the contract appears on pages 6–7; you have permission to modify and use this contract in whatever way you see fit.

Supplements for the Book

There are three supplements for the book:

1. An *Instructor's Edition,* which is identical to the student book except that it provides the answers to all of the practices and tests.
2. The combined *Instructor's Manual and Test Bank,* which you are now reading.
3. *Computer software,* in Windows and Macintosh formats, which contains two mastery tests for each skill plus two combined-skills tests—22 tests in all. These software tests are identical to those in the Second Test Bank in this *Instructor's Manual.* (Instructors planning to assign the software tests should **not** also give the tests in the Second Test Bank.)

If you've adopted the book for use in your reading classes, you're entitled to free copies of any of these supplements. Call 1-800-772-6410 or e-mail us at <**townsendcs@aol.com**> to get them shipped out to you immediately.

A Suggested Syllabus

Weeks 1–10:

One way to begin using the book is to have students work through the activities in "How to Become a Better Reader and Thinker" on pages 3–9. Then, as the first homework assignment, ask them to read the essay "The Professor Is a Dropout" on pages 423–436. Discuss the questions on page 436 in the next class.

I suggest then teaching one chapter a week, following the order in the book. Generally at the end of a chapter I give two mastery tests: one for practice and one that counts for a grade.

I go over the tests in class right after students take them. (I recommend collecting test papers as students finish and distributing them to students in other parts of the room. Some students resist putting X's on a paper that belongs to the person sitting right next to them.) That way students get immediate feedback on how they have done. Also, after class all I need to do is to check the grades quickly and transfer them to my grade book.

As the semester progresses, I use additional mastery tests, every so often, to review previous skills covered in the class.

Weeks 11–15:

In the last five weeks, students read two selections a week from Part II of the book. They also do the remaining mastery tests, including some of the tests in this manual, as well as the combined-skills tests in the book and in this manual.

Having done all of the reading of the materials in the book, as well as all of the thinking required to complete the many activities, students are, in my experience, better readers and thinkers. They are better equipped both to handle a standardized reading test at the semester's end and to go on to content courses in their college curriculum.

Suggested Answers to the Discussion Questions

Pages 22–41 in this manual provide suggested answers to the discussion questions that follow each of the twenty readings in Parts I and II of the book. There was simply no room in the Instructor's Edition for this material.

Writing Assignments

Writing and reading are closely related skills: practice at one will make a student better at the other. Also, writing about a selection is an excellent way of thinking about it. For these reasons, three writing assignments are provided (beginning on page 627 of the book) for each of the twenty reading selections in Parts I and II.

If you ask students to write about a selection, I suggest you first have them read the "Brief Guide to Effective Writing" that appears on pages 625–626.

Teaching Vocabulary

One basic change that I've made in my teaching of reading is that I now directly teach vocabulary. We all know that students don't know enough words. Because they don't, they have trouble understanding what they read, and they're limited in what they can write. (We have all seen how, in standardized reading tests, students are frustrated because they don't know enough of the words in a passage to understand it and to answer comprehension questions about it. And we all know that because of the vocabulary problem, the standardized tests that are intended to measure reading comprehension are often in fact serving as vocabulary tests.)

I teach vocabulary using a words-in-context approach (it is of no value to ask students to memorize isolated lists of vocabulary words). Specifically, I use a book titled *Advancing Vocabulary Skills, Short Version*, by Sherrie Nist and Carole Mohr. There are twenty chapters in this book, with ten words in each chapter. I do the first chapter in class, so that students understand how to use the pronunciation key for the words and understand just how the chapter works. I then assign one or two chapters a week for homework.

In class each week, I walk around and check students' books to see that they have worked through the four pages of material for each chapter. (After this quick check, I then return the focus of the class to reading skills.) Every third week, I give students one of the several tests that follow each unit of five chapters in the book. My vocabulary syllabus looks like this:

Week 2:   Vocabulary chapter 1 covered in class
Week 3:   Vocabulary chapters 2–3 for homework
Week 4:   Vocabulary chapters 4–5 for homework plus a test on Unit One in class
Week 5:   Vocabulary chapters 6–7 for homework
Week 6:   Vocabulary chapters 8–9 for homework
Week 7:   Vocabulary chapter 10 for homework plus a test on Unit Two in class
Week 8:   Vocabulary chapters 11–12 for homework
Week 9:   Vocabulary chapters 13–14 for homework
Week 10: Vocabulary chapter 15 for homework plus a test on Unit Three in class
Week 11: Vocabulary chapters 16–17 for homework
Week 12: Vocabulary chapters 18–19 for homework
Week 13: Vocabulary chapter 20 for homework plus a test on Unit Four in class

The Importance of Continual Reading and Thinking

Continual reading—coupled with thinking about what one has read—is the very heart of a reading class. *One improves the skills of reading and thinking by guided reading and thinking.* This statement is emphasized with good reason. If a teacher is not careful, he or she may play too participatory a role in the classroom, getting more reading and thinking practice than the student does. The teacher should serve as a manager, using the materials in the text to give students the skills practice they need. *Ten Steps to Advancing College Reading Skills* helps the teacher ensure that students do a great deal of active reading and thinking in the classroom.

The Importance of Constant Feedback

Along with continual reading, writing, and thinking, it is vital that students get frequent feedback. Here are ways they can secure such feedback:

- Small-group interactions
- Class discussions and reviews
- Short one-on-one sessions with the teacher
- Graded quizzes and tests
- The Limited Answer Key in the back of the book
- The software tests that accompany the book
- The online exercises available at **www.townsendpress.com**

In addition, since instructors using *Ten Steps to Advancing College Reading Skills* as a class text are permitted to reproduce any or all parts of this manual, you can selectively hand out copies of answers included here.

All of the exercises in the book are designed to make it easy to give clear and specific feedback. If students are going to learn to read and think more effectively, then they need clear, logical, specific responses to their efforts. This book enables teachers to provide such feedback.

Outlining, Mapping, and Summarizing

To take thoughtful, effective study notes, students need to learn three essential techniques: outlining, mapping, and summarizing. All three techniques often require students to identify the main idea and the major supporting details of a selection. But while educators agree that these three techniques are important for students to learn, they are all too seldom taught.

The book gives students instruction and practice in all three techniques. Passages in the "Supporting Details" and the two "Relationships" chapters, as well as all of the reading selections in Part II and the five additional readings in Part III, are followed by an outline, a map, or a summary activity. To complete many of these activities, students must look closely at the basic organization of the selection. They must think carefully about what they have read by asking two key questions: "What is the point?" and "What is the support for that point?" As students apply the techniques from one selection to the next and get specific feedback on their efforts, they will develop their ability to think in a clear and logical way.

Readability Levels . . . and Their Limitations

Below are the readability grade levels for the text of the book itself and the twenty reading selections. Because the book has been prepared on a computer, and there are now software programs that determine readability, it has been possible to do a complete readability evaluation for each reading, rather than merely sampling excerpts from the materials.

Please remember, however, that there are limits to the reliability and validity of readability scores. For instance, a readability formula cannot account for such significant factors as student interest, prior knowledge of a subject, the number of examples provided to explain concepts, and the overall clarity and logic of the writing.

Thus, while "How Dual-Earner Couples Cope" has a readability level of 13 and "The Influence of the Self-Fulfilling Prophecy" has a readability level of 12, their extremely clear organization makes them pieces that developmental students can understand. I respect readability levels, but I also take them with a grain of salt, and I have kept other factors in mind while determining the sequence of readings.

Material	*Word Count*	*Reading Level*
Text of *Ten Steps to Advancing College Reading Skills*		9
Part I		
1. The Quiet Hour	990	9
2. How Dual-Earner Couples Cope	927	13
3. Baby Love	1082	11
4. Personal Relationships in the Not-So-Good Old Days	816	10
5. Julia Burney: The Power of a Woman's Dream	3196	7
6. The Influence of the Self-Fulfilling Prophecy	1152	12
7. Managing Conflicts in Relationships	1831	10
8. A Legendary Moment	713	10
9. How to Become a Better Listener	1955	8
10. Obedience: Milgram's Controversial Studies	1081	10

Part II

A Final Note

Writing a book that contains hundreds of explanations and activities is a bit like being in a ball game where one steps up to the batter's box an almost countless number of times. One tries to get as many hits and extra-base hits as possible: to explain every concept so that students really understand it; to provide readings and practices that both interest students and teach the skills. One tries not to hit any foul balls. Hopefully there are not too many in this Fourth Edition of a book that has benefited from a great deal of teacher and student feedback.

Realistically, though, you might find that despite my best efforts, some items may not work. If they don't, and/or if you or your students are confused or uncertain about certain items, let me know so that I can consider making changes in the next printing or revision of the book. Send a note to me at Townsend Press, 1038 Industrial Drive, West Berlin, NJ 08091. Alternatively, call Townsend Press at its toll-free number: 1-800-772-6410; send a fax to 1-800-225-8894; or send e-mail to <**townsendcs@aol.com**>; your comments will be passed on to me. And if you have a question, a Townsend editor will get back to you with an answer very shortly. My thanks in advance for your help in my effort to keep improving the book!

John Langan

A PROFESSIONAL CONTRACT

FOR FIFTEEN WEEKS TOGETHER

between

_____

(Student's name here)

and

_____

(Instructor's name here)

Welcome to *(name of course)* _____. Counting today, we will be spending fifteen weeks together. How successful we are will depend on how well we follow a business contract that I would like you to read and sign, and that I will then sign and return to you. Here are the terms of the contract.

MY ROLE IN THE CONTRACT

My role will be to help you practice and master important reading and writing and thinking and learning skills. I will try to present these communication skills clearly and to give you interesting and worthwhile practice materials. I will conduct this as a skills course—not a lecture course where you could borrow a friend's notes afterward. Typically several skills will be explained briefly in class, and you will then spend most of the class time practicing those skills, making them your own. You will be learning in the best possible way: through doing.

Why learn these skills?

I promise you that the skills will be of real value to you in all the other courses you take in college. They will make you a better reader, writer, thinker, and learner, and they can dramatically increase your chance for success in school.

The skills can be just as valuable for the career work you are likely to do in the future. Consider that America is no longer an industrial society where many people work on farms or in factories. Instead, most jobs now involve providing services or processing information. More than ever, communication skills are the tools of our trade. This course will be concerned directly with helping you learn and strengthen the communication skills that will be vital for job success in the 21st century.

YOUR ROLE IN THE CONTRACT

Experiencing the course

Your role in this contract will be to come to every class and to give a full effort. Much of the value and meaning of this skills course will come from what happens in class, so you must be here on a steady basis. Imagine trying to learn another skill without being present: for example, imagine learning how to drive without the *experience* of actually being in the car and working with the controls and getting feedback from your instructor. How much would you learn about the skill of driving if you relied only on the notes of a classmate? In a similar way, to really learn communication skills, you need direct experience and practice. So if you miss classes, you are in effect missing the course.

Shaping your attitude

Some people start college with a "high-school mindset." They are passive; they do the minimum they need to get by; their attention is elsewhere; they are like the living dead—and the American high-school system (and watching thousands of hours of television) may be to blame. Gradually these people realize that college is not high school: they don't have to be in college, and they are no longer part of the sad game played out in many high schools, where they receive a free ride and promotion no matter how little they do.

If your attitude about learning has been hurt by what happened in high school, then part of your role is to change your attitude. You can do so, and this contract will help.

Understanding sick days and personal days

You should try not to miss *any* classes. But in the professional environment of this class, like in the work world, everyone is entitled to a set number of sick days as well as "personal days"—unexplained absences. In this course, you will have a total of *(insert number)* _____ such days—which can cover such real-world happenings as sickness, car breakdowns, or even the death of someone you know. If you missed more than this amount of time in a real-world job contract, you would be let go. (Only in some extraordinary situation, such as an extended illness confirmed by a doctor's report, might an exception apply.) The professional terms of the work world will apply here: if you miss more than _____ classes, you cannot pass the course.

YOUR ROLE IF YOU MISS CLASS

If you do miss a class, you are responsible for getting the homework for the following week's class. To do so, call a classmate. Write down the names and phone numbers of two people in the room. (For now, use the people sitting on either side of you; you can always change these names later.)

Classmate # 1: *Name* _____   *Phone* _____

Classmate # 2: *Name* _____   *Phone* _____

Note that you **must** turn in all homework assignments or you **cannot pass the course**.

If a test or tests are given on a day you miss class, you cannot ordinarily make up these tests. Instead, you will receive a grade of M (Missing) for each missed test. When all your grades are averaged at the end of the semester, three M's will be omitted; the rest will convert to zeros.

YOUR COMMITMENT

I've read this contract, and the terms seem fair to me. (I like the fact that this college class is being treated as a professional situation, and I'm learning the ground rules up front.) I accept the responsibility and the challenge to make this course worth my time and money.

_____   _____

Signed by (your name here)   *Date*

_____

Witnessed by the instructor

OR: If you don't want to sign this, please meet with me after this class to talk about why.

ANSWERS TO THE TESTS IN THE BOOK

Answers to the Review and Mastery Tests in Part I

VOCABULARY IN CONTEXT:
Review Test 1
1. context clues   4. C
2. B   5. examples
3. A

VOCABULARY IN CONTEXT:
Review Test 2
A. 1. A   B. 6. E. lack of
    2. D   essentials
    3. D   7. A. sociable
    4. B   8. C. insulting
    5. A   9. D. continuous
                  10. B. by chance

VOCABULARY IN CONTEXT:
Review Test 3
A. 1. repeat
    2. guess
    3. innocent
    4. relevant *or* applicable
    5. strong
B. *(Wording of answers may vary.)*
    6. negatively *or* unfavorably
    7. weakening
    8. despair
    9. false name *or* pen name
   10. judgments

VOCABULARY IN CONTEXT:
Review Test 4
1. C   6. C
2. C   7. D
3. A   8. A
4. D   9. B
5. B   10. B

VOCABULARY IN CONTEXT:
Mastery Test 1
A. 1. B   C. 6. B
    2. A   7. C
    3. A   8. B
B. 4. support D. 9. A
    5. prevent   10. C

VOCABULARY IN CONTEXT:
Mastery Test 2
A. 1. B   C. 6. A
    2. D   7. B
    3. C   8. B
B. 4. change   D. 9. D
    5. avoided   10. B

VOCABULARY IN CONTEXT:
Mastery Test 3
1. C   6. B
2. B   7. D
3. C   8. C
4. D   9. D
5. C   10. C

VOCABULARY IN CONTEXT:
Mastery Test 4
1. C   6. A
2. A   7. B
3. A   8. B
4. D   9. A
5. B   10. C

VOCABULARY IN CONTEXT:
Mastery Test 5
A. 1. D
    2. C
    3. D
    4. B
    5. A
B. *(Wording of answers may vary.)*
    6. main
    7. tell apart
    8. keeps in
    9. looking back
   10. somewhat changed

VOCABULARY IN CONTEXT:
Mastery Test 6
A. 1. death
    2. said to be caused by
    3. adjust
    4. loaded
    5. put forth as a theory
B. 6. excited
    7. strict
    8. something very popular
    9. had a strong desire
   10. unequaled

MAIN IDEAS:
Review Test 1

1. point
2. topic
3. C
4. list words
5. beginning

MAIN IDEAS:
Review Test 2

A. 1. a. S
    b. S
    c. P
    d. S
  2. a. S
    b. S
    c. S
    d. P

B. Group 1
    a. SD
    b. T
    c. SD
    d. MI
  Group 2
    a. SD
    b. MI
    c. T
    d. SD

MAIN IDEAS:
Review Test 3

1. 1
2. 2
3. 10
4. 2
5. 5

MAIN IDEAS:
Review Test 4

1. B
2. C
3. A
4. D
5. A
6. A
7. A
8. B
9. C
10. A

MAIN IDEAS:
Mastery Test 1

A. 1. a. S
    b. S
    c. P
    d. S
  2. a. S
    b. S
    c. S
    d. P
  3. a. S
    b. P
    c. S
    d. S

B. Group 1
    a. MI
    b. T
    c. SD
    d. SD
  Group 2
    a. SD
    b. T
    c. SD
    d. MI

MAIN IDEAS:
Mastery Test 2

A. 1. a. S
    b. P
    c. S
    d. S
  2. a. S
    b. S
    c. S
    d. P
  3. a. P
    b. S
    c. S
    d. S

B. Group 1
    a. T
    b. SD
    c. SD
    d. MI
  Group 2
    a. SD
    b. T
    c. MI
    d. SD

MAIN IDEAS:
Mastery Test 3

1. 2
2. 5
3. 1
4. 2
5. 3

MAIN IDEAS:
Mastery Test 4

1. 2
2. 7
3. 4
4. 1
5. 3

MAIN IDEAS:
Mastery Test 5

1. 2
2. 2
3. 1
4. 1
5. 8

MAIN IDEAS:
Mastery Test 6

1. 7
2. 1
3. 2
4. 1
5. 11

SUPPORTING DETAILS:
Review Test 1

1. details
2. details
3. main ideas
4. map
5. examples

SUPPORTING DETAILS:
Review Test 2

A. 1. B   2. A
   3. One
   4. *Any one of the following:* crime, pollution, overcrowding
   5. *Any one of the following:* smaller communities, opportunity to own a home and garden, better schools, status of living in an affluent suburb

B. 6–9. . . . functional illiteracy

Educational   Community   Home system

   10. Another

SUPPORTING DETAILS:
Review Test 3

A. *Main idea:* . . . disadvantages for advertisers.
   1. Advantages
     a. Ability to reach a mass audience
   2. Disadvantages
     c. VCRs allow viewers to pre-record shows and bypass commercials

B. *Main idea:* There are differing points of view on television violence.

Catharsis theory	Stimulation theory: Seeing violent scenes stimulates viewers to behave more violently.	Null theory: Fictionalized violence has no influence on real violence.

C. 10. B

SUPPORTING DETAILS:
Review Test 4

1. D
2. B
3. B
4. B
5. A
6. B
7. A
8–10. A. 1. C
        B.   A
        B. 2. B

(In all these tests, wording of main ideas and supporting details may vary.)

SUPPORTING DETAILS:
Mastery Test 1

A. 1. A   3. B
   2. C   4. B

B. *Main idea:* There are several explanations for why money is such a priority for people.
   1. Traditional reward in Western culture
     b. Reward for positive things—report card, success in competition, birthday
   2. Tangible
   3. Symbolic
     a. Measure of self-worth

SUPPORTING DETAILS:
Mastery Test 2

A. 1. D   4. B
   2. C   5. C
   3. A   6. quality

B. 1. Interview
     a. Can obtain a high response rate because people find it difficult to turn down a personal request
   2. Questionnaires
     a. Cheaper than interviews, especially when large samples are used

SUPPORTING DETAILS:
Mastery Test 3

A. 1. B   4. D
   2. D   5. C
   3. C

B. (6–10.)
Duration
Predictability
Frame of mind
Environmental setting
Attitude

(In all these tests, wording of main ideas and supporting details may vary.)

SUPPORTING DETAILS:
Mastery Test 4

A. 1. B   3. C
   2. B   4. also

B. *Main idea:* Today's college population has changed significantly in recent years.
   2. Difference in attendance patterns
     a. Enrollment in four-year colleges has remained steady.
     b. (2) Choice of students seeking career-based studies
   3. Difference in demographic background
     c. Age of students

SUPPORTING DETAILS:
Mastery Test 5

A. 1. A   3. B
   2. C   4. C
   5. *Ex.*—On a multiple-choice test, eliminate the obviously incorrect answers to each question.
   6. *Ex.*—Break down the writing of a paper into a series of separate tasks: choosing a topic, doing the research, preparing an outline, etc.

B. *Main idea:* Public speaking is very different from everyday conversation.

More structured	More formal language	Different method of delivery

SUPPORTING DETAILS:
Mastery Test 6

A. (1–3.)
— Global—stealing words and ideas
— Patchwork—stealing from several sources
— Incremental—stealing small portions from different parts of one source

B. (4–6.) *Main idea:* Most forgetting occurs because of interference from other information, which can take place in two ways.
   1. Proactive interference—prior information blocks new information
   2. Retroactive interference—new information blocks old information

C. (7–10.) *Main idea:* There are stages to children's play.
   1. Solitary play—individual play runs an independent course
   2. Parallel play—children play with similar materials near one another but hardly interact
   3. Cooperative play—direct interaction and cooperative role-taking

IMPLIED MAIN IDEAS AND THE CENTRAL POINT:
Review Test 1
1. imply   4. point
2. topic   5. implied
3. support

IMPLIED MAIN IDEAS AND THE CENTRAL POINT:
Review Test 2
1. B
2. C
3. B
4. There are several advantages for birds to stay in flocks rather than to live separately.
5. There are three stages to the birth process.

IMPLIED MAIN IDEAS AND THE CENTRAL POINT:
Review Test 3
A. 1. C
   2. A
B. 3. The hippo is a dangerous animal.
C. 4. 6

IMPLIED MAIN IDEAS AND THE CENTRAL POINT:
Review Test 4
1. C   8. D
2. B   9. A
3. C   10. B
4. A
5. D
6. C
7. The primary unit of society and attachment was the peer group.

IMPLIED MAIN IDEAS AND THE CENTRAL POINT:
Mastery Test 1
A. 1. C
   2. A
   3. B
B. 4. Sentence 2

IMPLIED MAIN IDEAS AND THE CENTRAL POINT:
Mastery Test 2
A. 1. B
   2. A
   3. A
B. 4. Sentence 2

IMPLIED MAIN IDEAS AND THE CENTRAL POINT:
Mastery Test 3
A. 1. B
   2. A
   3. B
B. 4. Sentence 4

IMPLIED MAIN IDEAS AND THE CENTRAL POINT:
Mastery Test 4
A. 1. D
   2. D
B. 3. In our daily lives, we use three kinds of memory.
C. 4. Sentence 2

IMPLIED MAIN IDEAS AND THE CENTRAL POINT:
Mastery Test 5
A. 1. C
   2. C
B. 3. A variety of reasons explain the declining voter turnout in U. S. elections.
C. 4. Sentence 9

IMPLIED MAIN IDEAS AND THE CENTRAL POINT:
Mastery Test 6
A. 1. D
   2. A
B. 3. Owning a dog can be beneficial to an elderly person.
C. 4. Sentence 25

(Note: Wording of answers to the implied main idea questions in the above tests may vary.)

RELATIONSHIPS I:
Review Test 1
1. Transitions
2. addition
3. time
4. supporting details
5. pattern of organization

RELATIONSHIPS I:
Review Test 2
A. 1. C. also   B. 6. B
   2. D. Before   7. After
   3. B. Another   8. Then
   4. E. last of all 9. Finally
   5. A. After   10. B

RELATIONSHIPS I:
Review Test 3
A. 1. First   B. 6. B
   2. Next   7. A
   3. until   8. B
   4. while   9. A
   5. B   10. B

RELATIONSHIPS I:
Review Test 4
1. A   6. B
2. C   7. A
3. B   8. B
4. A   9. B
5. D   10. A

RELATIONSHIPS I:
Mastery Test 1
A. 1. B. First of all B. 6. For one thing
   2. C. later   7. second
   3. A. another   8. Also
   4. D. In addition   9. final
   5. E. soon   10. A

RELATIONSHIPS I:
Mastery Test 2
A. 1. C. Before   C. 7. finally
   2. D. eventually   8. then
   3. B. Another   9. During
   4. A. After   10. B
   5. E. Also
B. 6. B

RELATIONSHIPS I:
Mastery Test 3
A. 1–4. 2, 3, 1, 4
   5. A
B. 6. B
C. 7. A
   8–10. *Main idea:* Many theories exist
         about what causes people to
         commit crimes.
         1. Celebration of violence in
            our culture
         3. Psychological reasons

RELATIONSHIPS I:
Mastery Test 4
A. 1–4. 4, 1, 3, 2
   5. C
B. 6. C
C. *Main idea:* Several types of
   marriage occur throughout the
   world.

Polygamy

Polygyny   Polyandry

RELATIONSHIPS I:
Mastery Test 5
A. 1. B
   2. *Any of the following:* first, Next,
      then, Finally
B. 3. A
   4. *Any of the following:* one,
      Another, also, further
C. 5. A
   6. final
   7–10. *Main idea:* There are three main
         ways of responding to offensive or
         annoying people.

Passive   Aggressive   Assertive
behavior   behavior   behavior

RELATIONSHIPS I:
Mastery Test 6
A. 1. A
   2. another
   3. B
B. 4. B
   5–7. *Any three of the following:* First,
        Then, Next, Eventually, Finally
C. 8. A
   9–10. 2. Strengthens the ties between
            insiders
         4. Gives members a sense of
            belonging and raises their
            self-esteem

RELATIONSHIPS II:
Review Test 1
1. A   4. C
2. B   5. examples
3. B

RELATIONSHIPS II:
Review Test 2
A. 1. E. For instance   B. 6. B
    2. C. Despite   7. C
    3. B. because   8. A
    4. D. even though   9. B
    5. A. Similarly   10. C

RELATIONSHIPS II:
Mastery Test 1
A. 1. B. For example   B. 6. A
    2. D. similar   7. D
    3. C. In contrast   8. C
    4. E. Therefore   9. B
    5. A. because   10. C

RELATIONSHIPS II:
Mastery Test 4
A. 1–4. 3, 4, 2, 1
        5. C
B.   6. B
       7. B
       8. in common *or* both *or* just as
          or similarly
C.   9. B
      10. effects *or* caused *or* Because of
          or due to *or* as a result

(In Tests 5 and 6, wording of main ideas and supporting details may vary.)

RELATIONSHIPS I and II:
Mastery Test 1
A. 1. C For instance   8. D result
    2. A Finally   9. A for instance
    3. B Later   10. C lastly
    4. E unlike
    5. D because
B. 6. E After
    7. B On the other hand

RELATIONSHIPS II:
Review Test 3
A. 1. C
    2. lead to / cause / produce /
       consequences / effects
B. 3. A
    4. for instance
C. 5. B
    6. opposite / similarities / likewise /
       just as / both / different / common
D. 7. C
    8. affect / effect / so
E. 9. B
   10. In contrast / but / However

RELATIONSHIPS II:
Mastery Test 2
A. 1. D
    2. Differences / On the other hand /
       Unlike / Instead of
B. 3. A
    4. Examples
C. 5. B
    6. effects / Therefore / cause
D. 7. C
    8. similarities / same / like / just as / as
E. 9. B
   10. reasons / led to / explanation /
       resulted in

RELATIONSHIPS II:
Mastery Test 5
A. 1. B
   2–5. Workers are less anxious and
        feel they are part of a community.
        Quality remains high because
        experienced workers are retained.
        Company is better equipped to
        meet increased demand when
        business recovers.
        Workers are more willing to
        put in long hours.
B. 6. C
   7–10. High-*achiever parents*
         Demand independence and
         self-reliance from their children
         at an early age.
         Low-*achiever parents*
         Children are thus less indepen-
         dent and often have low
         achievement needs.

RELATIONSHIPS I and II:
Mastery Test 2
A. 1. C   2. examples / include
B. 3. A   4. For one thing / furthermore
C. 5. B   6. First / Next / Then
D. 7. C   8. consequently / If / then /
                 therefore / because
E. 9. C   10. similar / differ / however /
                 In contrast / Unlike / but /
                 Although / difference

RELATIONSHIPS II:
Review Test 4
1. D   6. D
2. B   7. A
3. A   8. B
4. A   9. A
5. C   10. D

RELATIONSHIPS II:
Mastery Test 3
A. 1–4. 4, 3, 1, 2
        5. D
B.   6. C
       7. On the other hand / However
       8. On the other hand / However
C.   9. D
      10. For example / including

RELATIONSHIPS II:
Mastery Test 6
A. 1. C
   2–5. *Main idea:* Several reasons
        account for the sudden increase in
        the divorce rate.
            Greater social acceptance of
            divorce
            Increase in family income
            Greater opportunities for women
            (who are thus less dependent on
            their husbands)
B.   6. B
      7–10.

Indirect *development*	Direct *development*
	1. Juvenile is a sexually immature miniature version of the adult.
	3. Relatively few off-spring are produced.

RELATIONSHIPS I and II:
Mastery Test 3
A. 1. C
B. 2. A
C. 3. C
D. 4. B
E. 5. C

FACT AND OPINION:
Review Test 1
1. B
2. B
3. C
4. C
5. A

FACT AND OPINION:
Review Test 2
A. 1. F   6. F+O
   2. O   7. F
   3. O   8. F+O
   4. F   C. 9. F+O
B. 5. F   10. F

FACT AND OPINION:
Review Test 3
A. 1. O   B. 1. 11. O
   2. F+O   12. F
   3. F   13. F+O
   4. F   14. F
   5. O   15. O
   6. F+O   2. 16. O
   7. F   17. F
   8. F+O   18. F
   9. O   19. F+O
   10. F   20. O

FACT AND OPINION:
Review Test 4
1. A   6. C
2. B   7. C
3. A   8. C
4. B   9. A
5. B   10. B

FACT AND OPINION:
Mastery Test 1
A. 1. F   B. 11. F+O
   2. O   12. F
   3. F   13. F
   4. O   14. F+O
   5. F   15. F+O
   6. O   C. 16. F+O
   7. O   17. F
   8. F   18. F
   9. O   19. F
   10. F   20. O

FACT AND OPINION:
Mastery Test 2
A. 1. F   B. 11. F+O
   2. O   12. F
   3. F   13. F+O
   4. O   14. F
   5. O   15. F+O
   6. F   C. 16. F+O
   7. O   17. F
   8. F   18. O
   9. F   19. F
   10. O   20. O

FACT AND OPINION:
Mastery Test 3
A. 1. O   B. 11. F+O
   2. F   12. F
   3. O   13. F+O
   4. F+O   14. F+O
   5. F   15. F
   6. F   C. 16. F
   7. F+O   17. F+O
   8. F   18. F
   9. F   19. O
   10. O   20. O

FACT AND OPINION:
Mastery Test 4
A. 1. O   11. F+O
   2. F   12. F
   3. F   B. 13. F
   4. F   14. F
   5. O   15. F+O
   6. F+O   16. O
   7. O   17. O
   8. O   C. 18. O
   9. F   19. O
   10. O   20. F

FACT AND OPINION:
Mastery Test 5
A. 1. F   11. F
   2. F   12. F+O
   3. F+O   B. 13. F
   4. O   14. F
   5. F   15. F+O
   6. O   16. O
   7. F   17. O
   8. F   C. 18. O
   9. O   19. F
   10. F+O   20. O

FACT AND OPINION:
Mastery Test 6
A. 1. F   B. 11. F+O
   2. O   12. F
   3. F+O   13. O
   4. F   14. F
   5. F+O   15. O
   6. F   C. 16. O
   7. O   17. F
   8. F+O   18. F
   9. O   19. O
   10. F+O   20. F

INFERENCES:
Review Test 1
1. stated
2. D
3. inferences
4. metaphors
5. tables

INFERENCES:
Review Test 2
A. 1, 4, 5, 8
B. 1, 3, 5, 8
C. 2, 3

INFERENCES:
Review Test 3
A. 2, 4, 5, 7
B. 5. A
6. C
7. A
8. A
9. B
10. C

INFERENCES:
Review Test 4
1. C 6. A
2. D 7. A
3. F 8. D
4. D 9. C
5. C 10. D

INFERENCES:
Mastery Test 1
A. 1, 3, 6, 7
B. 1, 3
C. 7. C
8. B
9. B
10. A

INFERENCES:
Mastery Test 2
A. 2, 5
B. 2, 4, 6, 7
C. 7. A
8. C
9. B
10. C

INFERENCES:
Mastery Test 3
A. 1. C
2. A
3. C
4. B
B. 1, 3, 6, 7, 8, 9

INFERENCES:
Mastery Test 4
A. 1. C
2. A
3. A
4. B
5. A
B. 1, 3, 4, 7, 10

INFERENCES:
Mastery Test 5
A. 1. C
2. B
3. B
4. D
5. C
B. 1, 4, 6, 7, 9

INFERENCES:
Mastery Test 6
A. 1, 3, 4, 7, 8
B. 2, 4, 6, 9, 10

PURPOSE AND TONE:
Review Test 1
1. A
2. C
3. tones
4. ironic (*or* sarcastic)
5. T

PURPOSE AND TONE:
Review Test 2
1. P   4. P
2. I   5. I
3. E

PURPOSE AND TONE:
Review Test 3
1. C
2. F
3. D
4. H
5. A

PURPOSE AND TONE:
Review Test 4
1. C   6. B
2. C   7. B
3. B   8. A
4. D   9. B
5. D   10. C

PURPOSE AND TONE:
Mastery Test 1
A. 1. I   B. 6. E
   2. P   7. C
   3. E   8. D
   4. I   9. B
   5. E   10. A

PURPOSE AND TONE:
Mastery Test 2
A. 1. P   6. I
   2. E   7. P
   3. I   B. 8. D
   4. P   9. B
   5. E   10. F

PURPOSE AND TONE:
Mastery Test 3
A. 1. F   6. I
   2. G   7. E
   3. A   8. C
   4. D   B. 9. P
   5. J   10. E

PURPOSE AND TONE:
Mastery Test 4
A. 1. E   6. J
   2. I   7. B
   3. G   8. C
   4. F   B. 9. A
   5. A   10. B

PURPOSE AND TONE:
Mastery Test 5
A. 1. B   C. 5. B
   2. C   6. D
B. 3. B   D. 7. B
   4. B   8. A

PURPOSE AND TONE:
Mastery Test 6
A. 1. B   C. 5. B
   2. D   6. A
B. 3. B   D. 7. A
   4. C   8. B

ARGUMENT:
Review Test 1

    1. support *or* evidence
    2. F
    3. relevant
    4. adequate
    5. What is the support?

ARGUMENT:
Review Test 2

A. 1. B   B. 5–7. C, D, E
    2. C   8–10. A, C, F
    3. D
    4. A

ARGUMENT:
Review Test 3

A. 1. A
    2. D
    3. C
B. 4. D
    5. C

ARGUMENT:
Review Test 4

    1. B   6. A
    2. C   7. B
    3. B   8. C
    4. C   9. B
    5. D   10. A. S
                     B. X
                     C. P
                     D. S

ARGUMENT:
Mastery Test 1

A. 1. C   B. 5–7. B, D, E
    2. B   8–10. A, C, F
    3. D
    4. C

ARGUMENT:
Mastery Test 2

A. 1. D   B. 5–7. A, C, D
    2. D   8–10. A, B, D
    3. B
    4. B

ARGUMENT:
Mastery Test 3

A. 1–3. B, C, E
    4–6. A, B, E
B.   7. C
     8. C

ARGUMENT:
Mastery Test 4

A. 1–3. A, B, D
B.   4. A
     5. D
     6. Sentence 1
     7. B
     8. A

ARGUMENT:
Mastery Test 5

A. 1. A
    2. D
    3. A
    4. C
B. 5. C

ARGUMENT:
Mastery Test 6

A. 1. B
    2. B
    3. C
    4. D
B. 5. D

Answers to the Reading Selections in Part II

1 THE PROFESSOR IS A DROPOUT

Skills Questions

1. A	6. A	11. B	16. C
2. C	7. C	12. A	17. B
3. B	8. B	13. A	18. A
4. C	9. D	14. D	19. C
5. B	10. C	15. D	20. C

Summarizing (Note: Wording of answers may vary.)

— her grandfather became blind, and the family moved to Brownsville, Texas, hoping that doctors there could help him regain his eyesight

— a teacher and the principal shouted at her because she spoke in Spanish to a man asking for directions

— speaking English at home

— the success of her own children

2 TAMING THE ANGER MONSTER

Skills Questions

1. B	6. C	11. D	16. A
2. A	7. A	12. C	17. B
3. B	8. D	13. A	18. B
4. A	9. B	14. A	19. C
5. C	10. A	15. D	20. D

Outlining (Note: Wording of answers may vary.)

B. 1. Time
   2. Technology
   3. Tension
C. 1. Common sense and patience

3 HE WAS FIRST

Skills Questions

1. B	6. F	11. A	16. C
2. C	7. C	12. A	17. A
3. C	8. B	13. C	18. B
4. D	9. C	14. A	19. Paragraph 3
5. A	10. C	15. T	20. A. S
			B. P
			C. X
			D. S

Summarizing (Note: Wording of answers may vary.)

— not to fight back if anyone insulted him or attacked him with racial slurs

— accepted him and were friendly to both Jackie and his wife, Rachel

— Jackie had to stay in a "colored" hotel

— other team owners followed Branch Rickey's lead and hired black players, thereby changing major-league baseball forever

4 KEYS TO COLLEGE SUCCESS

Skills Questions

1. D	6. D	11. B	16. D
2. C	7. C	12. A	17. A
3. B	8. F	13. A	18. C
4. B	9. D	14. D	19. A
5. A	10. A	15. T	20. B

Outlining (Note: Wording of answers may vary.)

1. b. Prepare a weekly study schedule.
2. Attend class and take effective class notes.
   c. To save time, abbreviate while taking notes.
3. a. Preview the reading.
   b. Read the material and mark important parts.
   c. Write study notes.
     2) Write clearly.
     4) Organize your notes into a rough outline.
   d. 3) As you learn each bit of new information, go back and test yourself on the previous information.
4. Take responsibility for your studies.

5 MOTIVATION AND NEEDS

Skills Questions

1. C	6. B	12. B	17. T
2. A	7. T	13. F	18. A
3. C	8. C	14. D	19. C
4. D	9. D	15. C	20. A. S
5. A	10. C	16. D	B. X
	11. peak experience . . .		C. S
	five		D. P

Mapping

Self-actualization needs
Esteem and self-esteem needs
Love and belongingness needs
Safety and security needs
Stimulation needs

6 EFFECTS OF THE AUTOMOBILE

Skills Questions

1. B	6. B	11. B	16. C
2. C	7. D	12. C	17. A
3. A	8. D	13. B	18. D
4. A	9. C	14. A	19. P
5. A	10. D	15. B	S
			S
			20. C

Summarizing *(Note: Wording of answers may vary.)*
— horses and streetcar lines
— lower taxes
— parents
— women
— technology

9 BUSY AS A BEE?

Skills Questions

1. D	6. D	11. C	16. C
2. B	7. C	12. B	17. D
3. A	8. D	13. T	18. A
4. C	9. F	14. A	19. C
5. B	10. D	15. D	20. A. X
			B. S
			C. P
			D. S

Outlining
B

7 RABIES

Skills Questions

1. B	6. A	11. B	16. T
2. B	7. C	12. A	17. B
3. symptoms	8. C	13. A	18. A
4. B	9. D	14. C	19. D
5. D	10. D	15. C	20. C

Outlining

A. 2. A booster dose every two years, since antibody
levels fall with time
B. Prevention for people already bitten by an animal that
may have rabies
  1. For people not previously immunized
  2. b. Vaccine injections on days 0 and 2

10 THE LIFE OF THE URBAN WORKING CLASS

Skills Questions

1. A	6. A	11. C	16. D
2. D	7. A	12. D	17. D
3. A	8. C	13. B	18. A
4. C	9. F	14. A	19. D
5. A	10. B	15. B	20. D

Summarizing
A

8 BAD MANAGERS

Skills Questions

1. A	6. B	11. A	16. B
2. A	7. B	12. A	17. T
3. B	8. D	13. D	18. D
4. B	9. A	14. C	19. C
5. C	10. D	15. C	20. T

Mapping

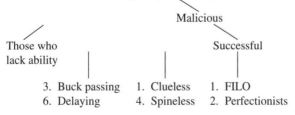

There are two types of bad managers.

Malicious

Those who lack ability

Successful

3. Buck passing
6. Delaying

1. Clueless
4. Spineless

1. FILO
2. Perfectionists

Answers to the Tests in Part III

COMBINED SKILLS:
Mastery Test 1

1. B	5. B		
2. C	6. F		
3. B	7. C		
4. D	8. A		

COMBINED SKILLS:
Mastery Test 2

1. C	5. D
2. D	6. A
3. B	7. C
4. A	8. C

COMBINED SKILLS:
Mastery Test 3

1. D	5. A
2. B	6. A
3. B	7. C
4. D	8. B

COMBINED SKILLS:
Mastery Test 4

1. C	5. A
2. C	6. D
3. D	7. B
4. A	8. A

COMBINED SKILLS:
Mastery Test 5

1. D	5. A
2. B	6. B
3. C	7. D
4. C	8. A

COMBINED SKILLS:
Mastery Test 6

1. D	5. B
2. D	6. D
3. A	7. B
4. B	8. A

COMBINED SKILLS:
Mastery Test 7

1. D	5. C
2. C	6. B
3. D	7. D
4. C	8. A

COMBINED SKILLS:
Mastery Test 8

1. D	5. D
2. C	6. C
3. D	7. D
4. B	8. C

COMBINED SKILLS:
Mastery Test 9

1. D	5. A
2. A	6. C
3. C	7. B
4. C	8. C

COMBINED SKILLS:
Mastery Test 10

1. D	5. B
2. B	6. B
3. D	7. C
4. B	8. B

COMBINED SKILLS:
Mastery Test 11

1. A	5. B
2. B	6. C
3. B	7. C
4. D	8. D

COMBINED SKILLS:
Mastery Test 12

1. B	5. C
2. B	6. D
3. D	7. B
4. C	8. A

COMBINED SKILLS:
Mastery Test 13

1. D	5. D
2. B	6. A
3. A	7. A
4. A	8. B

COMBINED SKILLS:
Mastery Test 14

1. D	5. C
2. C	6. A
3. B	7. B
4. D	8. C

COMBINED SKILLS:
Mastery Test 15

1. D	5. B
2. A	6. B
3. D	7. C
4. B	8. A

MORE ABOUT SUMMARIZING AND OUTLINING:
Review Test 1
   1. condense
   2. the main idea
   3. T
   4. F
   5. T

MORE ABOUT SUMMARIZING AND OUTLINING:
Review Test 2
A. 1–2. 3. S
          5. S
    3–4. 4. S
          6. S
    5–6. 4. S
          6. S
B. 7. D
C. 8. C

MORE ABOUT SUMMARIZING AND OUTLINING:
Review Test 3
A. 1–2. 1. S
          6. S
    3–4. 1. S
          5. S
    5–6. 2. S
          3. S
B. 7. B
C. 8. B

MORE ABOUT ARGUMENT:
Review Test 1
   1. B
   2. B
   3. A
   4. C
   5. C

MORE ABOUT ARGUMENT:
Review Test 2
A. 1. C   B. 6. C
   2. A   7. A
   3. B   8. B
   4. C   9. C
   5. A   10. A

MORE ABOUT ARGUMENT:
Review Test 3
A. 1. A   B. 6. C
   2. C   7. A
   3. B   8. B
   4. C   9. B
   5. A   10. A

UNDERSTANDING BIAS:
Review Test 1
   1. T
   2. F
   3. B
   4. C
   5. C

UNDERSTANDING BIAS:
Review Test 2
A. 1. B   C. 5. A
   2. B   6. C
B. 3. B   D. 7. B
   4. C   8. B

UNDERSTANDING BIAS:
Review Test 3
A. 1. B   C. 5. A
   2. A   6. A
B. 3. A   D. 7. C
   4. B   8. C

SUGGESTED ANSWERS TO THE DISCUSSION QUESTIONS IN PART I

Note: The numbers in parentheses refer to paragraphs in the reading. For some questions, additional related questions have been included to enhance class discussion.

1 "The Quiet Hour"

1. *What were family evenings like in your home as you grew up? Were they more like the images in paragraph 1 of the reading or more like the scenario in paragraph 2?*

   Answers will vary. Encourage students to comment on how their evenings resembled the ones described in paragraph 1 or 2.

2. *How many hours a day do you watch TV now? How might cutting down by an hour or so affect what you do each week? For instance, would you exercise, read, or study more?*

   Answers will vary.

   If you were unable to watch TV, what activities do you think you'd replace it with?

3. *Authors often strengthen their argument by raising possible objections to it and then showing the weaknesses of those objections. What objections does Mayer raise to his own point, and how does he show their weaknesses? (See paragraphs 12–15.) Do you agree or disagree with his analysis of each point?*

   Mayer indicates there would be objections to government involvement in TV scheduling. He counters these by saying the government is already involved because it licenses TV stations, and that the government would merely need to make those licenses inactive for an hour a day.

   He says the "quiet hour" would be criticized as an attack on personal freedom. His answer is that the effect of years of TV has been to actually limit our freedom, and that people would discover a more meaningful freedom without TV.

   He says that networks and advertisers would object because they would lose revenue. However, he feels that the welfare of the family is more important than business's desire to make money.

   In response to the idea that the quiet hour is "too radical," Mayer points out that the TV-dominated home is a relatively recent development, and that life without TV is a far more natural way to live.

   In terms of students' agreement or disagreement with Mayer's analysis, answers will vary.

4. *Mayer writes, "With time to kill and no TV to slay it for them, children and adults alike might discover reading." He suggests one way for children to enjoy books—by having them read aloud. In what other ways might parents help their children enjoy reading?*

   Parents can encourage their children to read by letting the children see them enjoying reading; by visiting libraries and bookstores with children; by helping children find books on topics that interest them; by subscribing to newspapers and magazines that are of interest to the children; by writing down stories that the children make up; by encouraging children to write to and receive letters from pen-pals.

   Can you think of additional ways that parents can help children learn to enjoy reading?

2 "How Dual-Earner Couples Cope"

1. *Discuss some of the challenges in a dual-income marriage. Draw upon your own experience if you are married, or use the example of a married couple you know.*

Students might mention some of the following:

- Dual-earner couples have less time and energy to devote to their home life. It may be more of a challenge to make a house feel like a home when they are both away so much.
- Parents who both work will have to arrange alternate care for their children. Children and parents can both lose out on valuable time spent together.
- The demands of two careers can create conflict. One partner may get an opportunity for advancement that requires a move away from where the other works.
- Partners who both work may become jealous and stressed if one makes more money or is more successful than the other.
- Partners may struggle over how to adapt traditional marriage roles when both partners work. For instance, a husband may continue to regard housework as "women's work" even though his wife is working outside the home.

2. *Discuss some of the benefits in a dual-income marriage. Again, draw upon your own experience if you are married, or use the example of a married couple you know.*

Some points that students may bring up:

- Financial pressure can be hard on a marriage. Having both partners working can relieve that pressure and thereby improve the marriage.
- In a traditional, one-income marriage, each partner may secretly suspect that he or she has the more difficult role. If both work outside the home and share chores at home, each may develop a new appreciation for what the other does.
- Women who have typically stayed home may find their self-esteem growing when they succeed in a job outside the home.
- Men may feel relieved from the stress of having to be a family's sole support.

3. *The author states, "Dual-income couples fall into three patterns: conventional, modern, and role sharing." What view of marriage did your family have as you grew up? How did that view affect your family's lifestyle? If you're married, which view do you and your spouse have?*

Answers will vary. Encourage students to give examples of how they or their families fall into a particular category.

4. *How do you think dual-earner marriages affect children?*

Some possible effects: Children may benefit if their family is better-off financially. If parents are challenged and satisfied by their work and not so worried about money, their sense of well-being will have a good effect on the home. Children of dual-income marriages grow up knowing that mothers as well as fathers are able to make their own living. If both parents work, children may lose some of the closeness and attention that is available from a stay-at-home parent. They may resent their parents' absence from the home. Parents who work outside the home may not as quickly notice children's problems as they would if they spent more time with the children. Children who are home alone as their parents work may be tempted to get involved in destructive activities.

How can parents take advantage of the good points of a dual-income marriage for their children while minimizing the bad points?

3 "Baby Love"

1. *Think about the babies you've known or know now. Who was the person each first formed an attachment to? In what ways could you observe that attachment?*

Answers will vary.

2. *What does the Harlows' experiment with a terry-cloth "mother" teach us about childcare?*

It teaches us the importance of warm physical contact between a baby and its caretaker. It demonstrates that babies have a tremendous need to be held and cuddled, especially when they are frightened or unhappy. Caretakers should learn from this experiment that lovingly touching a baby is as important as feeding and changing it.

How does reading "Baby Love" affect your sense of what a baby needs?

3. *If you were the head of an orphanage, how might you use the information in "Baby Love" to benefit the children?*

"Baby Love" indicates that children need individual loving attention and physical closeness from their caregivers in order to develop normally. Children in orphanages could easily miss out on that kind of attention, since employees are likely to concentrate on supplying their physical needs, such as feeding and dressing them. The head of an orphanage could correct that by bringing in additional staff, either paid or volunteer, whose job it was to play with, hold, cuddle, and talk to individual babies and children.

Do you think it would be better to have paid employees or volunteers come in to cuddle and play with the children? Why?

4. *The authors write, "You may have doubts about generalizing to humans from experiments with monkeys." Then they go on to present two reasons why they feel the experiments on monkeys raise issues important to humans. Explain these reasons. Do you think they are good reasons? Why or why not?*

The reasons presented are (1) apes and monkeys are closely related to humans and share many traits with us, and (2) like the monkeys in the experiments, children who are brought up in isolation do develop social and emotional difficulties. Answers as to whether these are good reasons will vary.

Why do you think the experimenters concentrated on monkeys rather than human beings?

4   "Personal Relationships in the Not-So-Good Old Days"

1. What is your reaction to this reading? Do its facts surprise you? Why or why not?

Answers will vary.

Before reading the selection, did you have an image of what family relationships in the old days might have been like?

2. The author writes that "when wives beat their husbands, it was the husband, not the wife, who was likely to be punished. . . . He had shamed the village by not controlling his wife properly." Do you think there are still men today who feel they are supposed to "control" their wives? Explain.

Answers will vary, but students should recognize that "control" can take many forms, from blatant physical control to more subtle emotional control.

3. In paragraph 7, Stark states that in the traditional family "the primary unit of society and attachment was not the family but the peer group." Does this statement apply at all to our society? At which stages or in what situations might people today feel closer to their peers than to their family members?

Teenagers are a group that is frequently strongly influenced by peers. For many teens, fitting into the social group is a more important need than almost anything else. People entering any new stage of life may look to their peers as examples. For instance, children beginning school, young people going away to college, or newlyweds might pay a lot of attention to their peer groups, because they are not sure of themselves in their new roles and believe the group can show them how they ought to behave.

At what points in your life have your peers been of special importance to you?

4. The author writes, "Only in modern times have most people married for love." Do you think love is the only thing people consider today when choosing a mate? What other factors might be important to consider when selecting a potential life partner?

The high divorce rate suggests that love alone is often not enough to make a good marriage. The ability of a couple to live together successfully depends on other factors as well, including their similar values regarding goals, having and raising children, managing conflict, handling finances, spending free time, planning for the future, and dividing up responsibilities in the marriage.

What are two or three points that you think will be especially important to you as you choose a spouse? (Or, if you are already married, what issues went into that decision for you?)

5 "Julia Burney: The Power of a Woman's Dream"

1. *Julia is passionate about the importance of reading. What is your attitude about reading? Explain. Do you read much in your everyday life? If not, what kinds of reading do you think you might like to do more of?*

Answers will vary.

2. *The story implies that her parents' example kept Julia from experimenting with drugs, alcohol, or tobacco. Based on your observation, what are the most important influences on children when it comes to making a similar decision? Is it their parents' example, for better or worse? The behavior of peers? Or something else?*

Children can be influenced from many directions, and students' answers will depend upon their own observations. As Julia's experience shows, parents' examples play a big role in many children's lives. But many studies show that peers have at least as much influence on children's behavior. (That raises the related question of why children select the friends that they do. Why do some children gravitate toward friends who will be negative influences in their lives, while others prefer friends who will encourage them in positive directions?) What children see on TV, in movies, and through other media can also influence them. Or children may copy the behavior of an older role model whose example, positive or negative, appeals to them in some way.

3. *Julia credits her Aunt Ruby with encouraging her to love reading. She says that through her work with the Cops 'n Kids Center, she is repaying a debt to her aunt. As a child, did you have an adult in your life who provided a special kind of support and encouragement? Explain. What effect did that adult's actions have upon you?*

Answers will vary. If students do not immediately think of a special adult, encourage them to go a little more deeply into their memories. Young people often do remember a supportive person— a Sunday school teacher, local merchant, coach, parent's friend, etc.—with whom they had a warm, positive contact, even if it was fleeting in nature.

4. *How can adults most effectively encourage children to become readers? If you eventually have children yourself or are in contact with young children, what do you think you might do to encourage them to read?*

Some possible answers: Read age-appropriate books to a child from birth onward (starting with picture books). Make reading together a special part of the day, so the child starts to think of reading as a favorite activity. Make sure there is plenty of reading material available in the home. Buy the child his or her own books, and put them in the child's bedroom. Make sure the child observes his or her parents reading for pleasure. Limit exposure to TV and other electronic forms of entertainment. Make family trips to the library a regular event. Ask the child questions about what he or she is reading.

6 "The Influence of the Self-Fulfilling Prophecy"

1. *In general, do you accept the premise of this reading: that our expectations have a great deal to do with what we later experience? What evidence have you seen that makes you agree or disagree with the author's premise?*

Answers will vary.

2. *Is it better to expect good things to happen, or to expect the worst and then be pleasantly surprised when things go well? Explain your answer.*

This question will divide the optimists and pessimists in the classroom. Optimists may say that we lose nothing by expecting good things to happen. Pessimists may call optimists unrealistic, pointing out that if we always expect the best, we aren't making alternative plans in case something bad happens.

3. *The authors write about people who are especially sensitive to rejection, and who seem to perceive it where it may not exist. Have you ever witnessed this happening? Why do you think it occurs?*

Probably everyone knows someone who is hypersensitive to rejection and who perceives rejection everywhere. Such people are usually unsure of their social skills. Their own nervousness and awkwardness may make others uncomfortable around them. At the first hint of other people's discomfort, they withdraw, feeling surer than ever that they've been "rejected."

4. *How might parents and teachers make use of what was demonstrated by* Pygmalion in the Classroom*?*

The *Pygmalion in the Classroom* experiment gives parents and teachers convincing evidence that children will rise, or fall, according to the expectations surrounding them. The lesson is clear: Parents and teachers should do all they can to communicate to kids that they believe the kids can be successful—and expect them to be successful.

7 "Managing Conflicts in Relationships"

1. Which of Verderber's five methods of dealing with conflict do you or people you know typically use? Give examples.

Answers will vary.

2. Why do you think Verderber regards discussion as "the most desirable means of dealing with conflict in a relationship"? And why might he feel that discussion "is often difficult to accomplish"?

Discussion is desirable because it focuses on the actual problem, rather than on the personalities of the people involved, their history together, or their fear of conflict. It involves looking at the problem fairly and objectively and coming to mutual agreement about the best solution. Both parties come away from the decision understanding why it was made and feeling that it was made fairly. Discussion is difficult because it demands that both parties go into the decision with an open mind, not trying to use manipulation, guilt, hurt, anger, or sulkiness to bring about the decision they want. It is human nature to want to prove that one is "right" rather than genuinely be open to considering alternative solutions.

Do you know anyone who seems to be particularly good at using discussion to resolve conflicts? What do you observe about his or her technique?

3. Verderber writes that conflict is sometimes useful because it forces us to make choices and test attitudes. When in your life has conflict been a good thing? What did you learn from it?

Answers will vary.

4. Suggest ways that someone you know could be encouraged to deal effectively with his or her specific conflict.

Answers will vary.

8 "A Legendary Moment"

1. *The author describes this incident as "a great, legendary moment" that she had heard about all her life. Why do you think the incident was so important to the family? Do you have any family stories that people tell over and over again? Why do you think they are important to your family?*

The incident was important in Kimmel's family because it was so unusual and dramatic. It also, as she writes, was "a touchstone moment" in her parents' marriage, which established that her mother would not be intimidated. Answers to the second part of the question will vary.

2. *Do you think it was acceptable that the author's mother slapped her husband? Why or why not? Would you feel differently if the husband had slapped his wife? Why?*

This question is likely to inspire student debate. Some students may be critical of Kimmel's mother, saying that a woman striking a man is just as unacceptable as a man hitting a woman. Others may say that this incident can't be compared to one in which the man was the aggressor. They may point out that the great majority of domestic violence cases involve a man hitting a woman, and that such violence is usually part of a pattern of abuse and intimidation. In this case, Kimmel describes the incident as a highly unusual one, not part of a pattern; she says that "afterward, there was never a threat of violence between them again."

3. *Within a marriage or other relationship, what would you say the rules for fair fighting should be? What kind of behavior is off-limits, in your opinion?*

Answers will vary. Many students will say that physical violence should always be off-limits. Other "fair fighting" rules they might mention are these: that the argument should be confined to the current incident (rather than bringing up things that have happened in the past); that the participants should admit it when they are wrong; that there should be no name-calling; that they should not involve other people (for example, complaining to a parent about the other person).

4. *The author's mother and grandmother let their husbands know very clearly how they expected to be treated. Do you let other people know how you want them to treat you? What advice would you give people who, perhaps because of self-esteem problems, have trouble communicating their feelings and expectations?*

Answers to the first part of the question will vary. Many people have trouble asking to be treated a certain way. They may be afraid that they will lose the other person's love or friendship if they demand too much. They may not believe they deserve to be treated well. They may have been told that the other person's hurtful behavior is just "teasing" and that they need to "lighten up." Whatever the reason, people who accept disrespectful or inconsiderate treatment are hurting themselves and (in the long run) their relationships. People who have trouble asking for what they want need to practice, beginning with small, non-threatening things. It is helpful if they can explain to the other person how a particular behavior makes them feel, and ask for a specific change. For instance, "When you leave your wet towel on the bathroom floor, it makes me feel that you see me as your maid. Would you please try to remember to pick it up yourself?" Then they can move on to more important issues.

9 "How to Become a Better Listener"

1. The author asserts that if you learn to be an active listener, you will be rewarded "in your schoolwork, in your personal and family relations, and in your career." What do you think might be some of the rewards of active listening in these areas? Be specific.

In school, students will have a better grasp of material they hear from a lecturer. They will be more able to distinguish between important and less significant points. They will be less likely to daydream and miss part of the instructor's message. Because they are actually thinking about what is being said, they will be more alert to points that are confusing and they can ask quickly for clarification.

Within personal relationships, active listening leads to a better understanding between people. Good listeners are aware of unspoken messages—for instance, a spouse may say, "Sure, it's fine with me if your father comes to live with us," while his or her body language or expression is suggesting something else. Active listeners are more able to quickly recognize and resolve problems than people who do not listen well.

On the job, an active listener does not merely receive instructions from a supervisor; he or she feeds back what the supervisor is saying so both parties are sure they understand one another. Because an active listener acts as a partner in the communication process, a supervisor is likely to view that person as a responsible worker who takes initiative to get the job done well.

2. Which of Lucas's suggestions for active listening are most relevant and valuable for you? Be specific.

Answers will vary.

3. The author claims that "aspects of modern life encourage us to listen passively." Do you agree? Is the "listening" you do when watching TV different from the listening you do in a conversation with someone? How?

Listening to television is different from listening in a conversation because it is one-sided. The TV does all the talking; we do all the listening. Even if we get so involved in a program that we "talk back" to the set, we have no effect on what is said or done. Many times we "listen" to TV but actually pay little attention as we go about other activities.

What do you think some effects would be if we listened to friends and family the way we listen to television?

4. In explaining how to be a better listener, the author also suggests how to be a good speaker. On the basis of the reading, what are some guidelines for making a good speech?

Pay attention to the unspoken messages you are conveying through your body language. Make sure that your appearance does not detract from your message—be neat and well-groomed. Organize your speech around two to four main points. Give an idea at the outset of your speech what your plan of development will be. Back up each of your main points with supporting evidence. Avoid making unfounded assertions and sweeping generalizations.

What aspect of speaking in public do you find most difficult?

10 "Obedience: Milgram's Controversial Studies"

1. Imagine that you were a subject in one of Milgram's experiments. How do you think you would have responded to the experimenter's commands? Why?

Students need to ask themselves how much they are swayed by the commands of people in authority; whether they would assume they should complete their assignment or whether they would feel justified in withdrawing from the experiment.

2. The authors write, "Presumably, obedience to legitimate authorities is something we learn early in life and retain throughout adulthood." Why do you think people develop an obedience to authority?

When we are young, we naturally look to older, more experienced people to teach us the things we need to know in life. We are taught from babyhood on up to obey our parents, teachers, and other authority figures.

If you have children someday (or have them now), will you be a fairly lenient parent or one who demands a good deal of obedience? Why?

3. What might the authors have been thinking of when they wrote that Milgram's experiments "stand out as . . . a warning for our society"? Can you think of any events that reflect unwise obedience to authority?

The authors mention two notorious examples: those of slaughter of the Jews by Nazi soldiers, and the mass suicide in Jonestown. Too often, children who are kidnapped, abused, and molested by adults do not fight back or reveal what has happened because they are convinced they must obey the adults involved. Otherwise honest people sometimes pretend not to notice unethical practices that their employers engage in, for fear of what will happen if they disobey the boss. People who are sexually harassed or exploited by their supervisors sometimes tolerate the behavior because of a sense of obedience to authority.

From your observations, would you say this sense of obedience to authority extends to groups of friends? Do members of the group tend to obey a leader within that group, even though he or she is their same age?

4. The reading refers to what is negative about obedience to authority. What do you think might be the positive aspects of such obedience?

A level of obedience is necessary for the survival of our species and the good of the community. Lack of obedience can lead to physical danger for the child, as well as chaotic conditions in the home and society.

Think of some scenarios at home, in school, or in the larger community, and imagine what would happen if obedience to authority was non-existent.

SUGGESTED ANSWERS TO THE DISCUSSION QUESTIONS IN PART II

1 "The Professor Is a Dropout"

1. *Lupe credits her fellow Hispanic students with being a great help to her in college. Is there anyone in your life—a teacher, family member, or friend—who has helped you through challenging times during your education? Explain what your obstacle was and how this person helped you to overcome it.*

   Answers will vary.

2. *Lupe found that her school responsibilities conflicted with her duties as wife and mother. What kinds of personal responsibilities have you had to juggle as a student? These may include parenthood, a job, a difficult home situation, extracurricular school activities, or anything else that poses a challenge to your academics. How have you balanced these obligations with your role as student?*

   Answers will vary.

3. *Lupe is an outstanding example of a person who took charge of her life. Would you say that you have taken charge of your life? Describe how, or describe what you think you must yet do to take charge of your life.*

   Answers will vary. Encourage students to recognize even small accomplishments along the road to "taking control."

4. *By the end of Lupe's story we see the serious mistakes made by those who called her "retarded" and her children "slow learners." Was there ever a time when you felt people misjudged you? What did they say about you that was wrong, and how did it make you feel? Explain how you reacted to their judgments—did you accept their remarks or did you fight to disprove them?*

   Answers will vary.

2 "Taming the Anger Monster"

1. *What kinds of things make you most angry? Is your anger directed mostly at others, or at yourself? What steps do you think you should take, or what steps have you taken, to control anger?*

   Answers to the first two parts of the question will vary. In answering the final part, students might discuss such strategies as counting to ten before they speak, trying to put themselves in the other person's place, employing a sense of humor, or walking away from an anger-producing situation.

2. *If you were teaching a class to students on what they should do to control anger, what would be your advice?*

   Students may suggest any of the techniques mentioned in the answer to question 1. They might also suggest that displays of anger are often counterproductive and even harmful, or that while an angry outburst may make a person feel briefly better, the person often feels ashamed or embarrassed later.

3. *Of the three sources of our anger identified in the reading—time, technology, and tension—which do you think is the greatest problem for you? Why?*

   Answers will vary.

4. *Do you agree with Carol Tavris, author of* Anger: The Misunderstood Emotion, *that almost no situation is improved by an angry outburst? Is anger ever helpful? Explain your answer.*

   Some students may agree with Tavris that angry outbursts are never appropriate. Others may disagree, saying that it is dishonest, unhealthy, or counterproductive always to suppress one's anger. Students may cite situations in which a person does something hurtful or offensive and say that they feel the need to "stand up and be counted" by showing their anger.

3 "He Was First"

1. *Kellmayer writes, "By 1944, the social climate had become more accepting of integration, in large part because of the contribution of black soldiers in World War II." Why do you think the contribution of black soldiers in World War II would be such an influence on the progress of integration in the United States?*

   World War II was a popular war, supported by the great majority of Americans. The soldiers who fought and died in it were regarded as heroes. Many of those soldiers were black. The realizations that black and white soldiers had fought side-by-side for the same cause, and that black soldiers had been American war heroes, were powerful ones for many white Americans, forcing them to re-evaluate their thinking on racial issues after the war was over.

2. *An ongoing question about history is whether individuals cause important changes in society or whether it is circumstances that lead to changes—once the circumstances are right, the right individuals will emerge. In the integration of baseball, how important do you think the times were? How important were the individuals involved?*

   Branch Rickey and Jackie Robinson were remarkable individuals whose dreams, drive, and talent are undeniable. But chances are good that those individuals could not have accomplished what they did a generation earlier. By the late 1940s, the contribution of black soldiers during World War II had given a huge boost to the growing sense that racial segregation could not survive in a democracy. Even under those circumstances, Robinson and the Dodgers faced enormous obstacles as the first integrated team. It is difficult to imagine that any individuals, no matter how gifted, could have made an integrated team succeed earlier.

3. *Do you think Branch Rickey was right to make Robinson agree "not to fight back"? Explain your answer.*

   Students may object to Robinson's pacifism as a sign of weakness, or as giving in to Rickey's desire to show Robinson as a "good Negro." They may believe that Robinson's right to defend himself outweighed Rickey's wishes. Alternatively, they may look at the outcome of Robinson's actions and defend his restraint as having been justified. They may point out that if Robinson had fought back, his actions, rather than the integration of the team, would have become the focus of attention.

   How do you think the Jackie Robinson/integration of baseball story would have been changed if Robinson had fought back against his tormenters?

4. *Robinson had to face a great deal of racism. Unfortunately, despite the greater integration of today, there is still racism. Have you experienced any racial insults yourself or seen anyone else treated badly because of the racial or ethnic group he or she belongs to? Tell what happened, and how you or the other person reacted.*

   Answers will vary.

4   "Keys to College Success"

1. *In general, would you say that your high-school experience prepared you adequately for the demands of college learning? Why or why not?*

   Answers will vary.

   How much responsibility should your school take for any lack of preparation you feel now? How much is your responsibility?

2. *Could your studying benefit from time-control measures? What steps do you already take to manage your time? When do you do most of your studying? Are there hours that slip away because you get distracted? Explain.*

   Answers will vary. Encourage students to think about specifically where, when, and how they study. If they respond that there is no predictable pattern to their studying, encourage them to think about how a more consciously planned approach to studying might benefit them.

3. *What study system or approach to studying textbooks do you use? How does it compare or contrast with the PRWR approach? Now that you have read about the PRWR approach, do you plan to use all or part of it? (Be honest.) Why or why not?*

   Answers will vary. Students may not see themselves as using a formal "system" of studying, but upon examining their usual routine they may find they actually have a more set pattern than they realize.

4. *The author states, "If you realize that earning a college degree is an important step you must take to achieve your career goals, you will take responsibility for your studies." What are your career goals, and how will a college degree help you achieve them?*

   Answers will vary.

5 "Motivation and Needs"

1. *Do you know a workaholic, a compulsive gambler, a television addict, or a joiner? Which of Maslow's needs do you think each of these people is trying to meet?*

Workaholics and gamblers may both be motivated by the need to achieve. However, workaholics seek personal accomplishments, while gamblers may seek achievement through luck. A person may be addicted to television as a means of fulfilling his or her stimulation needs; or perhaps a television addict fears success, and uses TV partly to avoid real-world challenges. Finally, a joiner may seek to fulfill his or her affiliation needs.

2. *What ads have you seen recently that appeal to our need for approval? Which ones begin with a "negative appeal," as Quinn describes it in paragraph 18?*

Answers will vary, but the following guidelines may help:

"Bandwagon" advertisements appeal to our desire to belong to a group. Ads that use this appeal imply that if we use the sponsor's product, we will be "jumping on the bandwagon." In addition, many ads for cosmetics and toiletries appeal to the desire to look and smell good— qualities intended to make us more lovable. Some ads show a "before and after" scenario in which someone is first shown negatively, then wins approval, popularity, even romance after using the product.

3. *On the basis of your own experience, why might some people fear success? And what reasons can you see for the fear of success being much more common among women than among men?*

As Quinn points out (paragraph 27), fear of success usually stems from the need for love and belongingness. Some younger students associate academic success with peer rejection—the "it's not cool to do well in school" syndrome. Similar feelings may cause workers to hold back on the job, fearful that their higher productivity, for example, especially if publicly recognized by the boss, might earn the resentment and disapproval of their colleagues. Women's fear of success could be due to a number of factors: the so-called "feminine" outlook that fosters cooperation over competition; the desire for approbation based (traditionally) on their appearance and social skills, not their achievements; the reluctance to appear too "masculine" by pursuing external, real-world goals; and the reluctance to compete and win against men, influenced by the childhood lesson that "boys don't like girls who beat them."

4. *According to the reading, achievements are a key way to satisfy the need for esteem and self-esteem. What achievements of yours have most strengthened your esteem and self-esteem? What achievement goals do you have for the future?*

Answers will vary, but students may wish to share their skills and talents with the class and the achievements those abilities have helped them both reach and aim for.

6 "Effects of the Automobile"

1. The author lists numerous effects of the automobile, but does he think any of those effects are positive or negative? Look at the reading and try to determine the author's opinion of the various effects he describes.

As the author describes how the automobile allowed people to leave the cities for the suburbs, and allowed farmers to travel easily from their villages to the city, he seems to suggest that the breakdown of the cities and "drying up" of the villages was a negative consequence.

An automobile-related change that the author seems to see as positive is the changed role of women in society. He notes that before the automobile, women were largely confined to their homes, making few decisions and having little independence. With the increased freedom that the cars provided, "[women] gained greater control over the family budget, and as their horizons extended beyond the confines of their home, they also gained different views of life."

The other effects the author describes seem to be ones he views in more neutral terms—as neither especially positive or negative.

2. Most people's lives would be different without the automobile and its automotive "relatives," such as the van, truck, bus, tractor, and motorcycle. How would your life change if there were suddenly no automobiles?

Answers will vary.

3. The selection explains that domestic chores were greatly changed with the introduction of the car and the electric refrigerator. Give some examples of other technological inventions that have changed domestic chores.

Electrical appliances such as the vacuum cleaner, stove, washing machines, toasters, microwave ovens, and dishwashers have all affected domestic life. The telephone and computer both make at-home shopping a reality.

What invention has had the greatest impact on your domestic life?

4. The passage argues that the automobile stands out as a candidate for the "single item that has had the greatest impact on social life in the twentieth century." Can you think of another item that has also had—or will have—a tremendous impact on society? What is it, and what are some of its more important effects?

Some candidates for "most important item" include the telephone, the TV, and the personal computer. The telephone allows instantaneous voice communication between all corners of the world. TV has had immeasurable influence, both because it keeps viewers informed of changes in their world, because popular programs influence our tastes, thoughts, and topics of conversation; and because watching TV has changed the ways families spend time together. The effect of the personal computer can only be guessed at as yet, but the storehouse of information, entertainment, shopping options, and social interaction it puts at a user's fingertips is sure to have a huge impact on future generations.

What are the drawbacks, if any, of the item you think of as "most important"? What negative effects has it had on society?

7 "Rabies"

1. *The tone of this essay can best be described as objective. Why has the author chosen to treat the subject matter in such a way?*

   The purpose of a medical reference book is to inform in a straightforward fashion, not to entertain, alarm, or persuade. More dramatic or exciting discussions of rabies are available, but they would not do as effective a job of simply presenting useful information.

2. *According to the article, many of the animals people typically associate with rabies—rats, mice, and other small mammals—rarely carry the disease. Have you ever had an idea about a disease, or a treatment for a disease, that you discovered to be false? Explain. What do you think causes people to believe false ideas?*

   Answers will vary. False, unproven, or exaggerated ideas about diseases are common (for instance, that leprosy is highly contagious, that wearing a copper bracelet will relieve arthritis, that a poison ivy rash can spread from one person to another, that colds or even pneumonia are caused by getting one's feet wet). Because the causes of disease are generally not visible to the naked eye, people from the beginning of time have looked for explanations for them. In an attempt to gain a sense of control over our bodies and health, we are willing to believe theories and treatments that are not necessarily factual.

3. *This essay appears in a current medical reference book designed for home use. Do you have such a medical reference book at home? How do you typically get medical information when you need it?*

   Answers will vary. Many resources are available for getting medical information: one's own doctor, friends and family members, encyclopedias and other reference books, publications available at clinics and other public places, health hotlines listed in the telephone book, health-related TV and radio shows, and the Internet.

   How do you distinguish between dependable medical information and medical information (or, for that matter, any information) that may be false?

4. *A major section of this essay concerns prevention. What steps, if any, do you take in your life to prevent general health problems? When did you become aware of the value of preventive medicine? If you take no everyday steps to prevent illness, why have you chosen not to protect yourself?*

   Answers will vary. A few common means people use to prevent health problems:
   - Eat a healthful diet
   - Take vitamins
   - Exercise daily
   - Stop smoking
   - Don't drink excessively
   - Practice safe sex
   - Monitor known health problems (such as high blood pressure or diabetes) and follow doctor's orders

8 "Bad Managers"

1. *Describe the worst boss you ever had. Which of the behaviors described in this selection did your boss exhibit? How did those behaviors affect you and other employees?*

Answers will vary.

2. *The reading describes problem managers but gives no advice on how workers should deal with them. Select one of the incompetent or malicious managers described in the reading. What advice would you give to someone who was trying to deal with such a boss?*

As the article says, bad managers are often poor because they are driven by fear: fear that they will make the wrong decision, they'll look foolish, they'll have to go out on a limb. In order to deal with such a manager (or any difficult person) it can be helpful to put oneself in his or her shoes and figure out how to relieve that fear. An employee who learns to understand and work around a manager's fear may have more success dealing with him or her. Eventually, of course, a employee may have to accept the fact that a manager is too much trouble to deal with and start looking for another job.

3. *On the basis of the information in this article and your own experience, describe the qualities of a person you would consider an ideal boss.*

Answers will vary. This article makes it clear that a common characteristic of a poor boss is refusal to take responsibility for decision-making. It can be assumed, then, that a willingness to make decisions is a desirable quality in a manager. Good humor, fairness, consistency, and the willingness to give recognition and praise are other qualities that many people would mention as highly desirable in a boss.

4. *What steps do you think companies should take to protect employees from incompetent or malicious bosses?*

It would be helpful if a company had clearly stated channels for an employee to go through when he or she had a complaint. For instance, a company might encourage workers to report problems to the board of directors, or the human resources director—in other words, to someone who is not under the supervision of the manager who is being complained about.

9 "Busy as a Bee? Then Who's Doing the Work?"

1. Books, articles, and television shows about animal behavior are often very popular. How would you explain the fascination that animal behavior holds for people?

One reason humans may be fascinated by animal behavior is that there seem to be two sides to animals. When animals are pets, we tend to view them as having "human" emotions and characteristics. We often think of our pets as gentle, kind, or mild-mannered. It is intriguing, then, to see animals in the wild, where survival is proportional to strength.

2. Do you have a pet? If so, how inactive is that animal? What do you think might be the similarities and differences between your pet's needs and the needs of animals living in the wild?

Answers will vary. In general, all animals have the same needs. However, pets have nearly all of these needs provided for them by their owners. For example, pets are not affected by seasonal changes nearly as much as animals in the wild are. Many wild animals must store food for the cold winter months; pets do not have this need. Further, wild animals must adapt in physical appearance for survival. For example, during the winter months, their fur often becomes thicker. As a result of these differences, it is not as much a matter of survival for pets to be inactive as it is for wild animals.

3. The article mentions that some scientists object to the term "laziness" being applied to animals and insects. The concept of laziness may apply only to humans. Can you think of any other human characteristics that are frequently attributed to animals? Do you believe the animals actually have those characteristics?

Answers will vary. There are a number of human characteristics that are frequently attributed to animals. Probably most common among these is human emotions. Humans tend to believe their pets are jealous, angry, or lonely when the humans themselves may actually be experiencing these emotions. Yet it is often said that only a pet can offer a human unconditional love.

4. In writing about the animal researchers and their work, the author could have used a formal, scientific tone or a lighter, more informal approach. Which tone did she use, and why do you think she made that choice? Find examples to support your opinion.

Angier uses a light, informal tone in this selection. This tone makes the article accessible to everyone, not just those in the science fields. It also changes what might have been a very dry subject to one which is vivid and interesting.

Some examples of Angier's informal tone include the following excerpts:

- "So while there may not be a specific gene for laziness, there is always a good excuse."

- The heading, "Flying Is So Draining"

- "Some species . . . fulfill the occasional social obligation, like picking fleas from a fellow creature's fur."

10 "The Life of the Urban Working Class"

1. *If you had lived in the period described in this article, what would have been the hardest parts of everyday life for you? What parts would be most different from your life in the world today?*

   Answers may focus on the cramped, unsanitary living conditions; the endless pregnancies and hard life of the women; the poverty; the anonymity of city life; the long days of heavy factory work; or the use of children as workers.

2. *The reading suggests that the demands of the urban environment had a dramatic effect on traditional family life. What details in the reading support the idea that family life was affected by the move to the industrial city?*

   In the villages, workers set their own hours and were generally employed in their home farms or workshops. Their work life and family life, then, were more integrated than that of a factory worker in the city, for whom the home was hardly more than a place to sleep. Village people were more self-sufficient, raising their own food, rather than having to rely on markets and unscrupulous merchants. Within the village, people kept tabs on one another's behavior, as demonstrated by the idea that premarital sex almost always led to marriage. In the city, people were far more anonymous and their behavior was less affected by what family or neighbors would think. While children in villages worked hard, they were employed helping their parents, rather than being sent out to work for strangers in dangerous factories or mines.

3. *Find details in the selection that suggest how children were regarded in the early 1800s. Judging from those details, how would you say the perception of childhood has changed between then and now? Explain your answer.*

   The selection points out that education was considered a luxury to most families. Children from a very young age were regarded as small adults, expected to work and help support the family. Today, childhood is generally seen as a time of special privilege, during which children are expected to play and learn, rather than take their place in the working world.

4. *The selection ends with the idea that by midcentury, the working class was beginning to see itself as having an identity of its own. Why do you think the workers saw themselves as "different from and in opposition to the middle class"?*

   Many of the men and women moving from the village to the city did so with dreams of making their fortune and having a better life. As the years went by, however, the workers became more realistic and embittered. They realized that no matter how hard they worked at their factory jobs, members of the middle class were born with greater opportunities, more money, and the expectation of better education. The workers understood that their own opportunities and those of their children were very limited, and they began to resent the middle-class people who were born into more privilege.

MODEL NOTES AND ACTIVITIES
FOR "FIVE ADDITIONAL READINGS"

Comments and Suggestions

- This section contains the following for each of the five additional reading selections on pages 592–602 of the text:

  1. An outlining, mapping, or summarizing activity.
  2. The completed outline, map, or summary of the reading. These activities can be copied and distributed for comparison purposes after students have completed the activity or taken their own notes.

- The five readings can be assigned one at a time throughout the semester after students have worked through "Supporting Details," Chapter 3 in Part I, in which outlining, mapping, and summarizing are explained.

- I suggest assigning the readings in terms of level of difficulty. From easiest to hardest, I would sequence the readings as follows:

  Labeling and the Onset of Old Age (easiest)
  Before You Begin Writing
  Nonverbal Communication
  Why Do Most Mothers Cradle Their Babies in Their Left Arms?
  Is Aggression a Response to Frustration? (hardest)

- Following are some notetaking guidelines you may wish to copy and pass out and/or briefly go over with students.

Some Notetaking Guidelines

- Before beginning to take notes, carefully read through and mark the material.

- Here's how to mark material: Circle definitions, set off examples with an *Ex,* and underline or bracket ideas that seem especially important. Use numbers (1, 2, 3 . . .) to mark off major items in a series.

- Then take notes by writing down each heading in turn and listing the important ideas that you find under that heading. Think carefully about each heading; it is often a key to main ideas and major details.

- Keep outlines simple. Often just one level of symbols (1, 2, 3 . . .) will do.

- Sometimes you may want two levels, and they can be labeled as follows:

1.
   a.
   b.
2.
   a.
   b.

- If you need three levels, they can be labeled as follows:

A.
   1.
      a.
      b.
   2.
      a.
      b.
B.
   1.
      a.
      b.
   2.
      a.
      b.
etc.

OUTLINING ACTIVITY: "WHY DO MOST MOTHERS CRADLE THEIR BABIES IN THEIR LEFT ARMS?"

Complete the following outline of the selection.

Why do mothers cradle babies in left arm?

1. Obvious explanation: _____

   _____

   However:

   a. 78 percent of left-handed mothers also favor holding babies on left.

   b. 84 percent of chimpanzees and 83 percent of gorillas, who are not predominantly right-handed, also hold babies on left side.

2. Most likely reason: _____

   _____

   a. Baby heard sound while in womb; associates it with peace, comfort, security.

   b. In an experiment, babies who heard recorded sound of heartbeat fell asleep twice as quickly as those who did not.

3. Another possible reason: _____

   _____

   a. Emotions are more strongly expressed on left side of face; mother gives baby a better chance to read her mood changes.

   b. Mother's left eye and ear are more tuned in to baby's emotional changes than her right eye and ear would be.

4. A fourth possible reason: _____

   _____

   a. 70 percent of newborns enter the world with a preprogrammed tendency to turn their heads to the right.

   b. Mothers about to feed their babies find babies' heads turned to right, so a mother will hold her baby in her left arm so they can be "face to face."

AN OUTLINE OF "WHY DO MOST MOTHERS CRADLE THEIR BABIES IN THEIR LEFT ARMS?"

Why do mothers cradle babies in left arm?

1. Obvious explanation: Majority of mothers are right-handed and want to keep right hand free.

   However:

   a. 78 percent of left-handed mothers also favor holding babies on left.

   b. 84 percent of chimpanzees and 83 percent of gorillas, who are not predominantly right-handed, also hold babies on left side.

2. Most likely reason: Mothers are bringing infants closer to sound of heartbeat.

   a. Baby heard sound while in womb; associates it with peace, comfort, security.

   b. In an experiment, babies who heard recorded sound of heartbeat fell asleep twice as quickly as those who did not.

3. Another possible reason: Mother is showing baby her "best side."

   a. Emotions are more strongly expressed on left side of face; mother gives baby a better chance to read her mood changes.

   b. Mother's left eye and ear are more tuned in to baby's emotional changes than her right eye and ear would be.

4. A fourth possible reason: The baby, not the mother, is responsible for the preference.

   a. 70 percent of newborns enter the world with a preprogrammed tendency to turn their heads to the right.

   b. Mothers about to feed their babies find babies' heads turned to right, so a mother will hold her baby in her left arm so they can be "face to face."

MAPPING ACTIVITY: "LABELING AND THE ONSET OF OLD AGE"

1. _____
_____

Ex.— wrinkles, balding, aches, difficulty in doing things that used to be taken for granted

2. _____
_____

Ex.— an accident, early motherhood or grandmotherhood

There are several factors that make people label themselves as "old."

3. _____
_____

Def.— _____
_____
_____

Ex.— _____
_____
_____

Ex.— U.S. television: older male news anchors are retained; older female anchors are not

Ex.— In movies, older men more likely to play romantic leads opposite much younger female stars

4. _____
_____

Def.— _____
_____
_____

Ex.— _____
_____
_____

A MAP OF "LABELING AND THE ONSET OF OLD AGE"

1. Biology

Ex.—wrinkles, balding, aches, difficulty in doing things that used to be taken for granted

2. Personal history or biography

Ex.—an accident, early motherhood or grandmotherhood

There are several factors that make people label themselves as "old."

3. Gender age

Def.— the relative value that a culture places on men's and women's ages

Ex.— On men, graying hair and wrinkles are signs of "maturing"; on women, they are signs of being old

Ex.— U.S. television: older male news anchors are retained; older female anchors are not

Ex.— In movies, older men more likely to play romantic leads opposite much younger female stars

4. Timetables

Def.— signals that societies use to inform their members they are old

Ex.— a particular birthday, the inability to perform productive social roles

OUTLINING ACTIVITY: "NONVERBAL COMMUNICATION"

A. Importance of nonverbal communication

   1. Accounts for 55 percent of our total communication.

   2. When verbal and nonverbal communication conflict, people believe nonverbal.

   3. _____

      a. If a coworker gives you an unusual glance, you wonder what it meant.

      b. Some employees avoid greeting others and instead show "frozen faces," which can be interpreted as displeasure.

      c. Some body language can be misleading: crossed arms may not mean lack of receptivity—only that the person feels cold.

B. _____

   1. Accenting: _____

      a. Poking finger into someone's chest

      b. _____

   2. _____: reinforcing verbal communication

      a. _____

      b. Standing four feet away from your boss and saluting her formally reinforces the message that she is of higher rank and has unchallenged authority.

   3. _____

      a. Often this is how people reveal true feelings or send an unintended message.

      b. For example, _____

      _____

      c. When verbal and nonverbal messages conflict, people believe the nonverbal ones.

   4. _____

      a. _____

      _____

      b. Tapping a coworker's shoulder while she is walking away means you want her to stop or wait for you.

      c. _____

      _____

   5. _____

      a. _____

      _____

      b. _____

      _____

AN OUTLINE OF "NONVERBAL COMMUNICATION"

A. Importance of nonverbal communication
   1. Accounts for 55 percent of our total communication.
   2. When verbal and nonverbal communication conflict, people believe nonverbal.
   3. Every gesture or glance communicates a message.
      a. If a coworker gives you an unusual glance, you wonder what it meant.
      b. Some employees avoid greeting others and instead show "frozen faces," which can be interpreted as displeasure.
      c. Some body language can be misleading: crossed arms may not mean lack of receptivity—only that the person feels cold.

B. Functions of nonverbal communication
   1. Accenting: punctuating verbal communication
      a. Poking finger into someone's chest
      b. Sweeping motion of hand to say that conversation is over
   2. Complementing: reinforcing verbal communication
      a. Standing four feet away from someone might indicate the person is a stranger.
      b. Standing four feet away from your boss and saluting her formally reinforces the message that she is of higher rank and has unchallenged authority.
   3. Contradicting: conveying messages opposite to the verbal messages
      a. Often this is how people reveal true feelings or send an unintended message.
      b. For example, people who give less eye contact than they receive send the message that they are bored.
      c. When verbal and nonverbal messages conflict, people believe the nonverbal ones.
   4. Regulating: controlling the course of a conversation
      a. Raising a hand with index finger extended means you want the other person to wait or to stop speaking.
      b. Tapping a coworker's shoulder while she is walking away means you want her to stop or wait for you.
      c. Touching someone's arm while he speaks means you want to speak.
   5. Substituting: replacing the verbal messages
      a. When we're in a hurry, we raise both eyebrows instead of asking how somebody is doing.
      b. We shake our heads while standing behind the boss to show we don't agree with what he is saying.

SUMMARIZING ACTIVITY:
"IS AGGRESSION A RESPONSE TO FRUSTRATION?"

Study notes:

Original frustration-aggression theory: _____

_____

_____

Frustration — anything that blocks _____

Displacement — _____

    Ex. — _____

    _____

    _____

Revised frustration-aggression theory: _____

_____

_____

One kind of aggressive cue — _____

_____

    Ex. — _____

    _____

    _____

    Ex. — Countries that ban handguns have lower murder rates. (The United States has about 10,000 handgun homicides per year; Britain has about 10.)

A SUMMARY OF
"IS AGGRESSION A RESPONSE TO FRUSTRATION?"

Study notes:

Original frustration-aggression theory: frustration always leads to some form of aggression, although the aggression need not be directed against the source of the frustration.

Frustration — anything that blocks our attaining a goal

Displacement — redirecting our aggression toward safer targets

> Ex. — A man who is humiliated by his boss takes it out on his wife; she yells at their son; the son kicks the dog; the dog bites the mail carrier.

Revised frustration-aggression theory: frustration produces anger, an emotional readiness to aggress, which is especially likely to explode when aggressive cues are present.

One kind of aggressive cue —the sight of a weapon perceived as an instrument of violence

> Ex. — Children who had just played with toy guns were more than willing to knock down another child's blocks.

> Ex. — Countries that ban handguns have lower murder rates. (The United States has about 10,000 handgun homicides per year; Britain has about 10.)

**MAPPING ACTIVITY:
"BEFORE YOU BEGIN WRITING"**

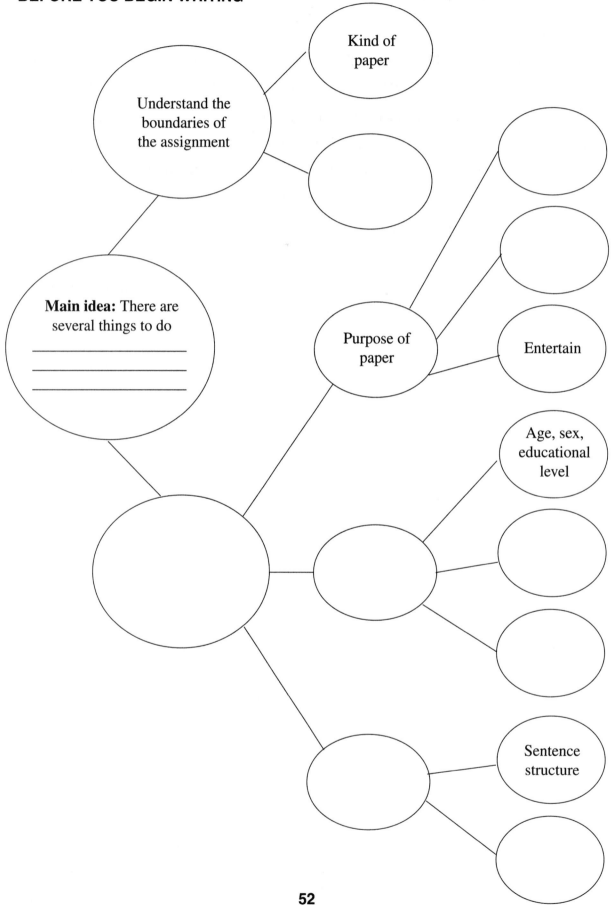

Understand the boundaries of the assignment

Kind of paper

Main idea: There are several things to do
_____
_____
_____

Purpose of paper

Entertain

Age, sex, educational level

Sentence structure

**A MAP OF
"BEFORE YOU BEGIN WRITING"**

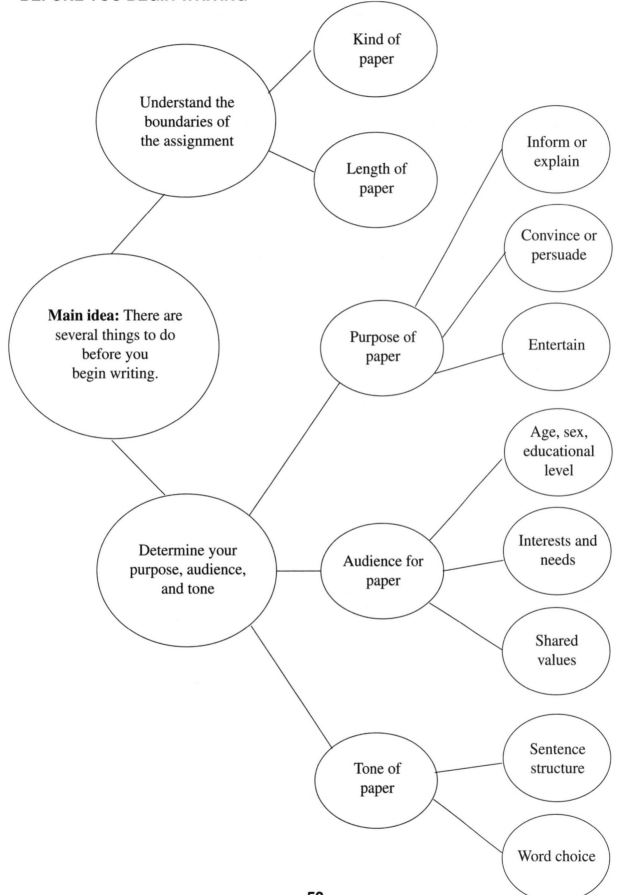

TEST BANKS

This section contains the following:

- A **First Test Bank** (pages 55–142) consisting of four additional Mastery Tests for each chapter in Part One of *Ten Steps to Advancing College Reading Skills*, Fourth Edition, as well as four additional Combined-Skills Mastery Tests;
- A **Second Test Bank** (pages 147–196) consisting of copies of the tests on the computer disks that are available with the book.

Instructors whose students are using *Ten Steps to Advancing College Reading Skills*, Fourth Edition, in class have permission to reproduce any of these tests on a photocopying machine as often as needed.

The answer key for the First Test Bank is on pages 143–146; for the Second Test Bank, on pages 197–198.

VOCABULARY IN CONTEXT: Test A

A. For each item below, underline the **examples** that suggest the meaning of the italicized term. Then, in the space provided, write the letter of the meaning of that term.

___ 1. Duane is the *antithesis* of his brother. For instance, Duane is very shy while his brother is outgoing. Also, Duane enjoys reading while his brother prefers playing sports.
    A. opposite   C. enemy
    B. imitation   D. hero

___ 2. Our neighbor has an *abrasive* personality. He can't seem to get along with people without frequent outbursts and quarrels.
    A. quiet and sweet   C. analytical
    B. cool   D. harsh and rough

B. Each item below includes a word or words that are a **synonym** of the italicized word. Write the synonym of the italicized word in the space provided.

_____ 3. Some actors are as *adroit* in business as they are skilled in performing.

_____ 4. Marie is a *meticulous* worker, but it's no surprise—her mother is also extremely careful and precise.

_____ 5. The mayor and the governor feel the same about each other—he *deplores* her as much as she disapproves of him.

C. Each item below includes a word or words that are an **antonym** of the italicized word. Underline the antonym of each italicized word. Then write the letter of the meaning of the italicized word.

___ 6. Jo left her term paper till the last minute and was able to do only *cursory* research. In contrast, Ian started his paper in plenty of time; his painstaking, thorough research earned him an A.
    A. hasty   C. careful
    B. rude   D. indirect

___ 7. Nina makes a big fuss about every little thing her children do, whether it's harmful or *innocuous*.
    A. loud   C. dangerous
    B. stubborn   D. harmless

(Continues on next page)

D. Use the **general sense of each sentence** to figure out the meaning of each italicized word. Then write the letter of the meaning of the italicized word.

___ 8. My old dented car looks *incongruous* among my neighbors' fancy new cars.
    A. useful   C. better
    B. appropriate   D. out of place

___ 9. It isn't *feasible* for me to attend the 12:30 meeting—I've got another important meeting that begins at noon.
    A. correct   C. noticeable
    B. possible   D. difficult

___10. It is usually obvious when someone has an *egocentric* personality. Ms. A., for instance, can talk of nothing but herself, and Mr. B. has no interest in anything that doesn't affect him directly.
    A. careless   C. caring
    B. violent   D. self-centered

Name _____

Section _____ Date _____

SCORE: (Number correct) × 10 = _____%

VOCABULARY IN CONTEXT: Test B

A. For each item below, underline the **examples** that suggest the meaning of the italicized term. Then, in the space provided, write the letter of the meaning of that term.

____ 1. To cheer up the hallway, Reba *embellished* her children's bedroom doors. She painted colorful circus pictures on her son's door and pasted seashells on her daughter's.
    A. replaced   C. decorated
    B. erased   D. recognized

____ 2. People in *sedentary* occupations, such as driving a taxi or writing books, need to make a special effort to exercise.
    A. high-stress   C. involving much sitting
    B. very well-paid   D. artistic

____ 3. My grandfather says that his teachers had students do *inane* things, such as spending hours on improving handwriting and memorizing the date each of the fifty states entered the union.
    A. wise   C. impossible
    B. foolish   D. expensive

B. Each item below includes a word or words that are a **synonym** of the italicized word. Write the synonym of the italicized word in the space provided.

_____ 4. Raheem has a *belligerent* nature. His friends can't explain why he faces the world with such a hostile attitude.

_____ 5. The houses along the river are in a *precarious* position, so they are often flooded. Yet afterward, the owners keep stubbornly rebuilding on the same risky sites.

C. Each item below includes a word or words that are an **antonym** of the italicized word. Underline the antonym of each italicized word. Then write the letter of the meaning of the italicized word.

____ 6. Ling is not self-praising, like her brother; in fact, she's self-*disparaging*.
    A. encouraging   C. knowing
    B. belittling   D. appealing

____ 7. On television, a speech may seem *impromptu* even though it's prepared. Speakers can read from a script that the audience cannot see.
    A. controversial   C. dull
    B. overly long   D. unrehearsed

(Continues on next page)

D. Use the **general sense of each sentence** to figure out the meaning of each italicized word. Then write the letter of the meaning of the italicized word.

___ 8. Unhappy with British rule, the American colonists fought to become *autonomous*.
    A. well-known   C. independent
    B. taxed   D. reasonable

___ 9. Our state representative *disseminates* useful information to residents in her district through letters, local interviews, and e-mail.
    A. collects   C. distributes
    B. believes   D. prevents

___10. Late for work because of a subway breakdown, Sean was afraid the boss wouldn't believe him. He was relieved when six coworkers came forward to *corroborate* his excuse.
    A. support   C. contradict
    B. listen to   D. ask for

VOCABULARY IN CONTEXT: Test C

Using context clues for help, write the letter of the best meaning for each italicized word or words.

___ 1. No one knows how humans acquired the concept of cooking food, but their first experience of cooking was probably *fortuitous:* very likely, some meat fell into a fire by accident.
   A. harmful
   B. planned
   C. lucky
   D. expensive

___ 2. Many husbands still find it difficult to *render* total support to their wives' careers, particularly if their wives earn more than they do.
   A. cook
   B. hide
   C. give
   D. delay

___ 3. The Amazonian forest in Brazil is so *expansive* that it influences weather and climate patterns.
   A. far
   B. broad
   C. green
   D. mysterious

___ 4. In the early 1900s, sums paid to widows with dependent children were *meager,* ranging from $2 to $14 a month for the first child and lesser amounts for the rest.
   A. slight
   B. old-fashioned
   C. harmful
   D. generous

___ 5. Running a *clandestine* operation—such as an underground newspaper in a dictatorship, a network of spies, or an undercover police investigation—is difficult and often highly dangerous.
   A. important
   B. expensive
   C. legal
   D. secret

___ 6. Good communication between marriage partners can often *mitigate* the stress caused by physical signs of aging, changes in work status or satisfaction, and the death of close relatives and friends.
   A. lessen
   B. hide
   C. cause
   D. add to

___ 7. Identifying the age of layers of rock also *fixes* the age of fossils that are within those layers.
   A. causes
   B. hides
   C. establishes
   D. casts doubt on

(Continues on next page)

___ 8. Government *entails* those political processes that have to do with the forming of rules and policies which are binding throughout a society.
- A. includes
- B. recognizes
- C. outlaws
- D. omits

___ 9. The elephant was deeply *enmeshed* in the fabric of Thai life. For centuries, it served as Thailand's main mode of transportation; its image graced temples, palaces, and the national flag.
- A. hidden
- B. harmed
- C. involved
- D. weakened

___10. When we interact, we behave like actors by following a script that we have learned. When someone enters a doctor's waiting room, for instance, he or she *assumes* the role of patient.
- A. meets
- B. contacts
- C. denies
- D. takes on

VOCABULARY IN CONTEXT: Test D

Using context clues for help, write the letter of the best meaning for each italicized word or words.

____ 1. In addition to getting a jail sentence, some criminals are required to pay *restitution*. One thief had to pay an elderly woman both the money he stole from her and several thousand dollars for her injuries.
    A. a fine   C. taxes
    B. payment to charity   D. repayment for loss

____ 2. In China, if you visit an acquaintance on a hot day and feel thirsty, you would not ask your host *point-blank,* "May I have a glass of water?" Instead, you would convey the same request by saying, "Isn't it hot today?"
    A. angrily   C. frequently
    B. directly   D. softly

____ 3. Measurement of population growth depends in large part on birth rates and *mortality* rates.
    A. marriage   C. death
    B. financial   D. education

____ 4. Contact, support, and encouragement between adult children and their parents are seldom one-way but are instead *reciprocal* interactions.
    A. selfish   C. give-and-take
    B. frequent   D. rare

____ 5. The Big Room at Carlsbad Caverns has an area equivalent to fourteen football fields and enough height to *accommodate* the U.S. Capitol Building.
    A. duplicate   C. easily reach
    B. find   D. contain

____ 6. *Turbulent* periods in nineteenth-century Europe included the Napoleonic wars, the revolutions of 1848, the Crimean War in the 1850s, and the Franco-Prussian War of 1870.
    A. violently disturbed   C. forgotten
    B. prosperous   D. extremely dull

____ 7. Why do we use *platitudes?* One theory is that remarks such as "Nice to see you," "Have a good day," and "Take care" save us the trouble of having to think of what to say.
    A. sad comments   C. questions
    B. commonplace remarks   D. reasons

(Continues on next page)

___ 8. "Quality circles" are small groups of employees that work together as equals. Practically all the companies that have *implemented* quality circles are in the manufacturing sector of the economy. Giving workers more control over their jobs can boost worker productivity.

    A. defined   C. seen often

    B. manufactured   D. put into effect

___ 9. During the 1920s, advertising agencies hired psychologists to design the first ad campaigns. They *touted* products by building up name-brand identification, creating memorable slogans, manipulating endorsements by doctors or celebrities, and appealing to consumers' hunger for prestige and status.

    A. manufactured   C. bought

    B. named   D. promoted

___10. President Nixon tried to keep the tapes from the Senate Watergate Committee by *invoking* executive privilege, insisting that a president had a right to keep confidential any White House communication.

    A. referring to for support   C. forgetting

    B. causing   D. fighting against

MAIN IDEAS: Test A

The following paragraphs have main ideas that may appear at various places within the paragraph. Identify the topic sentence of each paragraph by filling in the correct sentence number in the space provided.

___ 1. ¹Not that many decades ago, the entertainment world had a history of discrimination against black performers. ²For many years, for instance, radio listeners tuned in to *Amos 'n' Andy,* a popular situation comedy about two black men. ³But the actors who played Amos and Andy were both white. ⁴In those same years, before the start of the civil rights movement, talented black singers were hired to dub in movie songs for white actresses who couldn't sing. ⁵The singers' names, however, could never appear in the movie credits.

___ 2. ¹Actors are nervous before a play. ²Politicians are nervous before they give a campaign speech. ³Athletes are nervous before a big game. ⁴Surveys show that 76 percent of experienced speakers, such as novelists and lecturers, have stage fright before taking the floor. ⁵In other words, it is perfectly normal to be nervous at the start of a speech. ⁶Your body is responding as it normally would to any stressful situation—by producing more adrenaline. ⁷This sudden shot of adrenaline is what makes your heart race, your hands shake, your knees knock, and your skin perspire.

___ 3. ¹If you walk down just about any city street in America, you will encounter countless billboards, posters, bumper stickers, and bus and cab displays, each with a separate advertising appeal. ²Your kitchen cupboard is probably full of product packages and labels, each containing at least one sales message. ³Go to the racetrack and you will see two-hundred-mile-an-hour race cars carrying advertising worth $75 million per year. ⁴Go to a tennis tournament, a jazz festival, or a golf match, and you will find corporate sponsors, such as the makers of cigarettes, sodas, or blue jeans. ⁵Go to a movie and you will find that marketers have paid a handsome sum to have your favorite stars use their products in the film. ⁶Almost anywhere you go, you will encounter advertisements of all types and sizes reminding you to buy an endless stream of products.

(Continues on next page)

___ 4. [1]In almost every society in the world, couples have become engaged in some way before marrying. [2]Engagement serves a variety of functions for the couple. [3]It provides a clear indication that marriage is about to occur. [4]Due to the exclusive nature of the relationship, personal and interpersonal testing can continue with less threat from competitive forces. [5]A more thorough awareness of shared and nonshared values, marital-role expectations, and future aspirations can be examined. [6]Engagement provides the final opportunity prior to the legal union for each person to understand himself or herself in relation to the other. [7]It is likely that many couples view an engagement as a kind of trial marriage, including sexual intimacy, the sharing of certain financial obligations, and, in some instances, living together.

___ 5. [1]The pattern of life for most Europeans between 1600 and 1800 centered on the struggle to stay alive. [2]At least once a decade, climatic conditions—usually a long period of summer rainfall—would produce a devastatingly bad harvest, which in turn would result in widespread malnutrition, often leading to serious illness and death. [3]A family might survive for a time by eating less, but eventually, with its meager stocks exhausted and the cost of grain high, the human costs would mount. [4]The substitution of grass, nuts, and tree bark for grain on which the peasants depended almost entirely for nourishment was inadequate to sustain healthy life.

Name _____

Section _____ Date _____

SCORE: (Number correct) × 20 = _____%

MAIN IDEAS: Test B

The following paragraphs have main ideas that may appear at various places within the paragraph. Identify the topic sentence of each paragraph by filling in the correct sentence number in the space provided.

____ 1. ¹Hunger and thirst represent two of the most potent drives in our day-to-day lives. ²But psychologists have identified a number of secondary drives that are also extremely powerful forces. ³One such secondary drive is the need for achievement. ⁴Most of us are motivated by the satisfaction of striving for and attaining a level of excellence in our chosen endeavors. ⁵Another powerful secondary drive is the need for affiliation. ⁶Put simply, this is the widespread human need for friendship. ⁷A third type of secondary drive is the need for power. ⁸Some people are very much influenced by their need to have an impact on those around them.

____ 2. ¹When Chevrolet began to sell its Nova cars in Latin America, hardly anyone would buy them. ²The company finally learned that Spanish speakers read the car's name as the Spanish phrase "no va," meaning "doesn't go"! ³Like Chevrolet, many American companies have learned the hard way that they need to know their customers' language. ⁴When Pepsi-Cola ran its "Come Alive with Pepsi" ads in China, the consumers laughed. ⁵The company had not translated its slogan quite right. ⁶In Chinese, it came out as "Pepsi brings your ancestors back from the dead."

____ 3. ¹In the South, the Civil War destroyed half the region's farm equipment and killed one-third of its draft animals. ²The death of slavery also ended the plantation system. ³The number of farms doubled from 1860 to 1880, but the number of landowners remained the same. ⁴The size of the average farm dropped by more than half, as sharecropping and tenancy rose. ⁵A shortage of cash forced Southern farmers to borrow against future crops. ⁶Crop liens and high credit costs kept a lot of black and white farmers trapped in a cycle of debit and poverty. ⁷So at the very time the rest of the economy was consolidating after the Civil War, Southern agriculture was marching off in the opposite, less efficient direction.

(Continues on next page)

___ 4. ¹First the good news: Americans are definitely eating more healthful meals. ²We are consuming greater amounts of such high-fiber foods as whole-grain breads, fruits and vegetables, which are believed to help prevent certain cancers and other diseases. ³At the same time, we are substituting relatively low-fat foods for higher-fat ones—for example, eating fish instead of red meat, drinking skim milk instead of whole. ⁴The bad news is that our snack foods are not nearly as healthful. ⁵Between meals, we often revert to eating large amounts of fat. ⁶For instance, sales of ice cream and potato chips are going through the roof. ⁷Another drawback of the snack foods is that they have almost no fiber. ⁸As eating-behavior experts have concluded, we try super-hard to eat healthfully at mealtimes—but then undo some of the good work by "rewarding" ourselves with snacks that are bad for us.

___ 5. ¹What does it take to achieve extraordinary success? ²Educational psychologist Benjamin Bloom did a study of high achievers and found that drive and determination, not great natural talent, led to their success. ³The study included America's top performers in six fields: concert pianists, Olympic swimmers, sculptors, tennis players, mathematicians, and research neurologists. ⁴Development of Bloom's subjects began when parents exposed the child to music, swimming, scientific ideas, and so forth, "just for fun." ⁵At first many of the children were quite ordinary in their skills. ⁶One Olympic swimmer, for instance, remembers repeatedly losing races as a ten-year-old. ⁷At some point, however, the children began to get recognition for their abilities and pursued them more actively. ⁸After more successes and encouragement, the youngsters began "living" for their talent. ⁹Most spent many hours each day practicing their skills. ¹⁰This continued for many years before they reached truly extraordinary heights of achievement.

MAIN IDEAS: Test C

The following paragraphs have main ideas that may appear at various places within the paragraph. Identify the topic sentence of each paragraph by filling in the correct sentence number in the space provided.

___ 1. ¹All of us, at one time or another, have said something to someone that we regretted. ²It may have been something that embarrassed us or the other party, it may have had the effect of hurting someone, or it may have been a secret we were not supposed to tell. ³Some researchers have discovered that 75 percent of those "regrettable words" we say fall into five categories. ⁴The most common is the blunder—forgetting someone's name or getting it wrong, or asking, "How's your mother?" and hearing the reply "She died." ⁵The next category is direct attack—a generalized criticism of the other person or of his or her family or friends. ⁶The third category, negative group references, often contains racial or ethnic slurs. ⁷This is followed by direct and specific criticism, such as "You never clean house" or "You shouldn't go out with that guy." ⁸The fifth category of revealing or explaining too much includes telling secrets or telling hurtful things said by others.

___ 2. ¹Unlike women in other ancient societies, Egyptian women were not entirely subordinated to men. ²Although polygamy was permitted, it was not common; the basic social unit was the monogamous family. ³Even the pharaoh, who could keep secondary wives and concubines, had a chief wife. ⁴Women were not secluded. ⁵They could own and inherit property and engage in business. ⁶The Egyptians of the New Kingdom also permitted queens to act as royal regents, giving them the power to rule in the pharaoh's absence. ⁷For instance, Queen Hatshepsut of the Eighteenth Dynasty "controlled the affairs of the land." ⁸In monumental statues from the Eighteenth Dynasty, some queens were depicted on the same scale of size as their husbands, while statues of anyone else had to be much smaller.

___ 3. ¹Childhood experiences can influence how we feel about being touched. ²Little girls, for example, are generally kissed and cuddled more than little boys. ³As a consequence, women often are more comfortable with touching than men are. ⁴Also, Latin Americans and southern Europeans, for instance, casually touch each other far more than northern Europeans and most Americans. ⁵Furthermore, our willingness to touch and be touched is affected by the social circumstances. ⁶Even men who are generally uneasy about touching may hug one another at an exciting sporting event. ⁷Thus our feelings about physical contact with others are affected by our childhood experiences, cultural background, and social context.

(Continues on next page)

_____ 4. ¹Many bank robbers and home thieves are caught and convicted in this country. ²However, the American criminal justice system is not as well equipped to deal with white-collar crime as it is to handle street crime. ³Unlike a robbery, a stock or insurance fraud is complex and difficult to unravel. ⁴Local law enforcement officials commonly lack the skills and resources necessary to tackle crimes outside the sphere of street crime. ⁵Federal agencies will handle only the more serious white-collar crimes. ⁶And the handful of white-collar criminals who are prosecuted and convicted are given a slap on the wrist. ⁷Street criminals who steal $100 may find their way to prison, while the dishonest executive who embezzles $1 million may receive a suspended sentence and a relatively small fine. ⁸Federal statistics indicate that embezzlers at banks steal nine times more than bank robbers. ⁹Yet whereas 91 percent of bank robbers end up in jail, only 17 percent of the embezzlers go to jail.

_____ 5. ¹Andy and Sharon live in a small house with their two children in rural farm country. ²Andy farms and works part-time in the local grocery store, while Sharon works part-time as a cook in a diner. ³Although they earn only about $20,000 a year, they're happy, have the things they want, and think of themselves as doing pretty well. ⁴Leslie recently moved to the "big city" to attend a private college. ⁵Although her parents pay all her expenses and give her $750 a month for "extras," Leslie constantly complains about how difficult it is to be poor, and many of her affluent friends feel the same way. ⁶Keith, a struggling young actor, works part-time nights as a guard and supports himself on about $900 a month. ⁷It's a difficult task, but Keith is happy with his life and considers himself economically comfortable. ⁸By the government's economic measurement, all these people except Leslie would be considered poor. ⁹Yet it is Leslie who feels poor. ¹⁰To a great extent, whether or not people consider themselves poor depends upon their expectations and the economic conditions of those around them.

Name _____

Section _____ Date _____
SCORE: (Number correct) × 20 = _____%

MAIN IDEAS: Test D

The following paragraphs have main ideas that may appear at various places within the paragraph. Identify the topic sentence of each paragraph by filling in the correct sentence number in the space provided.

____ 1. ¹Technology revolutionized agriculture as inventions dramatically increased productivity on the farms. ²Eli Whitney's invention of the cotton gin in 1793 permitted an individual to clean three hundred pounds of cotton in a single day— three hundred times more than could be cleaned by hand. ³After the mechanization of wheat farming, the hours required to farm one acre dropped from sixty-one to three, and the per-acre cost of production fell from $3.65 to $0.66. ⁴Machines entered every phase of agriculture—by 1890 some 900 companies were manufacturing such items as hay loaders, cord binders, seeders, rotary plows, mowers, and combines.

____ 2. ¹Shame is a painful emotion resulting from a strong sense of guilt or unworthiness. ²It exists in all cultures. ³But in Western culture in general and the United States in particular, shame is self-oriented, while in a country like Japan, it is linked not to the self but to others. ⁴In America, if a child fails an exam, the child might feel terrible and be ashamed. ⁵A Japanese child, on the other hand, would be ashamed not because he or she failed but because the failure resulted in shame for the child's parents. ⁶Shame shows up in a similar way in the workplace. ⁷In Japan, if a company doesn't make a profit as a result of worker laziness, the worker will be ashamed. ⁸It's very hard to think of any American worker feeling ashamed that General Motors didn't make a profit. ⁹The Japanese corporation works because it is part of a social system in which the failure of the individual reflects upon the group. ¹⁰One feels shame for letting down the group, not the self.

____ 3. ¹In 1977, gypsy moths defoliated 1.3 million acres in Pennsylvania. ²Two years later, only 6,000 acres were defoliated. ³The sudden decrease in defoliation was due to the effectiveness of two parasitic flies introduced as biological control agents. ⁴One fly was imported from Europe and released in New England in 1908. It spread undetected in Pennsylvania for many years. ⁵The other fly was released as part of a control program of the Division of Forest Pest Management of the Pennsylvania Department of Environmental Resources. ⁶One species of fly lays eggs on the gypsy moth caterpillar, and when the eggs hatch, the maggots bore into the caterpillar. ⁷The other species lays eggs on leaves that the caterpillars eat. ⁸The eggs are then eaten along with the foliage and hatch inside the caterpillar.

(Continues on next page)

___ 4. [1]A growing sexual permissiveness in the early 1900s evoked a series of severe responses. [2]Purity forces crusaded against indecent styles of dancing, immodest dress, and impure books and films. [3]One religious journal denounced popular dance styles as "impure, polluting, corrupting, debasing, destroying spirituality, [and] increasing carnality." [4]A bill was introduced in the Utah state legislature to fine and imprison women who wore, on the streets, skirts "higher than three inches above the ankle." [5]In the Ohio legislature it was proposed that cleavage be limited to two inches and that the sale of any "garment which unduly displays or accentuates the lines of the female figure" be prohibited. [6]Four states and many cities established censorship boards to review films, and many other cities broke up red-light districts and required licenses for dance halls.

___ 5. [1]The palaces of the civilization of Minoan Crete (at its peak from about 2000 to 1500 B.C.E.) lacked fortification, and the art lacked angry warlords. [2]Women's clothing, at least for the upper class, was so elegant that it would be eye-catching at a modern Milanese fashion show. [3]Two circumstances help to account for what was so obviously a world of peace and prosperity in Minoan Crete. [4]One was that, living on an island in an age unfamiliar with seaborne invasions, the Minoans must have felt insulated from foreign attack. [5]The other was that a friendly climate and terrain suitable for pasturing and growing orchard crops (grapes, olives, nuts) freed the Minoans from heavy reliance on labor-intensive agriculture. [6]This meant that not only did people have more leisure than their counterparts in agricultural societies, but produce was more diverse, providing a greater hedge against famine and allowing for long-distance trade in goods that were less easily produced elsewhere. [7]To take but one example, the Minoans had plentiful wool and various kinds of natural dyes. [8]Since wool, unlike linen, is easily dyed, Minoans were exporting "exotic" multipatterned luxury cloths to Egypt as early as about 2000 B.C.E.

SUPPORTING DETAILS: Test A

A. (1–6.) Complete the outline of the following textbook passage by adding the main idea and the missing major or minor details. Read the entire passage before beginning work on the outline. You may wish to number or check the major details within the passage as you read.

[1]There are a few major reasons for family violence. [2]One is stress, which is highest among the urban poor, families with a jobless husband, and those with four to six children. [3]Stress by itself, however, does not necessarily cause violence. [4]Another important factor is "a culturally recognized script" for violent behavior under stress in U.S. society (Straus et al., 1988). [5]The violence on television, corporal punishment in schools, and the death penalty, for example, convey the idea that violence is an acceptable solution to problems. [6]Research suggests yet one more reason for family violence: the tendency for marital violence is transmitted from one generation to another. [7]It has been found that most of the violent married individuals have, as children, seen their parents hit each other.

Main idea: _____

_____

1. _____

    a. _____

    b. Families with a jobless husband

    c. People with four to six children

2. U.S. "culturally recognized script" for violent behavior under stress

    a. _____

    b. Corporal punishment in schools

    c. _____

3. _____

(Continues on next page)

B. Answer the supporting-detail questions that follow the textbook passage.

[1]At the beginning of the eighteenth century, the United States lacked a strong educational system. [2]Apprenticeship in a trade was a major form of education, and formal schooling was largely limited to those who could afford to pay. [3]Even "free" schools often required the payment of tuition, and primary schools often required entering students to be literate already, barring students who had not been taught to read by their parents. [4]Many schools admitted students regardless of age, mixing young children with young adults in their twenties, and classrooms could contain as many as eighty pupils. [5]Few textbooks were available, and most learning amounted to monotonous repetition of facts. [6]School buildings were generally unpainted, over-crowded, and lacked blackboards or windows.

___ 7. In general, the major supporting details of this paragraph are
  A. details of American life at the beginning of the eighteenth century.
  B. weaknesses of the American educational system at the beginning of the eighteenth century.
  C. problems with eighteenth-century America's school buildings.
  D. problems within the American educational system in previous centuries.

___ 8. The first sentence of the paragraph provides
  A. the main idea.
  B. major details.
  C. minor details.

___ 9. Sentence 5 provides
  A. the main idea.
  B. major details.
  C. minor details.

___10. The major details of the passage are
  A. stages in the educational system.
  B. elements of the educational system.
  C. results of the educational system.
  D. questions about the educational system.

SUPPORTING DETAILS: Test B

A. (1–5.) Complete the map of the following textbook passage by filling in the main idea and the missing major supporting details. Read the entire passage before beginning work on the map. You may wish to number or check the major details within the passage as you read.

[1]Pollster Louis Harris has divided suburbs into four distinct categories based on income level and rate of growth. [2]Higher-income suburbs are categorized as either affluent bedroom or affluent settled. [3]The affluent bedroom communities rank at the highest levels in terms of income, proportion of persons employed in professional and managerial occupations, and percentages of homeowners. [4]Affluent settled communities tend to be older, and perhaps even declining in population. [5]They are more likely to house business firms and do not serve mainly as a place of residence for commuters.

[6]Harris has recognized that certain suburban areas are composed of individuals and families with low or moderate incomes. [7]Low-income growing communities serve as the home of upwardly mobile blue-collar workers who have moved from central cities. [8]Low-income stagnant communities are among the oldest suburbs and are experiencing the full range of social problems characteristic of the central cities.

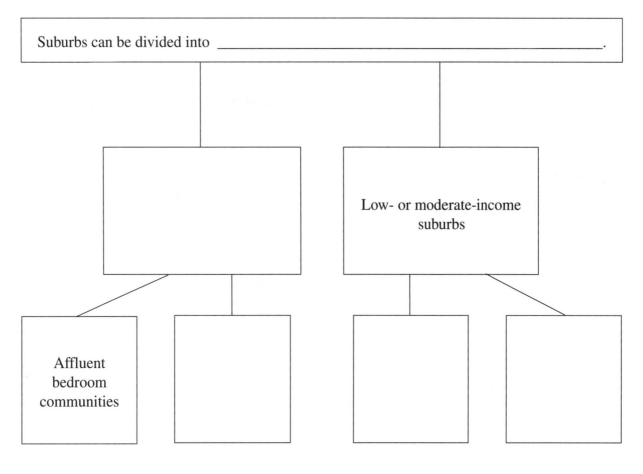

Suburbs can be divided into _____.

Low- or moderate-income suburbs

Affluent bedroom communities

(Continues on next page)

B. Answer the supporting-detail questions that follow the textbook passage.

¹Insomniacs may envy those who have no problem sleeping. ²However, too much sleep is also a sleep disorder. ³There are a couple of major causes of sleeping too much. ⁴One major cause of this problem is apnea, a condition associated with breathing difficulties during the night. ⁵In severe cases, the victim actually stops breathing after falling asleep. ⁶When the level of carbon dioxide in the blood rises to a certain point, apnea sufferers are spurred to a state of arousal just short of waking consciousness. ⁷Because this can happen hundreds of times in a night, apnea patients typically feel exhausted and fall asleep repeatedly the next day. ⁸Another cause of too much sleep is narcolepsy, a hereditary condition that causes victims to nod off without warning in the middle of a conversation or other alert activity. ⁹Narcoleptics will often experience a sudden loss of muscle tone upon expression of any sort of emotion. ¹⁰A joke, anger, sexual stimulation—all bring on a feeling of weakness. ¹¹Another symptom of the disorder is immediate entry into REM sleep, a state which produces frightening hallucinations that are in fact dreams that the narcoleptic experiences while still partly awake.

____ 6. In general, the major supporting details of the passage are
  A. types of insomniacs.
  B. causes of apnea.
  C. causes of getting too much sleep.
  D. symptoms of narcolepsy.

____ 7. Specifically, the major details are
  A. apnea and narcolepsy.
  B. insomnia and sleeping too much.
  C. exhaustion and repeated falling asleep during the day.
  D. a sudden loss of muscle tone, a feeling of weakness, immediate entry into REM sleep.

____ 8. Sentence 8 provides
  A. the topic sentence.
  B. a major detail.
  C. a minor detail.

____ 9. Sentence 11 provides
  A. the topic sentence.
  B. a major detail.
  C. a minor detail.

____10. According to the passage, apnea patients often fall asleep during the day
  A. when they experience any sort of emotion.
  B. because they have not slept at all at night.
  C. because of exhaustion from poor quality sleep.
  D. after they experience REM sleep.

SUPPORTING DETAILS: Test C

A. Answer the supporting-detail questions that follow the textbook passage.

[1]After a period of squabbling, domestic chickens sort themselves into a reasonably stable "pecking order." [2]Thereafter, when competition for food occurs, all hens defer to the dominant bird, all but the dominant bird give way to the second, and so on. [3]Conflict is minimized because each bird knows its place. [4]This process is an example of dominance hierarchy, a social arrangement in which animals establish a rank for members of the social unit, thereby eventually reducing aggression. [5]Dominance in male bighorn sheep is reflected in the size of their horns. [6]The larger the horn, the higher in the hierarchy a male bighorn sheep will be. [7]Wolf packs are organized so that each sex has a dominant or "alpha" individual to whom all others are subordinate.

____ 1. The main idea of the paragraph is expressed in sentence
   A. 1.
   B. 2.
   C. 4.
   D. 7.

____ 2. The major details of this paragraph are
   A. examples of the main idea.
   B. questions about the main idea.
   C. problems relating to the main idea.
   D. reasons for the main idea.

____ 3. The second major detail is introduced in sentence
   A. 1.
   B. 3.
   C. 5.
   D. 7.

4–5. Complete the following study notes that summarize the passage.

Dominance hierarchy _____

_____

Ex.— _____

_____

(Continues on next page)

B. (6–10.) Outline the following textbook passage. Read the entire passage before beginning work on the outline. You may wish to number or check the major details within the passage as you read.

¹All relationships, unless they remain at the casual, small-talk level, experience growth that usually goes through five specific levels. ²The first, called initiating, involves the participants assessing each other in various areas—such as their clothing, physical attractiveness, and beliefs and attitudes. ³From these observations, they begin to make judgments about each other. ⁴Experimenting, the second stage, involves making a conscious effort to seek out common interests and experiences. ⁵Participants express their ideas, attitudes, and values and observe how the other person reacts to them. ⁶At this stage of the relationship, everything is generally pleasant, relaxed, and uncritical. ⁷Many relationships stay at this particular stage—the participants enjoy the level of the relationship but show no desire to pursue it further. ⁸The third level is known as the intensifying stage. ⁹At this stage, participants have already decided that they like each other a lot. ¹⁰They tell each other private things about their families and friends. ¹¹And they begin to share their frustrations, imperfections, and prejudices. ¹²Participants begin to use nicknames for each other and develop a "shorthand" way of speaking. ¹³Trust becomes important. ¹⁴The fourth stage, integrating, is the point at which the participants' individual personalities begin to merge. ¹⁵People begin to expect to see them together. ¹⁶Each of them is able to predict and explain the behavior of the other. ¹⁷The final coming-together stage of a relationship is the bonding stage. ¹⁸In this stage the participants make some sort of formal commitment that announces their relationship to those around them.

Main idea: _____

_____

1. _____: Participants assess each other in areas such as looks, beliefs, and attitudes.

2. Experimenting: In an effort to seek out common interests and experiences, participants express their ideas, views, and values and are uncritical with each other.

3. _____: Participants know they like each other a lot, share private personal information, begin to use nicknames for each other; trust becomes important.

4. _____

_____

_____

5. _____

_____

SUPPORTING DETAILS: Test D

A. Answer the supporting-detail questions that follow the textbook passage.

[1]More and more companies are interested in international marketing of their products and services. [2]In developing a framework in which to conduct international business, managers have two general strategies to choose from. [3]A global strategy is a standardized, worldwide product and marketing strategy. [4]The firm sells the same product in essentially the same manner throughout the world. [5]In Ford's global strategy, it merges its United States, European, Asian, and Latin American operations into one huge organization. [6]The goal is to create cars in standardized categories to be sold worldwide. [7]Ford management hopes to reduce the company's costs dramatically by engineering products only once, rather than multiple times for different markets. [8]Under a multinational strategy, the firm treats each national market differently. [9]Products and marketing strategies are developed to appeal to the customs, tastes, and buying habits of specific national markets. [10]Software maker Microsoft pursues a multinational strategy by creating products for specific markets, such as software that can read Japanese characters. [11]Microsoft also staffs its overseas sales and distribution operations with local workers, who understand the culture and customer.

____ 1. The major details of the paragraph are types of
   A. companies.
   B. managers.
   C. general international strategies.
   D. buying habits of particular national markets.

____ 2. The main idea of the paragraph is best expressed in
   A. sentence 1.
   B. sentence 2.
   C. sentence 3.
   D. sentence 9.

____ 3. The second major detail of the paragraph is introduced in
   A. sentence 3.
   B. sentence 4.
   C. sentence 5.
   D. sentence 8.

____ 4. Ford is presented as an example of
   A. automotive marketing.
   B. a global strategy.
   C. reduction of costs.
   D. a multinational strategy.

(Continues on next page)

B. (5–10.) Complete the map of the following textbook passage by filling in the main idea and the missing supporting details. Read the entire passage before beginning work on the map. You may wish to number or check the major details within the passage as you read.

¹For more than thirty years, Lawrence Kohlberg studied the ways that young men arrived at moral judgments. ²On the basis of the thought processes shown for moral decisions, Kohlberg described three levels of moral reasoning. ³The first level is preconventional morality. ⁴People at this level, under external controls, obey rules to avoid punishment or harm to people or property; or they act in their own self-interest. ⁵This level is typical of children aged 4 to 10. ⁶Kohlberg's next level of morality is conventional role conformity. ⁷People at this level have internalized the standards of authority figures. ⁸They are concerned about being "good," pleasing and caring for others, and maintaining the social order. ⁹This level is typically reached after age 10; many people never move beyond it, even in adulthood. ¹⁰Kohlberg's last level is morality of autonomous moral principles. ¹¹At this stage, morality is fully internal. ¹²People now recognize conflicts between moral standards and make their own moral judgments on the basis of principles of right, fairness, and justice. ¹³People generally do not reach this level of moral reasoning until at least age 13, or more commonly in young adulthood, if ever.

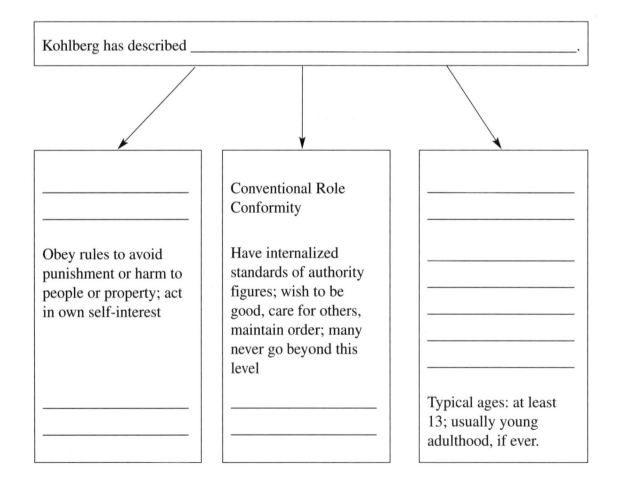

Kohlberg has described _____.

| _____
_____

Obey rules to avoid punishment or harm to people or property; act in own self-interest

_____
_____ | Conventional Role Conformity

Have internalized standards of authority figures; wish to be good, care for others, maintain order; many never go beyond this level

_____
_____ | _____
_____
_____
_____
_____
_____
_____

Typical ages: at least 13; usually young adulthood, if ever. |

IMPLIED MAIN IDEAS/CENTRAL POINT: Test A

A. In the space provided, write the letter of the sentence that best expresses the implied main idea of each of the following paragraphs.

___ 1. ¹Dolphins use a process called sonar to find their way and to find food. ²They emit sound waves that bounce off objects and return, giving the dolphin information about distance, size, and density. ³Some scientists think the dolphins can even "turn up" these sound waves and stun their prey. ⁴They know that certain levels of sound waves could easily kill a large squid in a matter of minutes. ⁵If these scientists are correct, dolphins could easily kill each other—yet they don't.

    A. Sea animals have wonderful skills at their disposal.
    B. Dolphins do not kill each other.
    C. Dolphin sonar is a powerful tool that appears to be used with skill and care.
    D. Sonar enables dolphins to find their way around by providing information on distance, size, and density.

___ 2. ¹Imagine a fundraiser comes to your door and asks for a five-hundred-dollar contribution. ²You laughingly refuse, telling her that the amount is way out of your league. ³She then asks for a ten-dollar contribution. If you are like most people, you'll probably be a lot more agreeable than if she hadn't asked for the huge contribution first. ⁴Similarly, college students were stopped on the street and asked to agree to a substantial favor—acting as unpaid counselors for juvenile offenders two hours a week for two years. ⁵Not surprisingly, no one agreed to such an outrageous request. ⁶But when they were later asked the considerably smaller favor of taking a group of juvenile offenders on a two-hour trip to the zoo, half the people complied. ⁷In comparison, only 17 percent of a control group of subjects who had not first received the larger request agreed.

    A. People are basically selfish and unwilling to help others.
    B. Only a small percentage of any group will agree to perform voluntary service.
    C. More people are willing to contribute money to a cause than donate their time.
    D. People are more willing to agree to a small favor after they have refused a large one.

___ 3. ¹In recent decades more young adults are returning to their parents' homes. ²Most parents express satisfaction with the arrangement, especially when it is temporary and when the adult child is under age 22. ³Parents appreciate help with household chores and with caring for younger children, and they enjoy sharing leisure activities. ⁴Usually everyone is active and healthy. ⁵But serious conflicts may arise, especially when a young adult is unemployed and financially dependent. ⁶Disagreements may center on household responsibilities and the child's lifestyle: dress, sex, alcohol, drugs, and choice of friends. ⁷The young adult is likely to feel isolated from peers and to have trouble establishing intimacy, while the parents may have to postpone renewing their own intimacy, exploring personal interests, and

(Continues on next page)

resolving marital issues. [8]The most difficult situation for parents seems to be the return of divorced or separated children with their own children.

A. Adult children who return to their parents' home should provide help with household chores and with caring for younger children.

B. A young adult who is unemployed and financially dependent makes life difficult for parents with whom he or she lives.

C. People who live together in the same household are likely to have both positive and negative experiences.

D. The return of adult children to their parents' homes can have both advantages and disadvantages.

B. (4.) The author has stated the central point of the following textbook selection in one sentence. Find and underline that sentence. Then, in the space provided, write the number of the sentence that contains the central point.

The Declining Birthrate in the United States

[1]In 1800, the American birthrate was higher than the birthrate in any European nation. [2]The typical American woman bore an average of seven children. [3]She had her first child around the age of twenty-three and bore children at two-year intervals until her early forties. [4]Had the American birthrate remained at this level, the nation's population would have reached 2 billion by 1990.

[5]Late in the eighteenth century, however, Americans began to have fewer children. [6]Between 1800 and 1900, the birthrate fell 40 percent, most sharply among the middle and upper-middle class. [7]Where the typical American mother bore seven children in 1800, the average number of children she bore had fallen to three and one-half in 1900. [8]Instead of giving birth to her last child at the age of 40 or later, by 1900 the typical American woman bore her last child at the age of 33. [9]The decline of the birthrate is such an important historical breakthrough that it has its own name: the demographic transition.

[10]What accounted for the declining birthrate? [11]In part, the reduction in fertility reflected the growing realization among parents that in an increasingly commercial and industrial society, children were no longer economic assets who would be productively employed in household industries or bound out as apprentices or servants. [12]Instead, children required significant investment in the form of education to prepare them for respectable careers and marriages. [13]The emergence of a self-conscious middle class concerned about social mobility and maintaining an acceptable standard of living also encouraged new limits on family size.

[14]The shrinking size of families also reflected a growing desire among women to assert control over their lives. [15]Much of the impetus behind birth control came from women who were weary of an unending cycle of pregnancy, birth, nursing, and new pregnancy.

[16]Thus, an important decline in the American birthrate began in the late 1800s because of the new advantages to limiting family size and the growing desire among women to gain control over their reproductive lives.

_____ is the number of the sentence that states the central point.

IMPLIED MAIN IDEAS/CENTRAL POINT: Test B

A. In the space provided, write the letter of the sentence that best expresses the implied main idea of each of the following paragraphs.

____ 1. [1]Intelligence is an ability to think logically and abstractly. [2]In contrast, wisdom is an ability to grasp paradoxes, reconcile contradictions, and make and accept compromises. [3]Because wise people weigh the effects of their acts on themselves and others, wisdom is particularly well suited to practical decision-making in a social context. [4]Whereas intelligence can figure out how to do something, wisdom asks whether it *should* be done. [5]Wise people, then, are better than others at solving social problems involving values—problems like easing racial tensions or deciding which divorcing spouse should have custody of the children.

    A. *Intelligence* is a word that describes our ability to think logically, allowing us to figure out how to do things.

    B. It is better to have wisdom than intelligence.

    C. Intelligence and wisdom are two different abilities, both important to human life.

    D. Humans have various natural abilities and skills that help them to understand and solve problems.

____ 2. [1]In the United States and other Western nations, service-related industries have increased greatly, while manufacturing has declined over the last few decades. [2]Older manufacturing industries, which have traditionally paid fairly well, have been closed as overseas competition has increased. [3]In addition, jobs today require more education and skills. [4]The workplace is changing faster than ever, with new industries, such as biotech and computer-related industries, growing. [5]These industries require more technical skills. [6]Furthermore, there is more insecurity in the workplace. [7]Only 55 percent of all workers in a recent study believed that their companies provided job security, a decline from earlier studies. [8]Some of this insecurity is caused by the downsizing of firms. [9]In an attempt to become more competitive, companies have laid off workers, requiring the remaining workers to become more productive. [10]Finally, the growth of temporary workers, part-time workers, and contract workers has changed the vocational landscape. [11]Some predict that within a few years, half of all jobs will be held by these temporary workers.

    A. The workplace of today differs substantially from the workplace of several decades ago.

    B. Based on current trends, the workplace of the twenty-first century will be largely composed of temporary workers.

    C. The last several decades have seen enormous changes in lifestyle throughout the world.

    D. Biotech and computer-related companies are growing and changing the nature of the workplace.

____ 3. [1]Verbs are the most important of all tools. [2]They push the sentence forward and give it momentum. [3]Active verbs push hard; passive verbs tug fitfully. [4]Most verbs also carry somewhere in their imagery or in their sound a suggestion of what they mean: *flail, poke, dazzle, squash, beguile, pamper, swagger, wheedle, vex.* [5]I would bet that no other language has such a vast supply of verbs so bright with color. [6]Don't choose one that is dull or merely serviceable. [7]Make active verbs activate your sentences. [8]Also, try to avoid verbs that end in a preposition; that preposition weakens the force of the verbs. [9]For example,

(Continues on next page)

don't "set up" a business that you can "establish." [10]Don't "come upon" an object that you can "discover," or "take hold of" one that you can "grab."

A. There are two types of verbs: active and passive.
B. Since verbs are the most important parts of sentences, writers should use active verbs, preferring colorful ones without prepositions.
C. In addition to having meanings, verbs sometimes have sounds that suggest what they mean.
D. A verb that ends in a preposition lacks the punch of a verb that carries all of the meaning itself.

B. (4.) The author has stated the central point of the following textbook selection in one sentence. Find and underline that sentence. Then, in the space provided, write the number of the sentence that contains the central point.

Aggression

[1]Aggression can be defined as physical or verbal behavior intended to hurt someone. [2]Scientists have learned there are various inborn and physical factors that influence the likelihood that an animal or human will be aggressive.

[3]Because aggression is a complex behavior, no one spot in the brain controls it. [4]But in both animals and humans, researchers have found neural systems that assist aggression. [5]When they activate those areas in the brain, hostility increases; when they deactivate them, hostility decreases. [6]Tame animals can thus be provoked into rage, and raging animals into submission.

[7]There are also genetic influences on aggression. [8]It has long been known that animals of many species can be bred for aggressiveness. [9]Sometimes this is done for practical purposes (the breeding of fighting cocks). [10]Sometimes, breeding is done for research. [11]Finnish psychologist Kirsti Lagerspetz took normal albino mice and bred the most aggressive ones together and the least aggressive ones together. [12]After repeating the procedure for twenty-six generations, she had one set of fierce mice and one set of placid mice. [13]Aggressiveness similarly varies among primates and humans. [14]Our temperament—how intense and reactive we are—is partly something we bring with us into the world, influenced by our sympathetic nervous system's reactivity. [15]Identical twins, when asked separately, are more likely than fraternal twins to agree on whether they have "a violent temper."

[16]Level of alcohol intake also influences neural sensitivity to aggressive stimulation. [17]Both laboratory experiments and police data indicate that when people are provoked, alcohol unleashes aggression. [18]Violent people are more likely (1) to drink and (2) to become aggressive when intoxicated. [19]In experiments, intoxicated people administer strong shocks or higher pain buttons. [20]In the real world, people who have been drinking commit about half of rapes and other violent crimes. [21]In 65 percent of homicides, the murderer and/or the victim had been drinking.

[22]Aggressiveness also correlates with the male sex hormone, testosterone. [23]Although hormonal influences appear much stronger in lower animals than in humans, drugs that diminish testosterone levels in violent human males will subdue their aggressive tendencies.

_____ is the number of the sentence that states the central point.

IMPLIED MAIN IDEAS/CENTRAL POINT: Test C

A. In the space provided, write the letter of the sentence that best expresses the implied main idea of each of the following paragraphs.

1. [1]In the summer of 1988, a forest fire destroyed over one-fourth of Yellowstone National Park. [2]Park officials had let the fire burn for several weeks before they took measures to put it out.

   [3]The let-burn policy is based on the idea that naturally occurring forest fires contribute to the overall long-term stability of the forest environment. [4]Small forest fires destroy fallen trees and leaves on the forest floor before large amounts of this debris can accumulate and cause larger and more destructive fires. [5]The earlier practice of suppressing all fires may have contributed to the intensity of the 1988 Yellowstone fires because large amounts of tinder had built up on the forest floor. [6]Forest fires also maintain the diversity of plant and animal life. [7]Small fires destroy some tall trees and thus allow for the growth of low bushes and grasses that attract small animal wildlife.

   [8]However, many people criticized the let-burn policy after the Yellowstone fire. [9]Local ranchers were concerned that elk and bison would be driven out of the park and compete with cattle herds for food. [10]Others questioned the safety of allowing a fire during a drought. [11]Many people were confused by a change in policy after a hundred years of anti-fire publicity. [12]Some ecologists pointed out the difficulty of determining what is "natural" in a forest that has been sustained by human activity.

   [13]In the meantime, Yellowstone officials have announced a return to the no-burn policy that existed before 1970, at least until experts agree that letting forest fires burn themselves out is justified.

   A. The Yellowstone fire of '88 resulted in a controversy about whether the let-burn policy had more advantages or disadvantages.
   B. The original no-burn policy for handling forests should never have been changed.
   C. The suppression of fire in forests leads to a buildup of possibly dangerous tinder on the forest floor.
   D. Managing natural resources should best be left in the hands of national park officials.

2. [1]The eighteenth century saw the introduction of two crops from the New World, maize (Indian corn) and the potato. [2]Since maize can be grown only in areas with a great deal of sunny and dry weather, its cultivation spread through Italy and the southeastern part of Europe. [3]Whereas an average ear of grain would yield only about four seeds for every one planted, an ear of maize would yield about seventy or eighty. [4]That made it a "miracle" crop, filling granaries where they had been almost empty before. [5]The potato was an equally miraculous innovation for the European North. [6]Its advantages were numerous: potatoes could be grown on the poorest, sandiest, or wettest of lands where nothing else could be raised; they could be fitted into the smallest of patches. [7]Raising potatoes even in small patches was profitable because the yield of potatoes was extraordinarily abundant. [8]Finally, the potato provided an inexpensive means of improving the human diet. [9]It is rich in calories and contains many vitamins and minerals.

(Continues on next page)

A. Both Indian corn and the potato originated in the New World.

B. Two New World crops—maize and the potato—have both advantages and disadvantages.

C. Two New World crops became important innovations in Europe, one in the sunny, dry south and the other in the north.

D. The discovery of the New World led to various new benefits for Europeans.

B. (3.) Write out the implied main idea of the following paragraph.

[1]An aquatic algae (seaweed) called *algin* is used often in salad dressings, ice cream, and other food products to keep the ingredients from separating. [2]Algae have also made an appearance in the beauty industry. [3]For example, a trendy treatment called thallassotherapy is a modern version of a treatment that was first used in France at the turn of the century. [4]In thallassotherapy, the body is smeared with a seaweed wrap that is the consistency of creamed spinach. [5]The desired result is to make the surface of the skin appear moist. [6]Algae are also used in a variety of cosmetics, including creams and astringents. [7]Extracts from some brown algae have antibacterial properties. [8]Manufacturers of creams and lotions containing these extracts advertise the antiseptic nature of their products. [9]Moreover, several types of seaweed have become popular staples at health-food stores for use in soups, stews, and salads.

Implied main idea: _____

C. (4.) The author has stated the central point of the following textbook selection in one sentence. Find and underline that sentence. Then, in the space provided, write the number of the sentence that contains the central point.

The Writing Process

[1]Writers describe the process of composing in different ways. [2]Some compose entirely in their heads, feeling no need to go through several drafts before approving what they have written. [3]The celebrated philosopher Bertrand Russell stated that after thinking intensely for an entire year about a series of lectures he had agreed to give, he called in a secretary and proceeded "to dictate the whole book without a moment's hesitation." [4]Similarly, the American poet Wallace Stevens composed many of his finest poems during his daily walk to his office, revising only for punctuation and spelling after he had dictated them to his secretary. [5]William Faulkner confessed that he put off writing as long as he could (owing to laziness, he admitted), but once he began, he found it fun, writing "so fast that somebody said my handwriting looks like a caterpillar that crawled through an inkwell and out onto a piece of paper."

[6]More often, however, writers struggle to get their ideas down on paper. [7]Impatient with the notion that writing is spontaneous joy, Wolcott Gibbs once observed that the only man he "ever knew who claimed that composition caused him no pain was a very bad writer, and he is now employed in a filling station." [8]S. J. Perelman confessed at the end of his career that unlike technicians "who are supposed to become more proficient with practice," he found "the effort of writing . . . more arduous all the time." [9]And the desire to escape from the labor of writing prompted the British novelist Anthony Trollope to advise all writers to attach a piece of cobbler's wax to the seat of their chairs to keep themselves securely fastened.

_____ is the number of the sentence that states the central point.

IMPLIED MAIN IDEAS/CENTRAL POINT: Test D

A. In the space provided, write the letter of the sentence that best expresses the implied main idea of each of the following passages.

1. [1]Antarctica represents one of the last resource frontiers left on the planet Earth. [2]It is 98 percent covered by ice, and its low annual precipitation of less than 8 centimeters makes it a virtual desert. [3]Its snow and ice hold 90 percent of the world's fresh water. [4]The ice-covered land is inhospitable to life, but the edge of the ice and the surrounding offshore areas have a rich fauna—whales, penguins, seals, seabirds, fish, and an economically important shrimplike species known as krill. [5]In the early 1900s, several nations claimed territory in Antarctica. [6]Scientific interest in the region grew, and research activities evolved into cooperative research agreements among twelve nations (the United States, the Soviet Union, the United Kingdom, Belgium, Japan, South Africa, New Zealand, France, Australia, Norway, Chile, and Argentina), who were joined by four others (Poland, the Federal Republic of Germany, Brazil, and India) in signing the Antarctic Treaty that took effect in 1961. [7]Sixteen more nations subsequently joined in the treaty. [8]The treaty established Antarctica as a demilitarized, nonnuclear area and guarantees freedom of scientific investigation. [9]The treaty also provides for free exchange of information among all researchers, and the participating nations agree not to assert any territorial claims while the treaty is in effect.

   A. Antarctica is a fascinating frontier with most of the world's fresh water and a rich variety of fauna.
   B. Antarctica has proven that the nations of the world can work together in peace.
   C. The Antarctic Treaty was originally agreed to by twelve nations who were then joined by four other nations.
   D. Since the early 1900s, scientific interest in resource-rich Antarctica led to cooperation among numerous nations.

2. [1]In a merger, two or more firms combine to form one company. [2]A vertical merger occurs between firms at different levels in a channel of distribution. [3]The primary reasons for a vertical merger are (1) to assure adequate raw materials and supplies for products or (2) to increase available distribution outlets for them. [4]In a backward vertical merger, a firm joins with a supplier; in a forward vertical merger, a producer buys a firm that distributes its products. [5]For instance, several Hollywood movie studios have acquired video rental companies in order to profit from that lucrative distribution outlet. [6]A horizontal merger joins firms in the same industry that wish to diversify and offer a more complete product line. [7]For example, two banks might combine to offer expanded services to a larger customer base. [8]A conglomerate merger combines unrelated firms. [9]The most common reasons for a conglomerate merger are to diversify, to spur sales growth, or to spend a cash surplus that might otherwise make the holder a tempting target for a takeover effort. [10]Conglomerate mergers may involve firms in totally unrelated industries. [11]Consider Metromedia International Group Inc., a venture that combines moviemaker Orion Pictures, several eastern European telecommunications companies, and Actava Group, the maker of Snapper lawn mowers.

   A. There are various reasons for firms of all types to merge.
   B. Mergers can be divided into three types, each with its own benefits.
   C. Hollywood movie studios that have acquired video rental companies illustrate the backward vertical merger.
   D. Companies must consider all the advantages and disadvantages of a merger before making a final decision to merge.   *(Continues on next page)*

B. (3.) Write out the implied main idea of the following paragraph.

¹Envy is a desire to acquire something that another person possesses. ²People are envious when they wish they could have a house or car that a friend owns, a promotion that a coworker received, the kind of close relationships enjoyed by other couples, or anything else that they currently lack in their lives. ³Typically, this occurs in situations in which people we like or associate with have things or take actions that threaten our definition of ourselves. ⁴Someone who defines himself or herself as successful might become envious if a coworker was given a larger raise, a close friend purchased a more expensive car, or a friend received a higher grade point average. ⁵On the other hand, jealousy is a fear of losing something to which we have become attached. ⁶We are jealous when we fear losing a dating partner or spouse to another person or when we feel excluded from the company of someone we like or love.

Implied main idea: _____

_____

C. (4.) The author has stated the central point of the following textbook selection in one sentence. Find and underline that sentence. Then, in the space provided, write the number of the sentence that contains the central point.

Preindustrial Childhood

¹The traditional preindustrial family was quick to send kids out on their own—at ages as young as 7 and 8. ²This reflected more than mere economic necessity or the fact that unskilled children could perform productive labor in preindustrial economics. ³In preindustrial families, indifference toward children and neglectful childcare practices were common. ⁴A good index of neglect and indifference is found in journals kept by local doctors. ⁵All of these doctors complained about parents leaving their infants and young children alone and untended for much of the day. ⁶Rashes and sores from unchanged swaddling clothes afflicted nearly all infants.

⁷Repeated accounts tell of children burning to death because they were left too close to an open hearth, and reports of unattended infants being eaten by barnyard pigs are frequent. ⁸In the part of France where silkworms were raised, a peasant proverb acknowledged that children were neglected during the busy season: "When the silkworms rise, the kids go to paradise." ⁹Indeed, throughout Europe, rural infants were most likely to die during the harvest season, when they were most neglected.

¹⁰Even when parents were around their infants, they ignored them. ¹¹Mothers rarely sang or talked to their infants when they tended them, nor did they play games with them as the children grew older. ¹²In fact, mothers didn't even refer to children by name, calling a child "it" or, in France, "the creature." . . .

¹³Because of the high rates of infant mortality, it might be understandable that parents were somewhat reluctant to form intense emotional bonds with their babies. ¹⁴But in some parts of France, parents typically did not attend funerals for children younger than 5, and there is widespread evidence that infant deaths often caused little if any regret or sorrow. ¹⁵Instead, parents often expressed relief at the deaths of children, and many proverbs reflected this attitude. ¹⁶Moreover, dead and even dying infants were often simply discarded like refuse and were frequently noticed "lying in the gutters or rotting on the dung-heaps."

¹⁷Large numbers of legitimate infants whose parents were still living were abandoned outside churches or foundling homes. ¹⁸Some scholars suggest that as many as half of the children abandoned in parts of France during the eighteenth century were abandoned by intact families.

_____ is the number of the sentence that states the central point.

RELATIONSHIPS I: Test A

A. Fill in each blank with an appropriate transition from the box. Use each transition once. Then, on the answer line, write the letter of the transition you have chosen.

A. also	B. first of all	C. other
D. third	E. until	

___ 1. [1]In Colonial America, washing clothing was so difficult that some households did it only four times a year. [2]The washing machine of the time was a "pounding barrel" containing a pole topped by a block of wood drilled with holes. [3]Moving the pole up and down caused water to suction through the clothes. [4]_____ the clothesline became common in the 1800s, wet clothes were spread on the ground or draped over a bush to dry.

___ 2. [1]Off-price stores are those stores that sell name-brand merchandise at prices below those in department stores. [2]They are able to do so for a couple of reasons. [3]_____, they take advantage of other people's mistakes and buy overstocked merchandise, irregulars, end-of-season items, and production overruns. [4]Second, they obtain merchandise at cut rates directly from manufacturers.

___ 3. [1]To get an image of an internal organ, a doctor sends an endoscope into the body, either through one of its natural openings or through one made especially for the purpose. [2]An endoscope is a flexible tube containing two separate bundles of fibers, each serving a different purpose. [3]One carries light into the opening, to illuminate the area being examined; the _____ picks up light reflected off the tissues and carries it back to the physician's eye or to the camera.

___ 4. [1]Even a quarrel can be done well or poorly. [2]According to some psychologists, there are several things to avoid when arguing. [3]One thing to avoid is bringing up unrelated issues from other situations. [4]You should also avoid using your knowledge of a person to humiliate him or her. A [5]_____ thing to avoid is pretending to agree with the other person while harboring resentment.

___ 5. [1]For most Americans, work is more than merely a means to food, shelter, and physical warmth. [2]When people work, they contribute to society. [3]The fact that they receive pay for their work indicates that what they do is needed by other people, and that they are a necessary part of the social fabric. [4]Work is _____ a major social mechanism for providing people with personal and social identities. [5]Much of who individuals are, to themselves and others, is interwoven with how they earn their livelihood.

(Continues on next page)

B. (6–9.) Fill in each blank with an appropriate transition from the box. Use each transition once. Then answer the question that follows.

also	another	eventually
for one thing		

[1]In the late 1800s, the lines between social classes tended to blur in the large cities, much to the discomfort of the wealthy who struggled to separate themselves from the hoi polloi in various ways. [2](6)_____, the rich moved to the suburbs and employed other methods of residential segregation to isolate themselves. [3](7)_____ tactic to protect their exclusive status was to allow their children only to marry within their narrow group of acquaintances. They [4](8)_____ used sports and athletic clubs to set themselves apart. [5]"Gentlemen and ladies," as they styled themselves, they wanted to compete only against opponents of similar dress, speech, education, and wealth. [6]One way to exclude the masses in sports was to engage in those that only the very rich could play. [7]Yachting and polo, for example, demanded nearly unlimited free time, expensive equipment, and a retinue of hired helpers. [8](9)_____, every major Eastern seaboard city had its exclusive yacht club.

___10. The main pattern of organization of the above selection is
    A. list of items.
    B. time order.

RELATIONSHIPS I: Test B

A. Fill in each blank with an appropriate transition from the box. Use each transition once. Then answer the questions that follow.

another	finally	one

[1]Cloning, the process of using genetic material to produce identical offspring, raises many difficult ethical questions which scientists have to answer. [2]These questions stem from the various possible uses of cloning. [3](1)_____ such use may be to assemble genetically a child with superior traits—even if parents lack those characteristics. [4](2)_____ possible use of cloning technology could be to give parents the ability to set aside duplicates of their children, so that if one died, they could produce another child who looked exactly the same. [5]Still another scenario predicts the possibility of using cloned embryos to produce a genetic duplicate if a child needed a bone marrow or kidney transplant, therefore eliminating any possible problem of immune rejection. [6](3)_____, cloning research may even make it possible someday for a woman to give birth to her own twin—a genetic copy of herself.

____ 4. The passage's main pattern of organization is
   A. list of items.
   B. series of events or stages.
   C. series of steps (directions).

____ 5. The total number of major details is
   A. two.
   B. three.
   C. four.

(Continues on next page)

B. (6–10.) Read the textbook passage below, and then answer the question and complete the map that follows. You may wish to number or check the major details within the passage before beginning to complete the map.

[1]Humanistic psychologist Carl Rogers believed that people are basically good and are endowed with tendencies to fulfill their potential. [2]Each of us is like an acorn, primed for growth and fulfillment, unless thwarted by an environment that inhibits growth. [3]Rogers theorized that a growth-promoting climate for people required three conditions. [4]The first of those conditions is genuineness. [5]According to Rogers, people nurture growth by being genuine—by dropping false faces and being open with their own feelings. [6]The second condition, said Rogers, is acceptance. [7]People also nurture growth, he said, by offering "unconditional positive regard"—an attitude of total acceptance toward another person. [8]We sometimes enjoy this gratifying experience in a good marriage, a close family, or an intimate friendship in which we no longer feel a need to explain ourselves and are free to be spontaneous without fear of losing another's esteem. [9]Finally, Rogers said that people nurture growth by being empathic —by nonjudgmentally reflecting feelings and meanings. [10]"Rarely do we listen with real understanding, true empathy," he said. [11]"Yet listening, of this very special kind, is one of the most potent forces for change that I know."

___ 6. The main pattern of organization of the above selection is
  A. list of items.
  B. time order.

7–10. Complete the map of the passage.

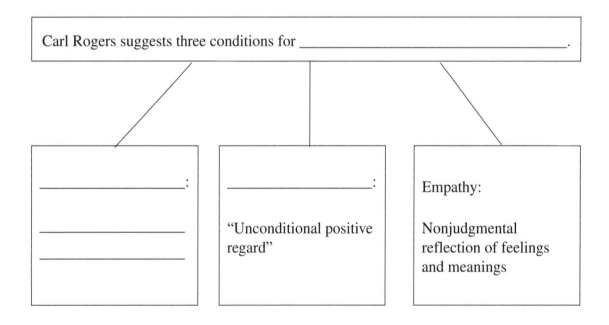

Carl Rogers suggests three conditions for _____.

_____:

_____

_____

_____:

"Unconditional positive regard"

Empathy:

Nonjudgmental reflection of feelings and meanings

RELATIONSHIPS I: Test C

Read each textbook passage and answer the questions or follow the directions provided.

[1]The history of treatment for psychological problems gives sufficient reason for appreciating modern therapies. [2]One of the more dramatic "cures" practiced by primitive "therapists" was a process called trepanning. [3]A hole was bored, chipped, or bashed into the skull of the patient, presumably to relieve pressure or release evil spirits. [4]Actually, trepanning may have simply been an excuse to kill people who were unusual, since many of the "patients" didn't survive the "treatment." [5]During the Middle Ages, treatment for the mentally ill in Europe focused on demonology. [6]Abnormal behavior was attributed to supernatural forces such as possession by the devil or the curses of witches or wizards. [7]Exorcism, which often took the form of physical torture, was used to drive out the evil. [8]The idea that the emotionally disturbed are "mentally ill" and that they should be treated compassionately emerged after 1793. [9]This was the year Philippe Pinel changed the Bicetre Asylum in Paris from a squalid "madhouse" into a mental hospital by personally unchaining the inmates.

_____ 1. The author presents the supporting details in
A. a list that could have been written in any order.
B. the time order in which the details occurred.

_____ 2. The supporting details are
A. modern therapies.
B. ways of treating psychological problems.
C. abnormal behaviors.
D. supernatural beliefs during the Middle Ages.

3. A transition that introduces a major detail of the paragraph is _____.

[1]Dr. Albert Merabian has researched interpersonal communications extensively, and he estimates that the majority of a message is composed of nonverbal communication. [2]His studies show that 55 percent of the total message sent is composed of factors such as facial expressions, gestures, posture, and territoriality. [3]Next most important is the tone used. [4]The tone may indicate that you are being sarcastic, serious, romantic, and so forth. [5]Tone is estimated to account for 38 percent of the total possible message. [6]That leaves just 7 percent for the _____ component—the verbal part. [7]The verbal message—the actual words—might be thought by many as the most important part of an message. [8]In reality the words themselves are not nearly as important as the tone with which they are spoken and the nonverbal cues that accompany them. [9]To focus on the words increases the chance of miscommunication.

_____ 4. The paragraph
A. lists and discusses types of nonverbal communication.
B. lists and discusses elements of a message.
C. describes stages of communication.
D. presents steps in good communication.

_____ 5. A transition that would fit the blank space is
A. *third.*
B. *fourth.*
C. *later.*

(Continues on next page)

[1]Most social movements aim to change society, but they seek varying degrees of change. [2]Social movements can be classified into four types on the basis of their goals. [3]The first type is revolutionary movements, which seek total, radical change in society. [4]Their goal is to overthrow the existing form of government and replace it with a new one. [5]Revolutionary movements typically resort to violence or some other illegal action. [6]Examples include the revolution for independence in the United States, the Chinese Communist revolution, and the Castro-led revolution in Cuba. [7]The second type of social movement is reform movements. [8]They seek only a partial change in society. [9]They support the existing social system as a whole and want to preserve it, but they aim to improve it by removing its blemishes, typically through legal methods. [10]Each reform movement usually focuses on just one issue. [11]The civil rights movement seeks to rid society of racial discrimination. [12]The women's movement seeks to eliminate gender inequality. [13]The ecology movement seeks to put a stop to environmental pollution.

[14]Third, resistance movements seek to preserve an existing system by resisting social change. [15]The Ku Klux Klan and the United States Nazi party, for example, try to stop racial integration. [16]In Muslim countries, the Islamic revolution seeks to protect the traditional Islamic ways of life against Western influences. [17]Finally, expressive movements seek to change the individual, not society. [18]Many are religious, aimed at converting individuals to a particular faith. [19]These movements enable their members to express their sense of guilt, their joy of redemption, and their devotion to their religion. [20]Examples include the Moonies, Hare Krishnas, and other sects.

____ 6. The main pattern of organization of the above selection is
    A. list of items.
    B. time order.

7–10. Complete the outline of the passage. You may wish to number or check the major details within the passage before beginning to complete the outline.

Main idea: _____

_____

1. Revolutionary movements
    a. Goal: Overthrow and replace government
    b. Methods: _____
    c. Example: American Revolution

2. Reform movements
    a. Goal: Improve society with a partial change, usually regarding one issue
    b. Methods: Typically legal
    c. Example: _____

3. Resistance movements
    a. Goal: Preserve existing system
    b. Methods: Resisting social change
    c. Example: Ku Klux Klan

4. _____
    a. Goal: Change individual, not society
    b. Methods: Often religious
    c. Example: The Moonies

RELATIONSHIPS I: Test D

Read each textbook passage and answer the questions or follow the directions provided.

[1]It was not until after World War II that most Southerners felt the impact of air conditioning. [2]As one historian on the subject commented, "The air conditioner came to the South in a series of waves, and only with the wave of the 1950s was the region truly engulfed." [3]Gradually air conditioning spread to department stores, banks, government buildings, hospitals, schools, and finally, homes and automobiles. [4]Home air conditioning soared _____ the introduction in 1951 of an inexpensive, efficient window unit. [5]By 1960, 18 percent of all Southern homes had either window units or central air conditioning. [6]That number topped 50 percent in 1970 and almost 75 percent by 1980. [7]"The South of the 1970s could claim air-conditioned shopping malls, domed stadiums, dugouts, greenhouses, grain elevators, chicken coops, aircraft hangers, crane cabs, off-shore oil rigs, cattle barns, steel mills, and drive-in movies and restaurants," wrote one historian.

___ 1. The main pattern of organization of the above selection is
   A. list of items.
   B. time order.

___ 2. A transition that would fit the blank space is
   A. *second.*
   B. *after.*
   C. *next.*

[1]Americans have long believed in the attainability of a just social and political order. [2]But at no time was the spirit of a just society stronger than during the 1820s, 1830s, and 1840s, when literally hundreds of utopian communities were created. [3]Shaker communities were one of the earliest utopian "experiments." [4]Aspiring to live like the early Christians, Shakers adopted communal ownership of property and a way of life emphasizing simplicity. [5]Dress was kept simple and uniform; architecture and furniture were devoid of ornament. [6]Robert Owen's experimental community at New Harmony presented a striking contrast to the Shaker colonies. [7]Owen sought to establish common ownership of property and abolish religion. [8]At New Harmony the marriage ceremony was reduced to a single sentence, and children were raised outside of their natural parents' homes. [9]Another utopian experiment was perhaps the most notorious and successful—John Humphrey Noyes's Oneida Community. [10]He established perfectionist communities that practiced communal ownership of property and "complex marriage." [11]Complex marriage meant that every member of the community was married to every member of the opposite sex. [12]The community also conducted experiments in eugenics—the selective control of mating in order to improve the hereditary qualities of children.

___ 3. The pattern of organization for the above selection is
   A. list of items.
   B. time order.

(Continues on next page)

4. A transition that introduces one of the major details of the paragraph is

_____.

_____ 5. The total number of major details is
A. two.
B. three.
C. four.

[1]Famous poets and writers have claimed for centuries that love stems from powerful emotions. [2]However, research has shown that feelings of love are at least in part influenced by various chemicals in the brain. [3]One group of chemicals that is just beginning to be understood are pheromones—substances that promote sexual attraction in the opposite sex. [4]Experiments show that males release a chemical in their sweat that has been shown to be highly appealing to women—particularly during ovulation. [5]Similarly, women produce their own pheromones that draw men's interest—one actually can raise the level of testosterone in a man's bloodstream.

[6]In addition to pheromones, another chemical, phenylethylamine (PEA), plays a crucial role in helping people fall "in love." [7]Related closely to the addictive stimulant drugs called amphetamines, PEA actually causes people to feel a high from their relationship. [8]The "heart-throbbing" sensations new lovers describe and the feelings of excitement and infatuation that are part of new relationships are directly attributed to this chemical. [9]As with many addictive drugs, eventually the body builds up a tolerance to PEA and the strong feelings begin to wear off, usually within two years. [10]This explains why infatuation cannot last forever.

[11]A third group of chemicals—endorphins—appears to be at work in long-term relationships. [12]Endorphins are the body's natural pain relievers. [13]In addition, they produce a sense of security, tranquility, and calm. [14]During physical intimacy, endorphins are released into the bloodstream, creating the feeling of satisfaction and security common to long-term successful relationships.

_____ 6. The main pattern of organization for the above selection is
A. list of items.
B. time order.

7. One transition that introduces a major detail of the selection is _____.

8–10. Complete the outline of the paragraph.

Main idea : _____

_____

1. _____

_____

2. Phenylethylamine (PEA)—Causes the high of new love, which wears off as the body builds up tolerance

3. _____—Are released into the bloodstream, creating a feeling of satisfaction, security, and calm

RELATIONSHIPS II: Test A

A. Fill in each blank with an appropriate transition from the box. Use each transition once. Then, on the answer line, write the letter of the transition you have chosen.

A. as a result	B. because of	C. even though
D. for instance	E. however	F. similarly

_____ 1. ¹Only boxing rivaled baseball in popularity during the late 1800s. ²Boxing began as a largely unstructured sport, but by 1900, businesspeople had reorganized the sport into a profitable activity. ³_____ boxing remained illegal in most parts of America, it produced some of the first national sports heroes.

_____ 2. ¹Sociologists have discovered that people seem to change their patterns of speech as social contexts change. ²_____, a woman asking her son to mow the lawn might give a direct order ("Get that lawn mowed!") but use an indirect phrasing when addressing her husband ("The lawn's getting awfully high").

_____ 3. ¹Can't get your ketchup out of the bottle? ²Here's a great way to get ketchup flowing easily. ³Simply insert an ordinary straw through the bottle's opening, pushing it straight down to the bottom. ⁴_____, air is forced through the ketchup, giving it the environment it needs to pour easily—rather than "avalanche" out.

_____ 4. ¹The increasing influence of the mass media contributes to the success of fast-food restaurants. ²Without saturation advertising and the influence of television and other mass media, fast-food restaurants would not have succeeded as well as they have. ³_____, the extensive advertising employed by such systems as H & R Block, Jenny Craig, and Pearle Vision Centers has helped make them resounding successes.

_____ 5. ¹The "witch hunts" conducted by Joe McCarthy that began in the late 1940s were narrow-minded searches for Communist sympathizers in the United States. ²These "witch hunts" took a heavy toll on the American movie industry. ³One effect was that the studios fired more than three hundred actors, writers, and directors suspected of Communist leanings. ⁴Many more were "blacklisted," which meant they weren't given work by the studios. Also, ⁵_____ the hysteria over Communism, studios avoided making politically liberal films for fear of being branded as Communist.

_____ 6. ¹When first produced, laundry bleach has no odor and is at its highest potency level. ²_____, being on the shelf for a length of time (five to eight days) causes the solution to begin to break down chemically. ³As it breaks down, the chlorine in the mixture gives off a gas, which is the reason certain bleaches exhibit a strong smell. *(Continues on next page)*

B. Label each item with the letter of its main pattern of organization.

- A Definition and example
- B Comparison
- C Contrast
- D Cause and effect

_____ 7. ¹The wealthy of ancient Egypt lived in splendid villas that opened onto fragrant gardens and shady groves. ²Their meals included many kinds of meat, poultry, cakes, fruit, wine, and sweets. ³They ate from vessels of alabaster, gold, and silver, and adorned themselves with costly jewels. ⁴However, the life of the poor was wretched. ⁵Laborers in towns lived in mud-brick hovels whose only furnishings were stools, boxes, and a few crude pottery jars. ⁶A surviving verse from the Middle Kingdom tells of the "weaver in the workshop, with knees against his chest," who "cannot breathe air," and who is "beaten fifty strokes" if he does not keep up with his work.

_____ 8. ¹Projection is an unconscious process of seeing one's own shortcomings in others. ²For example, a greedy shop owner may cheat many of his customers, yet consider himself a pillar of the community and a good Christian. ³How does he justify to himself his greed and dishonesty? ⁴He believes that everyone who enters his store is bent on cheating him any way he or she can. ⁵In reality, few, if any, of his customers share his motives, but he projects his own greed and dishonesty onto them.

_____ 9. ¹The rapid growth of industry in the United States resulted in a series of events that led to the Great Depression. ²Because of the success of industry, much of the country's wealth ended up in the hands of a few. ³As a result, the average American did not have enough money to buy all the products that were being manufactured. ⁴The lack of consumers caused companies to produce less. ⁵Needing fewer workers, they let old employees go and were unable to hire new ones. ⁶Workers therefore had less and less money, causing industry to collapse even more. ⁷As industries shut their plants and workers lost their jobs, banks across the country failed. ⁸In 1930, the first full year of the depression, 1,300 banks closed their doors. ⁹During the next two years, another 3,700 closed.

_____ 10. ¹History never repeats itself exactly, but there are close parallels, such as that between the American Revolution and the Vietnam War. ²In both cases, an extremely powerful country was fighting thousands of miles from home against a relatively small native army, which was supported and supplied by a third country. ³In the case of the Revolution, France was the third country; in the case of Vietnam, it was the Soviet Union. ⁴Just as the British, with their command of the sea, could land troops wherever they wished on the Atlantic coast, so could the United States, with its air superiority, airlift troops wherever it wished in Vietnam. ⁵Both wars were extremely unpopular at home. ⁶But the most striking of the resemblances between the two is that while both great powers often defeated their enemies in large battles, neither was eventually able to win the war.

RELATIONSHIPS II: Test B

Read each paragraph and answer the questions that follow.

A.   [1]When a person's position in society is derived primarily through inheritance, we call this ascribed status; that is, a person's position in society is fixed (or ascribed to him or her by others) on the basis of family background or genetic inheritance. [2]Racial, ethnic, and religious differences, as well as gender, often serve as the basis for ascribed status. [3]The caste system in India has long been an extreme example of a social structure based on ascribed status. [4]Each level in society is known as a caste. [5]Everyone is born belonging to a specific caste. [6]The caste of the parents thus generally determines the status of their children, regardless of ability or merit.

____ 1. The main pattern of organization of the selection is
   A. definition-example.
   B. cause-effect.
   C. comparison and/or contrast.

2. The transition that signals the pattern of organization is _____.

B.   [1]One of the factors that greatly influenced the development of the West was a simple product: barbed wire. [2]Cheap, easy to string for hundreds of miles, and able to contain aggressive range animals, barbed wire was the key to the success of the agricultural effort. [3]Because of that simple product, the once unlimited range was reduced to private holdings by barbed wire fences, and agriculture on newly protected lands grew. [4]Nomadic herds of wild animals were restricted and died out, and the cattle and sheep industries could no longer rely upon unobstructed access to public land for forage. [5]These changes in turn led to social and transportation system changes which tamed the West.

____ 3. The main patterns of organization of the selection are list of items and
   A. definition-example.
   B. cause-effect.
   C. comparison and/or contrast.

4. One transition that signals the pattern of organization is _____.

C.   [1]Capitalists say that market forces should determine both products and prices and that it is healthy for people to strive after profits. [2]They believe the potential for profit encourages people to develop and produce new products desired by the public, while workers are motivated to work hard so that they can make as much money as possible in order to purchase most goods. [3]In contrast, socialists believe that profit is immoral, that it represents *excess value* extracted from workers. [4]Karl Marx made the point that because an item's value represents the work that goes into it, there can be no profit unless workers are paid less than the value of their labor. [5]Profit, then, represents an amount withheld from workers. [6]To protect workers from this exploitation, socialists believe that the government should own the means of production, using them not for

(Continues on next page)

profit, but to produce and distribute items according to people's needs rather than their ability to pay.

_____ 5. The main patterns of organization of the selection are list of items and
   A. definition-example.
   B. cause-effect.
   C. comparison and/or contrast.

6. The transition that signals the pattern of organization is _____.

D. ¹There are three main sources of large-scale cultural change. ²The first is an alteration in the natural environment. ³A change in the climate, a shortage of wheat or gasoline or some other resource, a sudden rise or fall in population—all force people to adapt. ⁴They cannot go on living exactly as they did in the past. ⁵The second cause of cultural change is contact with groups whose norms, values, and technology are different. ⁶Cultural contact may be friendly or hostile, voluntary or involuntary, mutual (trade relations or a student exchange program) or one-sided (an invasion by military forces or technical advisors who impose their way of doing things). ⁷The third source of cultural change is *discovery* and *invention*. ⁸*Discovery* is uncovering of new knowledge about, or new uses for, something that already exists (such as oil in Mexico, the structure of genes, or the subculture of adolescents). ⁹*Invention* is a recombination of existing knowledge and materials to create something new (such as the steam engine, the airplane, the cubist style of painting, or democracy). ¹⁰Any one of these sources can lead to major change in a group's overall design for living.

_____ 7. The main patterns of organization of the selection are list of items and
   A. definition-example.
   B. cause-effect.
   C. comparison and/or contrast.

8. One transition that signals the pattern of organization is _____.

E. ¹When Charles Dickens told the story of the French Revolution in his classic novel *A Tale of Two Cities*, he based much of his tale on solid historical fact. ²History books mention the wastefulness of nobility; in like manner, Dickens tells of a French nobleman who required four servants just to bring him a cup of hot chocolate. ³History books detail the sorry conditions of the prisons; similarly, Dickens writes of dreadful diseases that overcame prisoners, who often died before their sentences could be carried out. ⁴But the most memorable features of *A Tale of Two Cities* are the characters, who are Dickens's own creations and have little to do with history. ⁵The villain Madame Defarge, for instance, never really existed. ⁶And history does not mention the heroic Sydney Carton or his famous sacrifice.

_____ 9. The main patterns of organization of the selection are list of items and
   A. definition-example.
   B. cause-effect.
   C. comparison and/or contrast.

10. One transition that signals the pattern of organization is _____.

RELATIONSHIPS II: Test C

A. Read the textbook paragraph below. Then answer the question and complete the outline that follows.

> ¹An invisible barrier keeps women from reaching the executive suite. ²What are the reasons for this barrier? ³Researchers have found that women tend not to be in the "pipeline" that leads to the top—marketing, sales, and production—positions related to the corporate bottom line. ⁴Instead, women are more likely to be working in human resources or public relations. ⁵Some say the reason women aren't in the "pipeline" positions is the male corporate culture. ⁶Men, who dominate the executive suite, tend to stereotype potential leaders as people who look like themselves. ⁷They also stereotype women as better at providing "support." ⁸Another fundamental reason for the barrier to women's entering the executive suite is that women—even those who are in pipeline positions—lack mentors, successful executives who will take an interest in them and teach them the ropes.

____ 1. The main organizational patterns of the paragraph are list of items and

    A. definition-example.

    B. cause-effect.

    C. comparison.

    D. contrast.

2–5. Complete the outline of the paragraph by writing in the heading and the missing supporting details.

Main idea: _____

_____

1. _____

_____

    a. Men tend to stereotype potential leaders as those who look like themselves.

    b. _____

_____

2. _____

_____

(Continues on next page)

B. Read the textbook passage below. Then answer the question and complete the map that follows.

¹Mutualism is a relationship in which two organisms live together or cooperate with each other for mutual benefit. ²For example, termites eat wood but are unable to digest its cellulose. ³The cellulose is digested by protozoa that live in the termite's gut. ⁴Termites benefit from the presence of the protozoa by getting food digested, and the protozoa benefit by being protected by the termite's body. ⁵In fact, under normal conditions the protozoa would be unable to live outside of the termite's body.

⁶Another interesting example of a mutualistic relationship is that of ants and acacia trees in Central and South America. ⁷For a long time, scientists knew that the bull thorn acacia housed large numbers of ants. ⁸Careful study of this relationship has revealed the reason. ⁹The acacia tree provides a home for ants in the form of large thorns on its stem. ¹⁰Sometimes ten or fifteen ants can fit into one thorn. ¹¹The tree also produces special growths on its leaves called beltian bodies. ¹²Chemical analysis of these structures revealed that they are full of glycogen, which is also called animal starch. ¹³The plant has a biochemical pathway that produces food used by ants. ¹⁴The acacia derives benefits too. ¹⁵Ants, protective of their food and housing, attack any predators that attempt to eat the acacia. ¹⁶In addition, the ants destroy other plants that, if allowed to grow, would shade the acacia and cut off its light. ¹⁷Bull thorn acacias are often found standing alone in open clearings because the ants have mowed down all the surrounding vegetation.

____ 6. The passage's main pattern of organization is
   A. definition-example.
   B. cause-effect.
   C. comparison and/or contrast.

7–10. Complete the map of the passage by writing in the main idea and the missing supporting details.

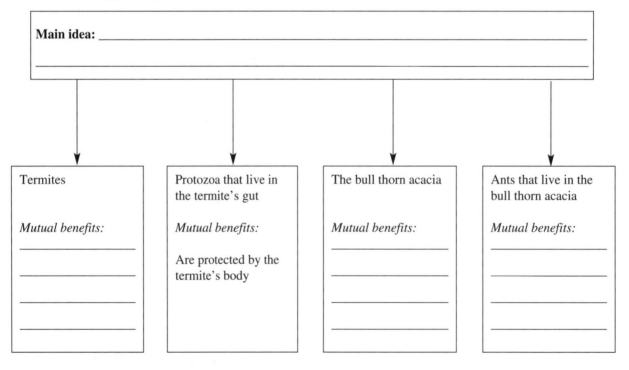

Main idea: _____
_____

Termites	Protozoa that live in the termite's gut	The bull thorn acacia	Ants that live in the bull thorn acacia
Mutual benefits: _____ _____ _____ _____	*Mutual benefits:* Are protected by the termite's body	*Mutual benefits:* _____ _____ _____ _____	*Mutual benefits:* _____ _____ _____ _____

RELATIONSHIPS II: Test D

A. Read the textbook passage below. Then answer the question and complete the outline that follows.

> [1]The population of Europe as a whole, estimated roughly at 205 million by 1800, had risen to 274 million by 1850, and to 320 million by 1870. [2]Various reasons for the rapid population growth in Europe have been suggested. [3]Several explanations support the notion of improved health. [4]One contributing factor to this continued growth may have been a decline in the virulence of certain fatal diseases as a result of the cyclical potency of microbes. [5]Certainly the curbing of cholera, through the adoption of sanitary reforms, and smallpox, as Edward Jenner's technique of vaccination gained gradual acceptance after 1796, help to explain the population trend. [6]Also, the availability of less expensive foods of high nutritional value—most notably the potato—and the ability to transport foodstuffs cheaply by rail meant European populations would not suffer as much from undernourishment as in the past. [7]The population increase was probably also the result of rising birth rates caused by earlier marriages. [8]As serfdom declined, peasants tended to set up households at a younger age. [9]The spread of cottage industries provided an alternate income source, allowing more rural couples to marry and set up households even without the inheritance of land.

___ 1. The organizational patterns of the passage are list of items and
   A. definition-example.
   B. comparison and/or contrast.
   C. cause-effect.

2–5. Complete the outline of the paragraph by writing in the main idea and the three missing supporting details.

Main idea: _____

_____

1. Less fatal illness
   a. Decline in certain fatal diseases due to cyclical potency of microbes

   b. _____

   c. Curbing of smallpox due to vaccination

2. _____
   a. Availability of less expensive foods of high nutritional value (especially the potato)
   b. Ability to transport food cheaply by rail

3. _____
   a. As serfdom declined, peasants tended to set up households at younger age
   b. Cottage industries allowed more rural couples to set up households even if they inherited no land to work

(Continues on next page)

B. Read the textbook paragraph below. Then answer the question and complete the map that follows.

[1]Whether a nation has a presidential or a parliamentary system makes a big difference in the identity and powers of the chief executive. [2]First of all, people become president by winning elections, and sometimes winning is easier if you can show the voters that you are not part of "the mess in Washington." [3]For instance, neither Jimmy Carter nor Ronald Reagan held national office before becoming president. [4]Prime ministers are selected from among people already in Parliament, and so they are always insiders. [5]They may or may not have any real personal following at the time they are appointed. [6]Margaret Thatcher was largely unknown to the country when she became prime minister in 1979.

[7]Presidents and prime ministers also differ in how they choose cabinet members. [8]Presidents choose cabinet members from outside Congress. [9]Under the Constitution no sitting member of Congress can hold office in the executive branch. [10]In contrast, the persons chosen by a prime minister to be in the cabinet are almost always members of Parliament. [11]This is one way by which the prime minister exercises control over the legislature. [12]If you were an ambitious member of Parliament, then you would not be likely to antagonize the person who appointed people to important posts.

[13]Finally, presidents have no guaranteed majority in the legislature. [14]A president's party often does not have a congressional majority. [15]In contrast, a prime minister's party (or coalition) always has a majority in Parliament; if it did not, somebody else would be prime minister.

___ 6. The organizational patterns of the passage are list of items and
   A. definition-example.
   B. comparison and/or contrast.
   C. cause-effect.

7–10. Complete the map of the paragraph by completing the main idea and filling in the missing major supporting details.

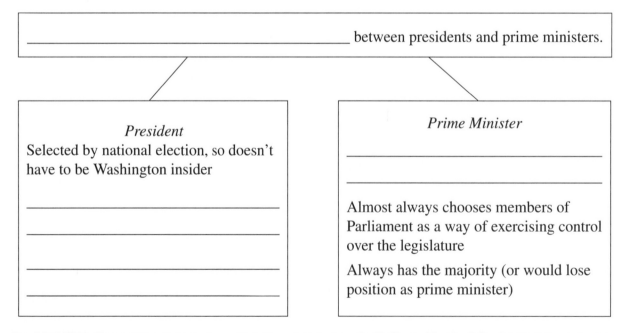

_____ between presidents and prime ministers.

President
Selected by national election, so doesn't have to be Washington insider

_____

_____

_____

Prime Minister

_____

_____

Almost always chooses members of Parliament as a way of exercising control over the legislature

Always has the majority (or would lose position as prime minister)

FACT AND OPINION: Test A

A. Five of the statements below are facts, and five are opinions. Identify statements of fact with an **F** and statements of opinion with an **O**.

_____ 1. According to one survey, the typical American adult spends an average of fourteen weekend hours on chores.

_____ 2. Weekends should be times for relaxing.

_____ 3. Baseball used to be exciting to watch, but now it's just big business.

_____ 4. In 1846, a New York Knickerbocker player was fined six cents for swearing at the umpire.

_____ 5. Elephants have been known to run as fast as twenty-four miles per hour for short distances.

_____ 6. African elephants are still being killed for their ivory tusks.

_____ 7. The elephant is a wonderful creature that should be protected.

_____ 8. No time in American history was more exciting than the settling of the West.

_____ 9. During the 1840s, tens of thousands of American families chalked "GTT" (Gone to Texas) on their gates or painted "California or Bust" on their wagons and joined the trek westward.

_____ 10. Those pioneers who traveled west in the 1800s were the last American heroes.

B. Here are short reviews taken from a newspaper movie guide. Some provide only factual reports; others contain opinions about the movie as well. Identify the factual reviews with an **F**; identify those that also contain the reviewer's opinion with an **F+O**.

_____ 11. **Dr. Doolittle, '98.** Eddie Murphy. A remake of the Hugh Lofting stories about the physician who can communicate with animals.

_____ 12. **Intolerable Cruelty, '03.** George Clooney, Catherine Zeta-Jones. A fast-moving comedy about a divorce lawyer and gold digger trying to get the best of each other. Laughs aplenty, and a sexy, goofy, irreverent charm.

_____ 13. **Radio, '03.** Cuba Gooding, Jr. and Ed Harris star in this story of a mentally challenged man and the high school football coach who decides to help him.

(Continues on next page)

_____ 14. **Death Takes a Holiday, '34.** Fredric March, Evelyn Venable. Lovely and interesting meditation on the supernatural. Death takes human form to visit Earth and learn why people fear him.

_____ 15. **Beloved, '98.** Oprah Winfrey, Danny Glover. Powerful performances hold together this somewhat uneven adaptation of Toni Morrison's novel about the legacy of slavery after the Civil War.

C. The book review below contains five sentences. Each sentence is fact or opinion. In addition, one sentence expresses both a fact and an opinion. Identify the facts with an **F**, the opinions with an **O**, and the statement of fact *and* opinion with an **F+O**.

[16]M. Scott Peck, M.D., has written more recent books, but none is as strong, persuasive, and encouraging as *The Road Less Traveled*. [17]First published in 1978, the book is still being sold in bookstores around the country. [18]Subtitled "A New Psychology of Love, Traditional Values and Spiritual Growth," it's about facing and solving life's problems. [19]A psychiatrist, Peck has drawn from his work with patients "as they struggled to avoid or to gain ever greater levels of maturity" as well as on his own life. [20]This book is sure to inspire every reader to reach a greater level of self-understanding.

16. _____   17. _____   18. _____   19. _____   20. _____

FACT AND OPINION: Test B

A. Five of the statements below are facts, and five are opinions. In addition, two statements include both fact and opinion. Identify facts with an **F**, opinions with an **O**, and each statement of fact *and* opinion with an **F+O**.

_____ 1. In 1939, there were fewer than two thousand private TV sets in the entire United States.

_____ 2. School-age children should watch television for no more than one hour a day.

_____ 3. Television is as addictive as any drug on the market today.

_____ 4. Despite the popularity of television, booksellers across the country have reported record sales in recent years.

_____ 5. The growing popularity of television and electronic books will eventually close all bookstores.

_____ 6. Games of chance should be made illegal everywhere except in casinos.

_____ 7. Poker is appealing because it is simple to learn; can be played by two to ten players; and, best of all, is played for serious money.

_____ 8. For over a century, a backstage game of poker has been going on during intermission at the Metropolitan Opera in New York City.

_____ 9. When abolitionist Abby Kelly requested permission to speak at the meeting of the Connecticut Anti-Slavery Society in 1840, the members voted to grant her permission.

_____ 10. The chairman of the Connecticut Anti-Slavery Society meeting immediately resigned his post with the declaration that he would not preside over a group that allowed women to speak.

_____ 11. To inspire pride and good citizenship in our nation's children, every student should travel to Washington, D.C., and visit the Smithsonian Museum at least once.

_____ 12. The Smithsonian, a national treasure, is a collection of museums that care for 140 million items, including such wonderful memorabilia as Dorothy's ruby slippers from *The Wizard of Oz*.

(Continues on next page)

B. The passage below contains five sentences. Identify each sentence with an **F** (for fact), an **O** (for the author's opinion), or **F+O** (for the one sentence that is a combination of fact *and* opinion).

   ¹³At the Old Bethpage Village Restoration in Old Bethpage, New York, baseball is played the nineteenth-century way. ¹⁴The program runs two leagues—one that plays by 1866 rules (including underhand pitching) and one that follows 1887 rules (which call for overhand pitching). ¹⁵In both cases, games are played on grass fields, foul balls don't count as strikes, and players are entitled to four strikes and five balls. ¹⁶Players make the games even more fun and realistic by using charming period expressions, such as "red hot" and "what the blazes!" ¹⁷Americans would be well served if more such instructive and entertaining programs were available throughout the country.

   13. _____   14. _____   15. _____   16. _____   17. _____

C. Below is an excerpt from "The Quiet Hour" (the first reading in Part I of the book). After reading the excerpt, identify each listed statement from the passage as either fact (**F**) or opinion (**O**).

   ¹Economically, the quiet hour would produce screams of outrage from the networks, which would lose an hour or so of prime-time advertising revenues; and from the sponsors, who would have that much less opportunity to peddle us deodorants and hemorrhoid preparations while we are trying to digest our dinners. ²But given the vast sums the networks waste on such pompous drivel as almost any of the TV "mini-series," I'm sure they could make do. ³The real question is, how long are we going to keep passively selling our own and our children's souls to keep Madison Avenue on Easy Street?
   ⁴At first glance, the notion of a TV-less hour seems radical. ⁵What will parents do without the electronic baby sitter? ⁶How will we spend the quiet? ⁷But it is not radical at all. ⁸It has been only about fifty years since television came to dominate American free time. ⁹Those of us 60 and older can remember television-free childhoods, spent partly with radio—which at least involved the listener's imagination—but also with reading, learning, talking, playing games, inventing new diversions, creating fantasylands.

   _____ 18. But given the vast sums the networks waste on such pompous drivel as almost any of the TV "mini-series," I'm sure they could make do.

   _____ 19. The real question is, how long are we going to keep passively selling our own and our children's souls to keep Madison Avenue on Easy Street?

   _____ 20. Those of us 60 and older can remember television-free childhoods.

FACT AND OPINION: Test C

A. Identify each of the following textbook excerpts as fact (**F**), the author's opinion (**O**), or a combination of fact *and* opinion (**F+O**). Three items combine fact and opinion.

_____ 1. Research to distinguish forced smiles from genuine ones indicates that different muscles are used in fake smiles.

_____ 2. The Edsel was introduced into the medium-price automobile market in 1957.

_____ 3. The idea for the Edsel was a very good one.

_____ 4. It would be impossible to find a more representative figure of the Italian Renaissance than Leonardo da Vinci, creator of *The Last Supper* and *Mona Lisa*.

_____ 5. American painting in the early nineteenth century was of a quality comparable to that of contemporary European work.

_____ 6. Daniel Webster projected a remarkable appearance of heroic power and moral strength.

_____ 7. The disgraceful conditions existing in mental asylums led Dorothea Dix, a woman of almost saintlike selflessness, to devote thirty years of her life to improve the care of the insane.

_____ 8. On March 12, 1938, as Hitler sent his troops into Austria, Edward R. Murrow described the scene live from Vienna for his radio audience.

_____ 9. The average soldier serving in Vietnam was 19 years old, compared with 26 for World War II.

_____ 10. No theory of socialization has had a greater impact on Western thought than that of Sigmund Freud.

_____ 11. When General Washington's Continental Army entered their Valley Forge winter campsite in December 1777, soldier Joseph Plumb Martin reported that their trail could "be tracked by their blood upon the rough frozen ground."

_____ 12. From 1866 to 1868 Cornelius Vanderbilt of the New York Central waged a futile battle to gain control of the Erie Railroad, headed by a trio of railroad sharks: the corporate buccaneer Daniel Drew, the flamboyant speculator James Fisk, Jr., and the subtle, calculating, and utterly unscrupulous Jay Gould.

B. Following are two textbook passages. Identify each listed statement from the passage as either fact (**F**), the author's opinion (**O**), or fact *and* opinion (**F+O**). Only one statement combines fact and opinion.

¹Some workplaces have instituted a casual day, often Fridays, when the official or unofficial dress code is relaxed or abandoned. ²This is not necessarily a blessing. ³Even though the standards of attire are supposedly lowered, what you wear will still be scrutinized. ⁴Now,

(Continues on next page)

instead of business wear and casual, you may need attire that falls in between these two—something that is now being called "business casual." [5]Also, although the dress restrictions have been eased, this is often done only for those with no client contact. [6]This means that people must check the calendar (to see if it is a casual day) and their schedules (to see if they have outside appointments) before getting dressed in the morning. [7]Although this is a concern, casual dress also has some problems. [8]For many companies, a large problem is that workers have taken the casual concept too far. [9]Workers have come to work in sweatsuits, shorts, and spandex. [10]Another drawback to casual dress, say some, is that it also leads to casual attitudes. [11]One firm found its sales staff felt that casual day was a "no sales call" day; instead of getting one relaxed dress day, the firm got one less work day. [12]The policy was soon reversed.

_____ 13. [A relaxed or abandoned dress code] is not necessarily a blessing.

_____ 14. Workers have come to work in sweatsuits, shorts, and spandex.

_____ 15. Another drawback to casual dress, say some, is that it also leads to casual attitudes.

[1]Ernesto Miranda was hardly the kind of person to influence legal history, but he did, in his own savage way, because of legal efforts on his behalf. [2]A high-school dropout with a criminal record dating to his teen years, Miranda abducted a teenage girl at a Phoenix movie house candy counter in 1963 and drove her into the desert, where he raped her. [3]After being picked up and making a written confession in which he stated that he had been informed of his rights, Miranda was convicted and sentenced to forty to fifty-five years in prison. [4]Society would have been better off if he had stayed there. [5]But at the trial, Miranda's court-appointed lawyer argued that his client had not been told of his right to legal counsel.

[6]The American Civil Liberties Union took the case of *Miranda v. Arizona* all the way to the Supreme Court, where it was heard by the Warren Court in 1966. [7]On June 13, 1966, the Court announced a five-to-four ruling in favor of Miranda that said a criminal suspect must be told of his right to silence, that his remarks may be used against him, and that he had a right to counsel during questioning, even if he could not afford one.

[8]Many citizens hailed this announcement as a great milestone for civil liberties and the protection of the rights of both the innocent and the criminal. [9]Yet it was hard to be happy when a convicted rapist had gone free.

[10]Fortunately, justice was eventually served in the *Miranda* case. [11]Based on new evidence, Miranda was convicted on the same charges of kidnapping and rape, and imprisoned. [12]He was eventually paroled, and ten years after the Court inscribed his name in legal history, Ernesto Miranda died of a knife wound suffered during a bar fight.

_____ 16. Ernesto Miranda was hardly the kind of person to influence legal history, but he did, in his own savage way, because of legal efforts on his behalf.

_____ 17. A high-school dropout with a criminal record dating to his teen years, Miranda abducted a teenage girl at a Phoenix movie house candy counter in 1963 and drove her into the desert, where he raped her.

_____ 18. Society would have been better off if he had stayed there.

_____ 19. The American Civil Liberties Union took the case of *Miranda v. Arizona* all the way to the Supreme Court, where it was heard by the Warren Court in 1966.

_____ 20. He was eventually paroled, and ten years after the Court inscribed his name in legal history, Ernesto Miranda died of a knife wound suffered during a bar fight.

FACT AND OPINION: Test D

A. Identify each of the following textbook excerpts as fact (**F**), opinion (**O**), or a combination of fact *and* opinion (**F+O**). (Two statements combine fact and opinion.)

_____ 1. In 1900 only 4 percent of Americans were age 65 and over; today the figure stands at almost 13 percent.

_____ 2. It's a sad fact that, in all industrialized nations, the lower one's social class, the shorter one's life span tends to be.

_____ 3. We should all work to provide equal health care to all social classes.

_____ 4. Nelson Mandela was given a life sentence in 1964 at age 45; in 1985, he rejected an offer of release in exchange for a promise to refrain from violent or illegal action.

_____ 5. Mandela has approached his job of president with the same cautious determination and moral courage he showed during his imprisonment.

_____ 6. Businesspeople should wake up to their social and environmental responsibilities and try to do the right thing.

_____ 7. Three out of four large companies have adopted a written code of ethics.

_____ 8. One of the best explanations of the relationship between interpersonal communication and self-concept is given by Evelyn Sieburg, who argues that whenever we communicate with people, we present to them a version of ourselves.

_____ 9. The grapevine is perhaps the most interesting of communication networks.

_____ 10. One study estimates that nearly 80 percent of the information acquired through the grapevine is basically accurate.

B. The passage below contains five sentences. Identify each sentence as fact (**F**), opinion (**O**), or a combination of fact *and* opinion (**F+O**).

[11]During the seventeenth to the nineteenth centuries, if a gentleman or occasionally even a lady was insulted, he or she was likely to challenge the offender to a duel. [12]Dueling was a much more efficient and dramatic method of challenging an enemy than the modern method of taking someone to court. [13]For many years duels were conducted with swords; in fact, young men came to Italian fencing schools from all over Europe to learn from masters. [14]Eventually, dueling was done with an even worse weapon—the gun. [15]Today's political squabbles would no doubt be more courteous if dueling with weapons were still in vogue.

11. _____   12. _____   13. _____   14. _____   15. _____

(Continues on next page)

C. Read the following textbook passage. Then identify each listed excerpt from the passage as either a fact (**F**) or an opinion (**O**).

¹Every new nation needs a hero to survive. ²George Washington's greatest contribution to the young United States was that he was a larger-than-life hero. ³Indeed, only in recent times have Washington's life and accomplishments been looked at in a new light.

⁴Washington was born into a modestly prosperous Virginia family. ⁵He spent about eight years in school, but never went to college. ⁶His early military career was remarkable mostly for the fact that he survived it. ⁷Even his ascent to power is suspicious. ⁸After volunteering to serve without pay, he was unanimously chosen commander of the Continental Army when it became apparent that for political reasons a Southerner had to fill the job.

⁹Traditionalists say that, as commander, Washington held together a ragged, ill-equipped army by sheer force of will, chose his commanders well, and became a master of the strategic retreat. ¹⁰But traditionalists have believed too many popular myths. ¹¹The revisionist view holds that Washington was an overly harsh leader who maintained brutal discipline in the ranks, nearly lost the war several times, and was saved only by greater incompetence on the part of the British.

¹²After serving as president for eight years, he returned to the gentleman's life at Mount Vernon, where he caught a chill on a cold December day. ¹³Left alone, he might have survived. ¹⁴Instead his physicians bled him, standard medical procedure in the day, and the treatment probably doomed him.

_____ 16. Every new nation needs a hero to survive.

_____ 17. George Washington's greatest contribution to the young United States was that he was a larger-than-life hero.

_____ 18. He spent about eight years in school, but never went to college.

_____ 19. But traditionalists have believed too many popular myths.

_____ 20. After serving as president for eight years, he returned to the gentleman's life at Mount Vernon, where he caught a chill on a cold December day.

INFERENCES: Test A

A. Read each passage below. Then write the letter of the **one** statement after each passage which is most logically supported by the information given.

¹Where does that road go? ²How does a television work? ³What is that tool used for? ⁴Answering these questions may have no obvious benefit for you. ⁵Exploration and curiosity appear to be motives directed toward no more specific a goal than "finding out." ⁶Even animals will learn a behavior just to be allowed to explore the environment. ⁷Animals also seem to prefer complexity, presumably because more complex forms take longer to know and are therefore more interesting. ⁸Placed in a maze that is painted black, a rat will explore it and learn its way around. ⁹The next time, given a choice between a black maze and a blue one, it will choose the blue one. ¹⁰Apparently the unfamiliarity of the unknown maze has more appeal.

_____ 1. The passage implies that curiosity
    A. occurs only to gain a practical benefit.
    B. is what separates people from animals.
    C. can lead to exploration.

_____ 2. The author implies that rats
    A. fear the challenge of a maze.
    B. are more curious than most other animals.
    C. can see color.

¹What is it about humor that makes us laugh? ²The clue can be found in the fact that almost all jokes contain a contradiction between two realities, usually a conventional and an unconventional one. ³These two realities represent conflicting definitions of the same situation. ⁴To make people laugh, we first make them clearly aware of their taken-for-granted conventional definition of a situation and then surprise them by contradicting that definition with an unconventional one. ⁵Look, for example, at the following joke from a study by one researcher:

⁶My wife comes home and says, "Pack your bags. ⁷I just won $20 million in the California lottery."

⁸"Where are we going? Hawaii? Europe?" I ask jubilantly.

⁹She says, "I don't know where you're going, Doug, as long as it's out of here."

¹⁰The first two sentences set up in our mind the conventional assumption that the married couple will share the joy of winning the lottery. ¹¹The punch line strikes down that assumption with the unexpected, unconventional reality that a presumably loving wife wants to be free from her husband.

_____ 3. The humor in the joke comes from the
    A. wife's good luck.
    B. husband's misunderstanding.
    C. places the husband suggested they might travel to.

_____ 4. Humor
    A. is never related to serious issues.
    B. involves hearing what we expect.
    C. involves surprise.

(Continues on next page)

B. (5–10.) Read the passage below, from *Long Walk to Freedom*, Nelson Mandela's autobiography. It's about events that took place in the Robben Island prison in South Africa, where Mandela spent eighteen of his twenty-seven years in prison. Then put a check (✓) next to the **six** statements which are most logically supported by the information given.

pap: mush   *warders:* guards

[1]Through a plastic-wrapped note hidden in our food drums, we learned in July of 1966 that the men in the general section had embarked on a hunger strike to protest poor conditions. . . . [2]Word was passed among us, and we resolved to initiate a sympathetic strike beginning with our next meal. [3]A hunger strike consists of one thing: not eating.

[4]Because of the time lag in communications, the general prisoners probably did not learn of our participation for a day or so. [5]But we knew that the news would hearten them. . . .

[6]During the first day of our strike, we were served our normal rations and refused to take them. [7]On the second day, we noticed that our portions were larger and a few more vegetables accompanied our pap°. [8]On the third day, juicy pieces of meat were served with supper. [9]By the fourth day, the porridge was glistening with fat, and great hunks of meat and colorful vegetables were steaming on top. [10]The food was positively mouthwatering. [11]The warders° smiled when we passed up the food. [12]The temptation was great, but we resisted, even though we were being driven especially hard at the quarry. [13]We heard that in the main section, prisoners were collapsing and being taken away in wheelbarrows.

[14]I was called to the Head Office for an interview with Colonel Wessels. . . . [15]Wessels was a direct man and demanded to know why we were on a hunger strike. [16]I explained that as political prisoners we saw protest to alter prison conditions as an extension of the anti-apartheid struggle. [17]"But you don't even know why they are striking in F and G," he said. [18]I said that did not matter, that the men in F and G were our brothers and that our struggle was indivisible. [19]He snorted, and dismissed me.

[20]The following day we learned of an extraordinary course of events: the warders had gone on their own food boycott, refusing to go to their own cafeteria. [21]They were not striking in support of us, but had decided that if we could do such a thing, why couldn't they? [22]They were demanding better food and improved living conditions. [23]The combination of the two strikes was too much for the authorities. [24]They settled with the warders and then, a day or two later, we learned the authorities had gone to the general section and asked for three representatives to negotiate changes. [25]The general prisoners declared victory and called off the hunger strike. [26]We followed suit a day later.

_____ 1. Mandela and others were in a special section of the prison.

_____ 2. Prisoners in Mandela's section had to communicate secretly with those in the general section.

_____ 3. Before the hunger strike, inmate dinners in Mandela's section usually contained big pieces of vegetables and meat.

_____ 4. The prisoners in Mandela's section were served tempting food to bring back their strength after the fast.

_____ 5. The prisoners in Mandela's section were served tempting food to get them to stop their sympathetic hunger strike.

_____ 6. The prison officials recognized that the sympathetic strike in Mandela's section strengthened the strike in the general section.

_____ 7. It was easy to stay on the hunger strike.

_____ 8. Mandela and his fellow prisoners were highly motivated to show their support of their fellow prisoners.

_____ 9. The warders were more clever than the prisoners.

_____ 10. A hunger strike is one tool the weak can use to influence those in power.

INFERENCES: Test B

A. Following are the first three stanzas of William Blake's poem "The Fly." Read the poem, and then write the letter of the best answer to each question.

The Fly

Little Fly,
Thy summer's play
My thoughtless hand
Has brushed away.

Am not I
a fly like thee?
Or art thou not
A man like me?

For I dance,
and drink, and sing,
Till some blind hand
Shall brush my wing.

William Blake

____ 1. The speaker has
   A. played with the fly.
   B. lightly brushed the fly away.
   C. killed the fly.

____ 2. The speaker compares himself to
   A. summer's play.
   B. a fly.
   C. a dance.

____ 3. The speaker feels his life is
   A. not worth living.
   B. enjoyable.
   C. not enjoyable.

____ 4. We can conclude that the image of a wing being brushed symbolizes
   A. dancing.
   B. drinking.
   C. dying.

____ 5. The speaker feels death comes
   A. according to a plan.
   B. at random.

(Continues on next page)

B. (6–10.) Read the following textbook passage. Then put a check (✓) next to the **five** statements which are most logically supported by the information given.

¹Without a native mythology, America had to manufacture its heroes. ²Thus, when America turned one hundred years old, the American media created a suitably heroic model in the cowboys of the Wild West. ³The image was of the steely-eyed cattle drivers living a life of reckless individualism, braving the elements, fighting off brutal Indian attacks; or of heroic lawmen dueling with sixguns in the streets at high noon. ⁴This image became so powerful that it entered the American political mentality. ⁵In fact, it shaped the images of Presidents Teddy Roosevelt, Lyndon Johnson, and Ronald Reagan. ⁶However, the heyday of the cowboy lasted only about twenty years, from 1867 to 1887, and wasn't as glamorous or as romantically dangerous as it had been portrayed. ⁷The modern politicians' comparison of drug-ravaged urban streets to the Wild West does a disservice to the West. ⁸The famed cow and mining towns of Tombstone, Abilene, Dodge City, and Deadwood had fewer shootouts and killings in their combined history than modern Washington, D.C., has in a few months.

_____ 1. American mythology is influenced only by fact.

_____ 2. The author implies that most or all cultures need or want a native mythology.

_____ 3. The author feels that the Wild West of the 1800s was more dangerous than urban areas of today.

_____ 4. Images in a culture's media—regardless of how true they are—can influence the mentality of the people.

_____ 5. The author feels Presidents Teddy Roosevelt, Lyndon Johnson, and Ronald Reagan should not have been elected.

_____ 6. The author suggests that the positive qualities of the cowboy of the American media were incorporated into the public images of Presidents Roosevelt, Johnson, and Reagan.

_____ 7. The passage suggests that lawmen of the 1800s were not brave.

_____ 8. We can deduce that the cowboy got his name from his work with cattle.

_____ 9. The occupation of cowboy totally disappeared from America in the late 1880s.

_____ 10. Industries of the American West in the 1800s included mining and cattle ranching.

INFERENCES: Test C

A. Read the graph below. Then put a check (✓) by the **five** statements that are most logically based on the graph.

Unemployment, 1929–1942

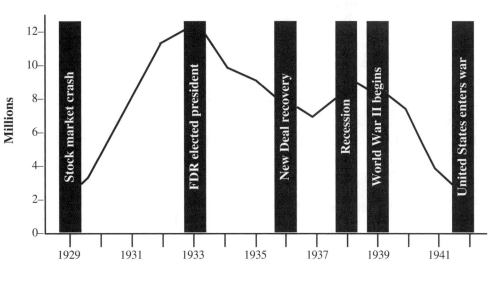

Source: *America and Its People*

_____ 1. In 1929, nobody was unemployed.

_____ 2. In the year after the stock-market crash, unemployment reached its highest point for the years 1929-1942.

_____ 3. It took about four years for unemployment to peak after the stock-market crash.

_____ 4. One problem FDR (Franklin Delano Roosevelt) faced after being elected president was great unemployment.

_____ 5. FDR had no success in lowering the unemployment rate.

_____ 6. The unemployment rate began to decrease after FDR became president.

_____ 7. By 1937, unemployment became as low as it had been before the stock-market crash.

_____ 8. The New Deal Recovery began to reverse in 1937.

_____ 9. Unemployment went up during World War II.

_____ 10. We can infer that during World War II, the unemployed found work in defense industries and the armed forces.

(Continues on next page)

B. (6–10.) Read the following passage from an essay on culture by American anthropologist Clyde Kluckhohn (1905–1960). Then put a check (✓) by the **five** statements which are most logically supported by the information given.

promiscuous: active sexually and relatively unselective about sexual partners
celibacy: going without sexual activity
reciprocities: exchanges

¹Every culture must deal with the sexual instinct. ²Some, however, seek to deny all sexual expression before marriage, whereas a Polynesian adolescent who was not promiscuous° would be distinctly abnormal. ³Some cultures enforce lifelong monogamy, while others, like our own, tolerate serial monogamy; in still other cultures, two or more women may be joined to one man or several men to a single woman. ⁴Homosexuality has been a permitted pattern in the Greco-Roman world, in parts of Islam, and in various primitive tribes. ⁵Large portions of the population of Tibet, and of Christendom at some places and periods, have practiced complete celibacy°. ⁶To us marriage is first and foremost an arrangement between two individuals. ⁷In many more societies marriage is merely one facet of a complicated set of reciprocities°, economic and otherwise, between two families or two clans.

_____ 1. In Polynesia, adolescent virginity is a virtue.

_____ 2. By "serial monogamy," the author means staying married to the same person until he or she dies.

_____ 3. By "serial monogamy," the author means staying married to one person at a time.

_____ 4. The sexual practices considered natural by a member of one society may be considered abnormal in another society.

_____ 5. Kluckhohn implies that marriage can be in part an economic decision.

_____ 6. Kluckhohn implies that homosexuality and celibacy are unnatural methods of expressing the sexual instinct.

_____ 7. The author suggests that all cultures should learn to express the sexual instinct in the same way.

_____ 8. The author suggests that a single human instinct may be expressed in a variety of ways.

_____ 9. The passage implies that the differences in sexual expression between societies are based on genetics.

_____ 10. The passage implies that the basis for the differences in sexual expression between societies is largely cultural.

INFERENCES: Test D

A. Read the following textbook passage. Then put a check (✓) by the **six** statements which are most logically supported by the information given.

¹Is eyewitness testimony, in fact, often inaccurate? ²Stories abound of innocent people who have wasted years in prison because of the testimony of eyewitnesses who were sincerely wrong. ³In the United States alone, some 80,000 trials a year hinge on eyewitness testimony. ⁴So even dozens of such cases would not prove that eyewitness accounts are unreliable. ⁵To assess the accuracy of eyewitness recollections, we need to learn their overall rates of "hits" and "misses." ⁶One way to gather such information is to stage crimes comparable to those in everyday life and then solicit eyewitness reports.

⁷This has now been done many times, sometimes with disconcerting results. ⁸For example, at California State University—Hayward, 141 students witnessed an "assault" on a professor. ⁹Seven weeks later, when asked to identify the assailant from a group of six photographs, 60 percent chose an innocent person. ¹⁰No wonder eyewitnesses to actual crimes sometimes disagree about what they saw.

¹¹Of course, some eyewitnesses are more confident than others—and it's the confident witnesses jurors find most believable. ¹²So it is disconcerting that unless conditions are very favorable, as when the culprit is very distinctive-looking, the certainty of witnesses bears only a modest relation to their accuracy. ¹³Intuitive confidence does correlate somewhat with accuracy, especially through people who make positive identifications. ¹⁴Yet some people—whether right or wrong—chronically express themselves more assertively. ¹⁵That explains why mistaken eyewitnesses are so often persuasive.

¹⁶This finding would surely come as a surprise to members of the 1972 United States Supreme Court. ¹⁷In a judgment that established the position of the U.S. judiciary system regarding eyewitness identifications, the Court, we now realize, goofed. ¹⁸It declared that among the factors to be considered in determining accuracy is "the level of certainty demonstrated by the witness."

¹⁹Errors sneak into our perceptions and our memories because our minds are not videotape machines. ²⁰Rather, we construct our memories based partly on what we perceived at the time and partly on our expectations, beliefs, and current knowledge.

_____ 1. Eyewitness testimony is useless.

_____ 2. More than just a few guilty people have probably gone free.

_____ 3. Eyewitnesses who are wrong are very likely to know that they are wrong.

_____ 4. Two sincere eyewitnesses may give contradictory evidence.

_____ 5. An eyewitness who is not confident may be more accurate than one who is.

_____ 6. Separating out truth from fiction in a trial must be relatively easy.

_____ 7. Jurors must sometimes make very difficult judgments.

_____ 8. The author feels that an ordinary-looking culprit is harder to identify.

_____ 9. Our memories are a mixture of correctly and incorrectly remembered events.

_____ 10. Memories we are quite sure about are very likely to be 100 percent true.

(Continues on next page)

B. The passage below from *The Writing Life*, by Annie Dillard, is about writing a book. After reading the passage, using the definitions as needed, write the letters of the inferences which are most logically supported by the details of the passage.

hie you: hurry   *cache:* a place where supplies are hidden

¹To find a honey tree, first catch a bee. ²Catch a bee when its legs are heavy with pollen; then it is ready for home. ³It is simple enough to catch a bee on a flower: hold a cup or glass above the bee, and when it flies up, cap the cup with a piece of cardboard. ⁴Carry the bee to a nearby open spot—best an elevated one—release it, and watch where it goes. ⁵Keep your eyes on it as long as you can see it, and hie you° to that last known place. ⁶Wait there until you see another bee; catch it, release it, and watch. ⁷Bee after bee will lead toward the honey tree, until you see the final bee enter the tree. ⁸Thoreau describes this process in his journals. ⁹So a book leads its writer.

¹⁰You may wonder how you start, how you catch the first one. ¹¹What do you use for bait?

¹²You have no choice. ¹³One bad winter in the Arctic, and not too long ago, an Algonquin woman and her baby were left alone after everyone else in their winter camp had starved. . . . ¹⁴The woman walked from the camp where everyone had died, and found at a lake a cache°. ¹⁵The cache contained one small fishhook. ¹⁶It was simple to rig a line but she had no bait, and no hope of bait. ¹⁷The baby cried. ¹⁸She took a knife and cut a strip from her own thigh. ¹⁹She fished with the worm of her own flesh and caught a jackfish; she fed the child and herself. ²⁰Of course she saved the fish gut for bait. ²¹She lived alone at the lake, on fish, until spring, when she walked out again and found people.

___ 7. In comparing writing a book to finding a honey tree (as described by Thoreau), Dillard implies that
   A. writing a book is like being in danger of getting stung.
   B. an author finds his or her way through a book one step at a time.
   C. to write a book, one must love nature.

___ 8. The comparison of writing a book to finding a honey tree suggests that writing a book, in the end, is
   A. a doubtful goal.
   B. an impossible goal.
   C. a desirable goal.

___ 9. In writing, "You may wonder how you start, how you catch the first one. What do you use for bait?" Dillard means
   A. Where does one get the very first idea with which to begin a book?
   B. What does one use for income while writing a book?
   C. How does one begin to write a book on fishing?

___ 10. With the anecdote about the Algonquin mother, Dillon implies that
   A. the Algonquin woman has great wisdom about writing.
   B. getting started with a book requires a painful digging within oneself.
   C. writing a book can be a life-or-death matter.

PURPOSE AND TONE: Test A

A. In the space provided, indicate whether the primary purpose of each sentence is to inform (**I**), to persuade (**P**), or to entertain (**E**).

_____ 1. Recent surveys reveal that the average daily television use per household is seven hours.

_____ 2. Our neighbor, the dentist, just got a new license plate for his car; it reads "DR-DKAY."

_____ 3. People convicted of drunk driving should automatically lose their licenses and get jail terms.

_____ 4. Angora sweaters are made from the long, silky hair of Angora goats or rabbits.

_____ 5. The old *Mary Tyler Moore Show,* featuring a cast of likable characters with real and endearing human qualities, should be honored as the best show in the history of television.

_____ 6. When the robot was buried, its owner wrote on its gravestone, "Rust in piece."

B. Each of the following passages illustrates one of the tones named in the box below. In each space provided, write the letter of the tone that applies to the passage. Two tone choices will be left over.

A. angry and impassioned	B. compassionate and caring	C. egotistical
D. apologetic and confused	E. critical but amused	F. objective

_____ 7. Barbie is an airhead. She is the material girl par excellence, the original mall rat. Introduced by Mattel at the Toy Fair in New York in 1959 as "The Barbie Doll: A Shapely Teenage Fashion Model," the long-limbed, 11½-inch-tall clotheshorse has no soul and barely a personality but has been the most successful doll in history. Like a handful of other famous women who need only a first name—Madonna, Jackie, Cher—Barbie has been at the vanguard of fashion for years. But unlike her human counterparts, she is a perpetually pubescent girl instead of a woman, and the only things on her mind are what she wears and the turning of Ken's vinyl head.

_____ 8. People think I have it so easy because my parents still support me. What they don't realize is that sure, I'd like to have a job. But nothing ever works out for me. I worked for a while at a restaurant, but they insisted on putting me on the breakfast shift. Face it, I'm a night owl, and getting up in time to

(Continues on next page)

work early in the day is just impossible for me. I want a job like my friend Alice, who wears nice suits and carries a briefcase to work. I've applied for a couple of jobs like hers, but the people who interview me say I'm not qualified. So what am I supposed to do? Until I'm offered a job that is worth my time, I'm not going to lower myself to accept something that's beneath me.

_____ 9. Mascara, eye shadow, and eyeliner may be part of every modern woman's makeup kit. But it was the ancient Egyptians who first thought of adorning the eyes with artificial cosmetics. Writings and pictures from more than 6,000 years ago demonstrate their interest in decorating the eyes. Ancient recipes survive for the Egyptians' favorite green eye shadows, created from powdered copper ore. Many Egyptian writings mention kohl, a black paste used to darken the lashes and eyebrows and to line the eyes. Fashionable Egyptian men and women also were the first to use eye glitter, made from the shells of beetles crushed to a fine powder.

_____ 10. Laws should be passed to limit the personal wealth of overly rich Americans. One percent of American families control 36 percent of the nation's wealth. Many of them play and prosper while everyday folks struggle to survive. Hundreds of thousands of Americans are homeless, and many poor children suffer from malnutrition. Middle-class families, too, are affected by America's unequal distribution of wealth, with many parents unable to afford to send their children to college. We must join the many ordinary, hard-working Americans all across the country that are speaking out in favor of a more just and appropriate system of distribution of wealth. After all, the spoiled rich don't deserve to be rich.

Name _____

Section _____ Date _____

SCORE: (Number correct) × 10 = _____%

PURPOSE AND TONE: Test B

A. Eight quotations in the story below are preceded by a blank space. Identify the tone of each italicized quotation by writing in the letter of one of these tones. (Two tone choices will be left over.)

A. angry	B. annoyed	C. apologetic
D. confused	E. frightened	F. grateful
G. ironic	H. matter-of-fact	I. optimistic
J. pleading		

The line for course registration wound nearly around the college gymnasium. Barbara and Carol, sophomores at the college, had been waiting in line an hour. During that time they had introduced themselves and swapped information on the teachers they liked and the courses they planned to take.

_____ 1. "*I just don't understand why we have to wait in line so long,*" Barbara said, frowning at the long line ahead of them.

_____ 2. "*It shouldn't be too much longer. The line seems to be moving with more speed now,*" Carol said cheerfully. "*Besides, the wait has given us the chance to get to know each other.*"

When Carol reached the registration table, she signed up for four courses, including Psychology 201. Then she stood to the side to wait for Barbara.

_____ 3. "*I'd also like to register for Psych 201,*" Barbara told the man at the registration table.

_____ 4. "*I'm very sorry,*" the man said sincerely. "*I hate to tell students that they won't be able to take a course, but that one has already been filled. I am sorry.*"

_____ 5. "*What do you mean it's been filled?*" Barbara asked. "*This is the first day of registration. How can it be filled already? That really stinks! What do I pay college tuition for when I can't register for a course I really need this semester?*"

"I'm sorry, but the course is closed," the man insisted.

_____ 6. "*Oh, can't you put just one more student down?*" Barbara asked. "*Please. Just one more?*"

The man shook his head no.

"Can she take my place in the class?" Carol asked the man. "After all, I only just signed up for it a minute ago. And I can easily take it another semester."

_____ 7. "*Well, I . . . Let me see . . . It's a little irregular, but . . . Well, I don't know,*" he said.

(Continues on next page)

"I'm equally interested in other courses," Carol added. "I really don't mind signing up for something else."

"Well, all right," the man agreed.

_____ 8. *"Thanks, Carol. Thanks a lot,"* Barb said. "After all, I'd say an hour is a short time to wait—for a new friend."

B. In the space provided, indicate whether the primary purpose of each passage is to inform (**I**), to persuade (**P**), or to entertain (**E**).

_____ 9. [1]Contrary to popular opinion, fish can drown! [2]Here's how: Fish must extract oxygen from the water in order to live, the same way that we must get oxygen from the air. [3]Therefore, if fish are in an aquarium, ocean, lake, or any other body of water that is poor in oxygen content, they can die. [4]Remember the definition of "drowning" is dying from suffocation in water because access to oxygen is limited or cut off. [5]So, even though fish live in water, they can also die in it—if the water is oxygen-poor.

_____ 10. [1]In the eyes of some, legalizing narcotics is a tantalizing cure-all for America's drug problem. [2]It's time, they say, to stop pouring enormous resources into the war on drugs. . . .

[3]True, the war on drugs is not being won. [4]The courts are overflowing with cases waiting to be tried. [5]Huge seizures of narcotics stop only a small fraction of the drugs coming into the country. [6]Countless dragnets snare only the small-time pusher, not the drug kingpin. [7]Clearly, as it is being waged now, the national fight against drug abuse is futile.

[8]The only thing more costly than continuing the current war on drugs would be the legalization of narcotics; such a measure would claim innumerable human lives. [9]Government figures estimate that crimes involving drug use cost society more than $58 billion a year. [10]Substance abuse is linked with 52 percent of rapes committed, 49 percent of murders, 62 percent of assaults, and 50 percent of traffic fatalities and incidents of spousal abuse. [11]The legalization of narcotics could only push those figures higher.

PURPOSE AND TONE: Test C

Read each of the selections below. Then carefully consider the questions that follow, and write the letters of the best responses.

A. [1]Violence, of course, is rampant in the media. [2]But it is usually set in some kind of moral context. [3]It's usually only the bad guys who commit violent acts against the innocent. [4]When the good guys get violent, it's against those who deserve it. [5]Dirty Harry blows away the scum; he doesn't walk up to a toddler and say, "Make my day."

[6]But in some rock songs, it's the "heroes" who commit the acts. [7]The people we are programmed to identify with are the ones being violent, with women on the receiving end. [8]In a society where rape and assaults on women are endemic, this is no small problem, with millions of young boys watching on their TV screens and listening on their Walkmans.

[9]I think something needs to be done. [10]I'd like to see people in the industry respond to the problem. [11]I'd love to see some women rock stars speak out against violence against women. [12]I would like to see disc jockeys refuse air play to records and videos that contain such violence. [13]At the very least, I want to see the end of the silence. [14]I want journalists and parents and critics and performing artists to keep this issue alive in the public forum.

____ 1. The primary purpose of this paragraph is to
   A. inform readers about violence in the media in the United States today.
   B. persuade readers that rock lyrics that promote violence should be opposed.
   C. entertain readers with descriptions of dramatic media images.

____ 2. The tone of this paragraph can be described as
   A. indignant and determined.
   B. superior and mocking.
   C. understanding and tolerant.
   D. hurt and revengeful.

B. [1]Geologists study rocks. [2]Archaeologists study old civilizations. [3]And atmospheric chemists—the newest breed of scientist—study old air, the kind trapped in bubbles found in glaciers left over from the last ice age or in the ice sheets of Greenland or Antarctica. [4]By studying the history of our atmosphere, these scientists can tell what the air was like in prehistoric times and measure how human activity over two thousand years has changed it. [5]First the ice is cut into cubes, and then the air is sucked out into a vacuum chamber where it is stored in tubes. [6]Finally, the carbon dioxide level is analyzed by a laser beam. [7]It is believed that rising levels of carbon dioxide foretell a rise in temperatures around the world. [8]Thus these scientists may be able to predict dangerous changes in climate and possibly the next ice age.

____ 3. The primary purpose of this paragraph is to
   A. inform.
   B. persuade.
   C. entertain.

(Continues on next page)

_____ 4. The author's tone is
  A. straightforward but disbelieving.
  B. excited and cheerful.
  C. solemn and sympathetic.
  D. straightforward and matter-of-fact.

C. ¹I have a relative who never throws anything away. ²This woman (in the interests of protecting her privacy, I won't tell you who she is. ³Just let me say that I've known her forever and she shares a bedroom with my father) has a stack of _Reader's Digest_ magazines five feet high. ⁴"Someday I'm going to take all the 'It Pays To Increase Your Word Power' quizzes," she says when I suggest it's time to say goodbye to issues from, oh, say, 1974 to 1987. ⁵In her garage are roughly four million cardboard tubes from rolls of toilet paper and paper towels. ⁶"They're so useful for children's art projects," she says, ignoring the fact that her children are all in their mid-twenties. ⁷Her kitchen cupboards are jammed with little aluminum foil pans from chicken pot pies. ⁸"I could make individual lemon-meringue pies for a special dessert," she says. ⁹"You've been saying that for fifteen years," I say. ¹⁰"Well, someday I'm going to," she answers. ¹¹"Just as soon as I've gotten through all those 'Word Power' quizzes."

_____ 5. The primary purpose of this paragraph is to
  A. inform.
  B. persuade.
  C. entertain.

_____ 6. The author's tone is
  A. serious and critical.   C. informal and humorous.
  B. sentimental and optimistic.   D. surprised but compassionate.

D. ¹Young men who have committed minor crimes are generally locked up in jail with older, more hardened lawbreakers. ²There the younger men merely learn to be better criminals. ³A far better idea is to send young offenders to "boot camp." ⁴Such camps have been set up in scattered areas around the country, and more should be established. ⁵In the boot camps, modeled after the ones Army recruits go through, young offenders serve their time as they become more disciplined, increase their self-confidence, and learn to work as part of a team. ⁶Instead of sitting in jail cells all day, the men cooperate in work projects, undergo a tough physical training program, and see other men functioning as positive role models. ⁷"Graduates" of prison boot camp are more likely to become productive citizens than men who have spent their sentences in jail.

_____ 7. The primary purpose of this paragraph is to
  A. inform.
  B. persuade.
  C. entertain.

_____ 8. The author's tone is
  A. direct and concerned.   C. contemptuous and sarcastic.
  B. bitter and cynical.   D. outspoken but ambivalent.

PURPOSE AND TONE: Test D

Read each of the paragraphs below. Then carefully consider the questions that follow, and write the letters of the best responses.

A. ¹There is something as inevitable as labor that takes over around Christmas. ²I feel impelled to the kitchen. ³I feel deep hungers for star-shaped cookies and tangerine ices and caramel cakes, things I never think of during the rest of the year. ⁴Even when I have vowed to keep it simple, I have found myself making the deadly Martha Washington Jetties my mother made every year on the cold back porch. ⁵You have to make them in the cold because the sinful cream, sugar, and pecan fondant balls are dipped by toothpick into chocolate and held up to set before being placed on the chilled wax-papered tray. ⁶The chocolate dip, of course, constantly turns hard and must be taken into the kitchen and heated. ⁷My mother made Jetties endlessly because her friends expected them. ⁸We professed to find them too rich but ate them until our teeth ached. ⁹I still have the cut-glass candy jar they spent their brief tenures in.

____ 1. The purpose of this paragraph is to
A. give readers tips on celebrating a holiday.
B. persuade readers to make Martha Washington Jetties.
C. entertain readers by sharing a sweet experience.

____ 2. The tone of the paragraph can be described as
A. matter-of-fact and solemn.
B. ironic and self-mocking.
C. uncertain and bewildered.
D. nostalgic and affectionate.

B. ¹The differences between complaints and personal criticisms are simple. ²In a complaint, a wife states specifically what is upsetting her, and criticizes her husband's *action*, not her husband, saying how it made her feel: "When you forgot to pick up my clothes at the cleaner's, it made me feel like you don't care about me." ³It is an expression of basic emotional intelligence: assertive, not belligerent or passive. ⁴But in a personal criticism, she uses the specific grievance to launch a global attack on her husband: "You're always so selfish and uncaring. ⁵It just proves I can't trust you to do anything right." ⁶This kind of criticism leaves the person on the receiving end feeling ashamed, disliked, blamed, and defective—all of which are more likely to lead to a defensive response than to steps to improve things.

____ 3. The primary purpose of this paragraph is to
A. inform the reader of two ways to communicate a problem: complaints and personal criticisms.
B. persuade readers that complaints are a better way of communicating a problem than personal criticism.
C. entertain readers with the drama of a husband-wife conflict.

____ 4. The tone of the paragraph can be described as
A. critical but understanding.
B. superior and detached.
C. explanatory and caring.
D. distressed but optimistic.

(Continues on next page)

C. ¹It's easy to see why a lot of people aren't as successful at losing weight as I'm going to be. ²They go for some crazy scheme that doesn't work. ³Not me. ⁴I'm going to do it the old-fashioned way and simply cut down on everything. ⁵After I've lost twenty pounds, I may write a book about it.

⁶Come to think of it, later today I may call my publisher and ask if there'd be any interest in a book about my weight loss. ⁷*How I Lost 20 Pounds in 20 Days,* I may call it. ⁸That would be a good title, give or take a few days.

⁹It might even be a good idea if I started a diary the same day I start losing weight. ¹⁰Maybe I'll start the diary tomorrow, too; then I'll have the book done at the same time I'm twenty pounds lighter.

¹¹Of course, I don't want to get too thin. ¹²I don't want to look drawn. ¹³Doctors advise against going up and down too fast, so I don't want to overdo it. ¹⁴Maybe I'll have an occasional dish of ice cream. ¹⁵It might be better if I didn't try to get too thin too soon. ¹⁶If I lose weight gradually, it might be a good idea if I didn't start the book right away, either. ¹⁷I wouldn't want to finish the book before I'm finished losing weight.

____ 5. The purpose of this paragraph is to
  A. inform readers about a personal decision.
  B. persuade readers of the importance of a healthy weight.
  C. entertain readers by poking fun at an all-too-human approach to dieting.

____ 6. The tone of the paragraph can be described as
  A. serious and caring.   C. warm and respectful.
  B. playful and self-mocking.   D. analytical and instructive.

D. ¹Words can be more powerful, and more treacherous, then we sometimes suspect; communication more difficult than we may think. ²We are all serving life sentences of solitary confinement within our own bodies; like prisoners, we have, as it were, to tap in awkward code to our fellow men in their neighboring cells. ³Further, when A and B converse, their dialogue involves not two characters, as they suppose, but six. ⁴For there is A's real self—call it A_1; there is also A's picture of himself— A_2; there is also B's picture of A—A_3. ⁵And there are three corresponding personalities of B. ⁶With six characters involved even in a simple one-on-one conversation, no wonder we fall into muddles and misunderstandings.

⁷Perhaps then, there are five main reasons for trying to gain some mastery of language:

⁸We have no other way of understanding, informing, misinforming, or persuading one another.

⁹Even alone, we think mainly in words: if our language is muddy, so will our thinking be.

¹⁰By our handling of words we are often revealed and judged. ¹¹"Has he written anything?" said Napoleon of a candidate for an appointment. ¹²"Let me see his *style*."

¹³Without a feeling for language, one remains half-blind and deaf to literature.

¹⁴Our mother tongue is bettered or worsened by the way each generation uses it. ¹⁵Languages evolve like species.

____ 7. The primary purpose of this paragraph is to
  A. inform readers about how to communicate.
  B. persuade readers of the importance of language skills.
  C. entertain readers with interesting observations about people.

____ 8. The tone of this paragraph can be described as
  A. serious and analytical.   C. ambivalent but optimistic.
  B. critical and ironic.   D. joking and affectionate.

ARGUMENT: Test A

A. (1–4.) In each group, one statement is the point of an argument, and the other statements are support for that point. Write the letter of the point of each group.

___ *Group 1*

   A. My boss expects me to work overtime on a moment's notice.

   B. Driving to work now takes me an hour.

   C. I think I ought to look for another job.

   D. I've worked at the restaurant for over a year, and I still haven't gotten a raise.

___ *Group 2*

   A. Couples are marrying later than ever before.

   B. Legal abortion and birth control devices are available.

   C. Dropping fertility rates can be explained by changes in American society.

   D. Fewer couples are opting for large families.

___ *Group 3*

   A. A good, zestful laugh has a positive effect on various systems of the body.

   B. During a hearty laugh, your muscles release tension as they tighten up and relax again.

   C. One psychological effect of laughing is a feeling of well-being—like a "runner's high."

   D. When you laugh, heavy breathing creates a vigorous air exchange in your lungs and a healthy workout for your respiratory system.

___ *Group 4*

   A. The ultraviolet rays of the sun can cause skin cancer, particularly in fair-skinned people.

   B. Up to 90 percent of all wrinkles are caused by the sun.

   C. While people are out in the sun getting a tan, their skin is losing much of its natural moisture, causing the skin to look dry.

   D. A suntan may not be so healthy or good-looking in the long run.

(Continues on next page)

B. Each point is followed by three statements that provide relevant support and three that do not. In the spaces, write the letters of the **three** relevant statements of support.

Point: The county should require residents to recycle newspapers, cans, and bottles.

 A. When the county had a "Clean Up Our Streets" day, everyone pitched in.

 B. By selling the materials to be recycled, the county could gain much-needed funds.

 C. County residents should be taught to buy products that are not wastefully packaged.

 D. Recycling contributes to a stronger environment by making the best use of limited resources.

 E. It wouldn't be difficult for the county to give every home a recycling bin to use.

 F. Recycling will help solve the problem of limited space in landfills.

5–7. *Items that logically support the point:*   _____   _____   _____

Point: Many insects and spiders are beneficial.

 A. By eating insects, crickets and spiders help to maintain the balance of nature.

 B. Most spiders are not harmful.

 C. Ants improve the soil by breaking down organic materials.

 D. In regions of the Amazon River that flood each year, ants avoid drowning by building their nests in trees.

 E. It is unknown why female black widow spiders sometimes kill and eat their mates after sex.

 F. Bees not only produce honey; they also help to pollinate various crops.

8–10. *Items that logically support the point:*   _____   _____   _____

ARGUMENT: Test B

A. For each paragraph, write the letter of the sentence that does **not** support the point of the argument.

[1]Our prisons do an inadequate job of rehabilitating prisoners. [2]Our recidivism rate—the percent of those released from prison who are later arrested for other crimes—runs somewhere between 30 and 80 percent, depending on the study. [3]The crime rate among former prisoners is actually much higher, for the recidivism rate represents only those who are rearrested. [4]To top it all off, for one reason or another, many guilty people are never even sent to jail. [5]Part of the reason for recidivism is a penal system that produces contempt and hatred—attitudes hardly conducive to law-abiding behavior.

___ 1. Which sentence is **not** relevant support for the argument that our prisons do an inadequate job of rehabilitating prisoners?
   A. Sentence 2
   B. Sentence 3
   C. Sentence 4
   D. Sentence 5

[1]Trappers should not use the steel-jaw leghold trap, used to trap animals for their fur. [2]In snapping shut on an animal's leg, the trap tears muscle and shatters bone. [3]Commonly, animals caught in leghold traps die slowly and painfully—from exposure, starvation, or lack of water. [4]Those who manage to break free, by chewing off part of their leg, are likely to die from infection. [5]Those still trapped and alive when the trapper returns are strangled or clubbed to death. [6]In any case, with the warmth of modern fabrics, it's absolutely unnecessary to make any fur coats at all.

___ 2. Which sentence is **not** relevant support for the author's argument that the steel-jaw leghold trap should not be used to trap animals?
   A. Sentence 2
   B. Sentence 3
   C. Sentence 4
   D. Sentence 6

[1]We need better police protection on campus. [2]So far this year, a dozen dorm rooms have been broken into; in each instance, valuables were stolen. [3]Within the past two months, several students have been mugged when they returned to their cars in campus parking lots. [4]If there were more plentiful parking near the center of campus, students wouldn't have to park in the more isolated lots at the outskirts of campus. [5]While walking back to their dorms from evening classes, several other students have been raped. [6]When I walk across the campus at night, I usually fail to see a single police officer or security guard. [7]There may be plenty of security guards protecting the equipment inside the college's buildings, but people are more important than property.

(Continues on next page)

___ 3. Which sentence is **not** relevant support for the author's conclusion that better police protection is needed on campus?

    A. Sentence 2

    B. Sentence 3

    C. Sentence 4

    D. Sentence 5

B. For each group, read the three items of support (the evidence). Then write the letter of the point that is adequately supported by that evidence.

Group 1

Support:

- Car phones allow businesspeople to do two jobs at once—go to an appointment and make a business phone call.
- If a car occupant is going to be late for a business or family event because of traffic, he or she can call and change the time of the meeting.
- People with car phones can report accidents the minute they happen.

___ 4. Which of the following conclusions is best supported by the evidence above?

    A. Every car should have a car phone.

    B. Car phones can be an asset.

    C. A car phone can distract the driver and cause an accident.

    D. All companies should be required to buy car phones for their employees.

Group 2

Support:

- The added lifetime earnings value of a college degree versus a high-school diploma is $329,000 for men and $142,000 for women.
- A college degree increases intellectual curiosity and the ability to think logically.
- Persons with a college degree tend to have increased interest in and responsiveness to the arts.

___ 5. Which of the following conclusions is best supported by the evidence above?

    A. People without a college degree do not appreciate the arts.

    B. College's benefits are mainly academic.

    C. A college degree can have valuable financial and intellectual benefits.

    D. Everyone in our society should go to college for four years.

ARGUMENT: Test C

A. Each of the two points below is followed by six items, three of which logically support the point and three of which do not. In the spaces provided, write the letters of the **three** items that logically support each point.

Point: A stoplight should be put in at the intersection of Broad and Walnut.

    A. That intersection has one of the highest accident rates of all the intersections in town.

    B. A police officer should be stationed there during the early morning and later afternoon, when traffic is heaviest.

    C. At Broad and Walnut, a driver cannot see the road in all directions without starting to pull out into the intersection.

    D. Our town seems to care more about park equipment than it does about the safety of its intersections.

    E. Many children have to cross the intersection at Broad and Walnut in order to get to school, so the safety of that intersection is especially important.

    F. We pay plenty of taxes in this township.

1–3. *Items that logically support the point:* _____ _____ _____

Point: There should be a law requiring motorcycle riders to wear helmets.

    A. Of the many motorcyclists who have had accidents, those not wearing helmets sometimes end up brain-dead.

    B. The government should not pass laws to protect people in every area of their lives; otherwise, we'd need numerous other types of laws as well—prohibiting drivers from buying even one drink, prohibiting people from eating too many saturated fats, and so on.

    C. Motorcyclists should sign organ donor cards so that if they have an accident and become brain-dead, at least someone will benefit.

    D. It's the taxpayers who pay when motorcyclists without adequate insurance refuse to wear helmets and end up with horrible head injuries.

    E. Even motorcyclists who wear helmets are sometimes greatly injured.

    F. There's a precedent for requiring people to protect themselves—many states require people to use seatbelts.

4–6. *Items that logically support the point:* _____ _____ _____

B. Read the following three items of support (the evidence). Then write the letter of the point that is adequately supported by that evidence.

Support:

- Yoga improves a person's posture, resulting in more energy and greater lung capacity.
- Stretching and relaxing muscles through yoga postures releases tension and helps the body to align properly.
- Holding yoga postures helps increase strength and balance.

(Continues on next page)

_____ 7. Which of the following conclusions is best supported by the evidence above?
   A. Yoga is one of the most popular forms of exercise today.
   B. Practicing yoga benefits the body in several ways.
   C. Yoga is not as beneficial as working out with weights.
   D. There are a number of ways to practice yoga.

C. Read the paragraphs below, and then write the letter of the best answer to each question that follows.

[1]Much of the surgery performed in United States hospitals is unnecessary. [2]For one thing, there are more than twice as many surgeons per capita in the United States as in England—and twice as much surgery. [3]Yet there is no reason to believe that Americans need twice as much surgery as the British. [4]Perhaps it's the American surgeons' bank accounts that "need" all those extra operations. [5]At least one-third of all hysterectomies performed in the United States are thought to be unnecessary, yet the operation is the fourth most common in the country. [6]Fifteen years ago, only 6 percent of births in the United States were accomplished through Caesarean sections; today that figure is close to 25 percent. [7]Yet there is no evidence that women have more difficulty bearing children than they did fifteen years ago.

_____ 8. Which statement is **not** relevant support for the argument that much of the surgery done in U.S. hospitals is unnecessary?
   A. Sentence 3
   B. Sentence 4
   C. Sentence 5
   D. Sentence 6

[1]Poverty is one important cause of shoplifting, as suggested by the evidence that poor people are more likely than others to shoplift and that shoplifting becomes more common when unemployment is high. [2]Another economic reason for shoplifting is frugal customers, ones who can afford to buy the things they need but are driven to steal them by a desire to stretch their budget. [3]In addition to economic motivations for shoplifting, there are also social-psychological ones. [4]The most common psychological cause is the sense of excitement and fun that shoplifters experience. [5]Young shoplifters should be pointed toward other exciting, more wholesome activities, such as sports. [6]Another social-psychological cause is the desire for social acceptance; youngsters in particular when asked why they shoplift say, "Because my friends are doing it."

_____ 9. Which statement is the point of the argument?
   A. Poverty is an important cause of shoplifting.
   B. Young people have different motives for shoplifting than adults.
   C. Economic and social-psychological motives are behind shoplifting.
   D. Shoplifting is a big and complicated problem in our society.

_____ 10. Which statement is **not** relevant support for the point of the argument?
   A. Sentence 1
   B. Sentence 2
   C. Sentence 5
   D. Sentence 6

ARGUMENT: Test D

A. Each of the two points below is followed by six items, three of which logically support the point and three of which do not. In the spaces provided, write the letters of the **three** items that logically support each point.

Point: It is better for environmentalists to work with, not against, timber companies.

    A. One conservation group has purchased forests to keep them out of the hands of timber companies.

    B. By working with timber companies, environmentalists can encourage less-damaging harvesting methods, such as leaving some trees to hold soil in place and shelter songbirds.

    C. In previous years, the timber companies and conservationists have strongly opposed each other.

    D. Timber companies that work with conservationists agree to avoid building steep logging roads, which encourage erosion.

    E. Environmentalists are working to preserve such endangered ecological sites as sand dunes in Florida's panhandle and prairies in the Midwest.

    F. Conservation groups are helping companies to maintain forests with selective cutting, instead of cutting them all down, and thereby gaining the support of communities, which welcome the continuation of timber-related jobs.

    1–3. *Items that logically support the point:*   _____   _____   _____

Point: Animal tests do not necessarily reveal whether a drug will be safe or effective for humans.

    A. Penicillin, one of the safest drugs for humans, kills guinea pigs and hamsters.

    B. Computers can analyze a drug's chemical structure.

    C. A survey of two hundred drugs that had tested safe and effective for animals showed that 80 percent of the drugs proved harmful or ineffective for humans.

    D. Currently, the law requires that all drugs be tested on animals.

    E. Before being marketed, all drugs are tested on human volunteers.

    F. After testing safe for rats, mice, and other animals, the drug thalidomide caused serious birth defects in humans.

    4–6. *Items that logically support the point:*   _____   _____   _____

B. Read the following three items of support (the evidence). Then write the letter of the point that is adequately supported by that evidence.

Support:

- Among the Tasmanians of the South Pacific, the most dangerous type of hunting—swimming out to remote rocks in the sea to stalk and club sea otters—was assigned to women.
- Women formed the bodyguard of Dahomeyan kings because they were thought to be particularly fierce fighters.
- In most prominent American families of the eighteenth and nineteenth centuries, girls' education centered on needlework, music, dancing, and languages.

(Continues on next page)

_____ 7. Which of the following conclusions is best supported by the evidence above?
A. There were very few men among the Tasmanian and the Dahomeyan tribes.
B. The women in those tribes were slaves.
C. Women's roles have varied greatly from society to society.
D. Tasmanian and Dahomeyan women had unnatural societal roles.

C. Write the letter of the sentence in each paragraph that does **not** support the point of the argument.

[1]Age at marriage is an important predictor of a marriage's success. [2]Teenagers have high divorce rates for various reasons. [3]Early marriage may lock a couple into a relationship neither one is mature enough to handle, restricting both partners' potential for growth. [4]This in turn makes the young husband and wife less able to deal successfully with the challenges all marriages face. [5]Studies show that remarriage at any age is also a challenge leading to more frequent divorce. [6]Studies also show that people who wait until their late twenties or later to marry have the highest chances of success at marriage.

_____ 8. Which sentence is **not** relevant support for the author's argument that age at marriage is an important predictor of a marriage's success?
A. Sentence 2   C. Sentence 5
B. Sentence 3   D. Sentence 6

[1]Kübler-Ross's five stages of dying should not be overemphasized. [2]The recognition of those five stages is very important to an understanding of the dying process. [3]However, though the emotions that Kübler-Ross describes are common, not everyone goes through all five stages, and people may go through the stages in different sequences. [4]A person may go back and forth between stages—anger and depression, for example—or may feel both at once. [5]Instead of the orderly progression in Kübler-Ross's theoretical model, dying people may show "a jumble of conflicting or alternating reactions running the gamut from denial to acceptance, with a tremendous variation affected by age, sex, race, ethnic group, social setting, and personality" (Butler & Lewis). [6]Unfortunately, some health professionals feel that they have failed if they cannot bring a patient to "the ultimate goal, the big number _five_—'acceptance' of death" (Leviton).

_____ 9. Which sentence is **not** relevant support for the argument that Kübler-Ross's five stages of dying should not be overemphasized?
A. Sentence 2   C. Sentence 5
B. Sentence 4   D. Sentence 6

[1]Genetic testing should be very limited. [2]Genetic information may be disseminated in a way that violates privacy. [3]Although medical data are supposed to be confidential, it is almost impossible to keep such information private. [4]A study at the University of Minnesota found that at least fifty people had access to each patient's medical charts. [5]Secondly, a genetic profile may be used to deny a job, insurance, or other benefits. [6]In fact, discrimination on the basis of genetic information has already occurred. [7]An informal survey found fifty cases in which people had been denied jobs, insurance claims, and other benefits because of their genes. [8]In addition, it might be extremely anxiety-producing for a person to learn that she or he has the gene for an incurable disease. [9]What is the point of knowing you have a potentially debilitating condition when you cannot do anything about it, especially if the financial costs of testing are very high? [10]At the same time, determining a person's genetic makeup may lead to early detection or prevention of a disorder.

_____ 10. Which sentence is **not** relevant support for the argument that genetic testing should be limited?
A. Sentence 1   C. Sentence 8
B. Sentence 6   D. Sentence 10

COMBINED SKILLS: Test A

After reading the passage, write the letter of the best answer to each question.

¹The eyes themselves can send several kinds of messages. ²Meeting someone's glance with your eyes is usually a sign of involvement, whereas looking away often signals a desire to avoid contact. ³This is why solicitors on the street—panhandlers, salespeople, petitioners—try to catch our eye. ⁴Once they've managed to establish contact with a glance, it becomes harder for the approached person to draw away. ⁵Most of us remember trying to avoid a question we didn't understand by glancing away from the teacher. ⁶At times like these we usually became very interested in our textbooks, fingernails, the clock—anything but the teacher's stare. ⁷Of course, the teacher always seemed to know the meaning of this nonverbal behavior, and ended up calling on those of us who signaled our uncertainty.

⁸Another kind of message the eyes communicate is a positive or negative attitude. ⁹When someone glances toward us with the proper facial expression, we get a clear message that the looker is interested in us—hence the expression "making eyes." ¹⁰At the same time, when our long glances toward someone else are avoided by that person, we can be pretty sure that the other person isn't as interested in us as we are in him or her. ¹¹(Of course, there are all sorts of courtship games in which the receiver of a glance pretends not to notice any message by glancing away, yet signals interest with some other part of the body.)

¹²The eyes communicate both dominance and submission. ¹³We've all played the game of trying to stare somebody down, and in real life there are also times when downcast eyes are a sign of giving in. ¹⁴In some religious orders, for example, subordinate members are expected to keep their eyes downcast when addressing a superior.

____ 1. The word *solicitors* in sentence 3 means
  A. panhandlers.
  B. people who pass by.
  C. people who wish to ask for something.
  D. people who wish to help us.

____ 2. The word *subordinate* in sentence 14 means
  A. below another in rank or power.
  B. more powerful than another.
  C. disrespectful.
  D. playful.

____ 3. According to the author, avoiding the eyes of someone who is giving us long glances
  A. is a sure sign of interest.
  B. is always an indication of lack of interest.
  C. indicates respect for someone with greater rank or power.
  D. usually, but not always, indicates a lack of interest.

(Continues on next page)

___ 4. The relationship of sentence 8 to the sentences that precede it is one of
   A. time.   C. illustration.
   B. comparison.   D. addition.

___ 5. The relationship of sentence 14 to sentence 13 is one of
   A. addition.   C. illustration.
   B. contrast.   D. comparison.

___ 6. The main pattern of organization of this passage is
   A. series of steps.
   B. list of items.
   C. comparison and/or contrast.
   D. definition and example.

___ 7. From this passage, you could infer that
   A. people should communicate verbally more often.
   B. eye messages can reflect our desires and relationships.
   C. we should try to avoid communicating with our eyes.
   D. eye messages are more likely to be negative than positive.

___ 8. Which is the most appropriate title for this selection?
   A. The Human Eye
   B. The Role of Eyes in Courtship
   C. The Eyes As Messengers
   D. Using the Eyes to Establish Dominance

___ 9. The topic sentence of the second paragraph is sentence
   A. 8.   C. 10.
   B. 9.   D. 11.

___10. Which of the following best outlines the passage?
   A. Types of messages sent by the eyes
       1. An interest or lack of interest in involvement
       2. A positive or negative attitude
       3. Dominance and submission

   B. 1. Meeting someone's glance
          a. A sign of involvement
          b. Lack of involvement
       2. Positive attitude
          a. Making eyes
          b. Lack of interest—avoidance of glance
          c. Dominance—"staring somebody down"
          d. Submission—giving in

   C. Nonverbal behavior
       1. Meeting someone's glance
       2. Avoiding someone's glance
       3. Staring others down
       4. Giving in

COMBINED SKILLS: Test B

After reading the passage, write the letter of the best answer to each question.

[1]When the *Mayflower* left Plymouth, England, in September 1620 on its historic journey to the New World, three of its 102 passengers were pregnant. [2]The fates of the three pregnant women and their children illustrate the fears that early American women facing childbirth must have held for themselves as well as for their children's survival. [3]One of the passengers, Elizabeth Hopkins, gave birth at sea to a baby boy she named Oceanus. [4]Oceanus Hopkins died during the Pilgrims' first winter in Plymouth. [5]Two weeks after Oceanus's birth, *Mayflower* passenger Susanna White bore her son, Peregrine, who lived into his eighties. [6]The spring after the *Mayflower* arrived in Plymouth, passenger Mary Norris Allerton died giving birth to a stillborn baby.

[7]During the seventeenth and eighteenth centuries, nearly one and one-half percent of all births resulted in the death of the mother from exhaustion, infection, dehydration, or hemorrhage. [8]Since the typical mother gave birth to between five and eight children in her lifetime, her chances of dying in childbirth ran as high as one in eight. [9]Even when the mother survived childbirth, she had reason to be anxious about the fate of her child. [10]In even the healthiest seventeenth-century communities, one in ten children died before the age of 5. [11]Less healthy settlements saw three out of ten children dying in their early years.

____ 1. According to the author, the experience of the three pregnant *Mayflower* passengers and their babies
   A. was very unusual for that time period.
   B. demonstrated how safe ocean travel was in that era.
   C. was typical for that time period.
   D. is similar to the experience of today's women and infants.

____ 2. During the seventeenth century, childbirth in America was
   A. rare.
   B. dangerous.
   C. avoided.
   D. easy.

____ 3. According to the passage, early childhood in colonial America was a time of great
   A. health risk.
   B. hope.
   C. learning.
   D. exhaustion.

(Continues on next page)

___ 4. The first paragraph
    A. discusses a series of causes.
    B. lists the fates of three early American pregnant women and their children.
    C. discusses the similarities between three pregnant travelers and their children.
    D. narrates the events of the *Mayflower*'s journey.

___ 5. This passage is made up mainly of
    A. facts.
    B. opinions.

___ 6. From this passage, you could infer that
    A. all settlements were equally unhealthy.
    B. early American families tended to be smaller than they are now.
    C. antibiotics to control infection were not available in seventeenth-century America.
    D. all of the above.

___ 7. From the passage, you can conclude that in seventeenth-century America
    A. it was not unusual for men to become widowers.
    B. mothers were likely to have at least one child die by the age of five.
    C. women experienced frequent pregnancies.
    D. all of the above.

___ 8. The author's primary purpose in the passage is to
    A. question.
    B. praise.
    C. inform.
    D. entertain.

___ 9. The author's attitude toward the facts is
    A. fearful.
    B. shocked.
    C. objective.
    D. sorrowful.

___10. Which sentence best expresses the central point of the passage?
    A. Traveling on the *Mayflower* was dangerous for pregnant women and their babies.
    B. There were great health dangers involved with childbirth and childhood in early America.
    C. Women's health suffered greatly in colonial America.
    D. In the early American colonies, infant mortality was great.

COMBINED SKILLS: Test C

After reading the passage, write the letter of the best answer to each question.

[1]Modern crowds that flood museums to view fabled treasures of Egyptian art are still captivated by the spell of one of the oldest and most alluring civilizations in history. [2]Almost as old as the civilization founded in Mesopotamia during the fourth millennium B.C.E., Egyptian civilization provides a fascinating contrast to that of Mesopotamia because it was characterized by stability and serenity as opposed to the turmoil and tension of Mesopotamia. [3]Not only were the Egyptians peaceful for long periods of their ancient history, but surviving Egyptian statuary and painted human figures often seem to smile and bask in the sun as if they were on summer vacation.

[4]Environmental factors best explain the striking differences. [5]Since the Mesopotamian climate was harsh, and since the Tigris and Euphrates flooded irregularly, the Mesopotamians could not view nature as dependably life-enhancing. [6]Furthermore, since Mesopotamia, located on an open plain, was not geographically protected from foreign incursions, its inhabitants were necessarily on continual military alert. [7]Egyptian civilization, on the other hand, was centered on the dependably life-enhancing Nile. [8]Not only did the richly fertile soil of the Nile valley provide great agricultural wealth, but the Nile flooded regularly year after year during the summer months and always receded in time for a bountiful growing season, offering Egyptians the feeling that nature was predictable and benign. [9]In addition, since the Nile valley was surrounded by deserts and the Red Sea, Egypt was comparatively free from threats of foreign invasion.

_____ 1. The word *enhancing* in sentences 5 and 7 means
   A. harming.
   B. improving.
   C. creating.
   D. questioning.

_____ 2. The word *incursions* in sentence 6 means
   A. invasions.
   B. languages.
   C. supporters.
   D. delays.

_____ 3. According to the passage, the Nile was
   A. more beautiful than the Tigris and Euphrates rivers.
   B. larger than the Tigris and Euphrates.
   C. more predictable than the Tigris and Euphrates.
   D. deeper than the Tigris and Euphrates.

(Continues on next page)

____ 4. Sentence 5 expresses a relationship of
   A. addition.
   B. time.
   C. contrast.
   D. cause-effect.

____ 5. The main pattern of organization of the passage is
   A. list of items.
   B. time order.
   C. comparison.
   D. contrast.

____ 6. Sentence 1 is
   A. all fact.
   B. all opinion.
   C. a mixture of fact and opinion.

____ 7. The passage suggests that the environment can affect
   A. war and peace.
   B. art.
   C. diet.
   D. all of the above.

____ 8. We can conclude that civilizations grew up in river valleys because
   A. the valleys kept out foreign invaders.
   B. rivers provided water, which was essential for good crops.
   C. clothing could easily be washed in the nearby river.
   D. people could better defend themselves over water.

____ 9. In sentence 1, the author's tone can be described as
   A. enthusiastic and admiring.
   B. serious and solemn.
   C. tolerant and hopeful.
   D. warm and affectionate.

____ 10. Which sentence best expresses the central point of the passage?
   A. Museums are a doorway to fascinating ancient civilizations.
   B. Ancient civilizations tended to settle and flourish in fertile river valleys.
   C. While the Tigris and Euphrates flooded irregularly, the Nile River flooded regularly during the summer months.
   D. The Mesopotamians and Egyptians built two very different civilizations in large part because of the differences in their environments.

COMBINED SKILLS: Test D

After reading the passage, write the letter of the best answer to each question.

^{1}Cells, like any factory, need energy to operate. ^{2}Two different kinds of cellular power plants have evolved: some cells absorb energy directly from the sun, while others gather energy by eating other organisms that have stored it. ^{3}Plants acquire energy directly from sunlight through the process of photosynthesis. ^{4}In this process, molecules of chlorophyll or related pigments absorb photons from the sun. ^{5}The photons' energy is converted into chemical energy that the plant can use to grow and reproduce. ^{6}In the course of this rather complicated chemical process, carbon dioxide and water from the cell's surroundings are converted into glucose plus oxygen. ^{7}The net effect of photosynthesis, then, is to remove carbon dioxide from the air, produce energy for the cell, and give off oxygen as a waste product. ^{8}Animals, unlike plants, cannot convert the sun's energy directly to food, and therefore must get theirs by eating plants or by eating animals that eat plants. ^{9}The food you eat contains energy in the form of the bonds that hold its molecules together. ^{10}After the food has been broken down, it is taken into the cells, where its energy is released by a process called respiration. ^{11}This process allows molecules like glucose to combine with oxygen, thereby releasing the energy tied up in the molecular bonds. ^{12}Its waste product is carbon dioxide, which you breathe out.

_____ 1. The word *net* in sentence 7 means
    A. final.
    B. negative.
    C. unlikely.
    D. sensible.

_____ 2. The energy in the food you eat
    A. is contained in the bonds that hold its molecules together.
    B. is absorbed into your body by photons.
    C. is released by your body in a process called photosynthesis.
    D. results in a waste product of oxygen, which you breathe out.

_____ 3. TRUE OR FALSE? While plants give off carbon dioxide as a waste product of photosynthesis, animals give off carbon dioxide as a waste product of respiration.

_____ 4. From sentence 4, we can deduce that the sun gives off
    A. chlorophyll.
    B. pigments.
    C. photons.
    D. all of the above.

(Continues on next page)

_____ 5. From sentences 10–12, we can deduce that respiration requires
   A. oxygen.
   B. photosynthesis.
   C. carbon dioxide.
   D. chlorophyll.

_____ 6. It can be inferred that glucose is
   A. important in the energy processes of both plants and animals.
   B. produced during photosynthesis.
   C. sometimes combined with oxygen during respiration.
   D. all of the above.

_____ 7. From the paragraph, we can infer that houseplants benefit humans by
   A. giving off oxygen.
   B. taking oxygen from the air.
   C. adding carbon dioxide to the air.
   D. adding both oxygen and carbon dioxide to the air.

_____ 8. The author's primary purpose is to
   A. entertain.
   B. persuade.
   C. inform.
   D. question.

_____ 9. The topic sentence of the passage is
   A. sentence 1.
   B. sentence 2.
   C. sentence 7.
   D. sentence 8.

_____ 10. Which outline best organizes the material in the passage?
   A. Kinds of cellular "power plants"
      1. Plant cells
      2. Animal cells

   B. Different kinds of cellular power plants
      1. Animals
      2. Plants
      3. Photosynthesis
      4. Respiration
      5. Glucose combined with oxygen

   C. Cells, like any factory, need energy to operate.
      1. Photons' energy is converted into chemical energy.
      2. Carbon dioxide is removed from the air.
      3. Animal cells release energy through respiration.

ANSWERS TO THE TESTS IN THE FIRST TEST BANK

VOCABULARY IN CONTEXT: Test A

1. Examples: *Duane is very shy while his brother is outgoing; Duane enjoys reading while his brother prefers playing sports;* A
2. Examples: *outbursts, quarrels;* D
3. skilled
4. careful and precise
5. disapproves
6. Antonym: *painstaking, thorough;* A
7. Antonym: *harmful;* D
8. D
9. B
10. D

VOCABULARY IN CONTEXT: Test B

1. Examples: *painted colorful circus pictures, pasted seashells;* C
2. Examples: *driving a taxi, writing books;* C
3. Examples: *spending hours on improving handwriting, memorizing the date each of the fifty states entered the union;* B
4. hostile
5. risky
6. Antonym: *praising;* B
7. Antonym: *prepared;* D
8. C
9. C
10. A

VOCABULARY IN CONTEXT: Test C

1. C	6. A
2. C	7. C
3. B	8. A
4. A	9. C
5. D	10. D

VOCABULARY IN CONTEXT: Test D

1. D	6. A
2. B	7. B
3. C	8. D
4. C	9. D
5. D	10. A

MAIN IDEAS: Test A

1. 1	4. 2
2. 5	5. 1
3. 6	

MAIN IDEAS: Test B

1. 2	4. 8
2. 3	5. 2
3. 7	

MAIN IDEAS: Test C

1. 3	4. 2
2. 1	5. 10
3. 7	

MAIN IDEAS: Test D

1. 1	4. 1
2. 3	5. 3
3. 3	

SUPPORTING DETAILS: Test A

A. (1–6.) *(Wording of answers may vary.)*
   Main idea: There are a few major reasons for family violence.
   1. Stress is highest among certain groups.
      a. Urban poor
   2. a. Violence on TV
      c. Death penalty
   3. Tendency for marital violence to be transmitted from one generation to the next
B. 7. B
   8. A
   9. B
   10. B

SUPPORTING DETAILS: Test B

A. (1–5.) *(Wording of answers may vary.)*
   Main idea: Suburbs can be divided into four distinct categories.

Higher-income suburbs

Affluent settled communities   Low-income growing communities   Low-income stagnant communities

B. 6. C
   7. A
   8. B
   9. C
   10. C

SUPPORTING DETAILS: Test C

A. 1. C
   2. A
   3. C
   4–5. *(Wording of answers and example may vary.)*
      . . . is a social arrangement in which animals establish a rank, eventually reducing aggression. *Ex.*—Chickens establishing a "pecking order"

B. (6–10.) *(Wording of answers may vary.)*
   Main idea: Relationships develop through five levels.
   1. Initiating   3. Intensifying
   4. Integrating: Personalities begin to merge; people expect to see them together; each is able to predict other's behavior.
   5. Bonding: Participants make a formal commitment.

IMPLIED MAIN IDEAS/CENTRAL POINT: Test A

A. 1. C   B. 4. Sentence 16
   2. D
   3. D   -

IMPLIED MAIN IDEAS/CENTRAL POINT: Test C

A. 1. A
   2. C
B. 3. Seaweed has a number of surprising uses.
   (Note: Wording of answer may vary.)
C. 4. Sentence 1

RELATIONSHIPS I: Test A

A. 1. Until   B. 6. For one thing
   2. First of all   7. Another
   3. other   8. also
   4. third   9. Eventually
   5. also   10. A

(Note: Wording of main ideas in Tests B–D may vary.)

RELATIONSHIPS I: Test C

   1. B   7–10. *Main idea:* Social movements
   2. B   can be classified into four types.
   3. during *or*   1b. Violent, illegal
      after   2c. Civil rights movement *or*
   4. B   women's movement *or*
   5. A   ecology movement
   6. A   4. Expressive movements

SUPPORTING DETAILS: Test D

A. 1. C   3. D
   2. B   4. B
B. (5–10.) *(Wording of answers may vary.)*
   Main idea: Kohlberg has described three levels of moral reasoning.

Preconventional morality	Autonomous moral principles
	Fully internal; recognize conflicts between moral standards; make own judgments on basis of right, fairness, justice
Typical ages: 4–10	Typical ages: after 10

IMPLIED MAIN IDEAS/CENTRAL POINT: Test B

A. 1. C   B. 4. Sentence 2
   2. A
   3. B

IMPLIED MAIN IDEAS/CENTRAL POINT: Test D

A. 1. D   2. B
B. 3. Envy and jealousy are two different emotions.
   (Note: Wording of answer may vary.)
C. 4. Sentence 3

RELATIONSHIPS I: Test B

A. 1. One   7–10. *Main idea:* Carl Rogers
   2. Another   suggests three condi-
   3. Finally   tions for promoting
   4. A 5. C   personal growth.
B. 6. A   Genuineness: Acceptance
               Being open
               with feelings

RELATIONSHIPS I: Test D

   1. B   7. one *or* in addition *or* third
   2. B   8–10. *Main idea:* Various chemicals
   3. A   in the brain stimulate love.
   4. Another   1. Pheromones—Promote
   5. B   sexual attraction in the
   6. A   opposite sex
               3. Endorphins

144

RELATIONSHIPS II: Test A

A. 1. Even though
    2. For instance
    3. As a result
    4. Similarly
    5. because of
    6. However
B. 7. C
    8. A
    9. D
    10. B

RELATIONSHIPS II: Test B

A. 1. A
    2. example
B. 3. B
    4. Because [of] *or* led to
C. 5. C
    6. In contrast
D. 7. B
    8. cause *or* lead to
E. 9. C
    10. in like manner *or* similarly *or* but

RELATIONSHIPS II: Test C

(Wording of answers 2–5 and 7–10 may vary.)

A. 1. B
2–5. *Main idea:* There are two main reasons that keep women from reaching the executive suite.
    1. Women tend not to be in the "pipeline" positions that lead to the top because of the male corporate culture.
        b. Men stereotype women as better at providing "support."
    2. Women lack mentors to teach them how to reach the top.
B. 6. A
7–10. *Main idea:* Mutualism is a relationship in which two organisms live together or cooperate for mutual benefit.

| Are able to digest food | Predators are attacked; competing plants are destroyed | Are housed in thorns; get food |

RELATIONSHIPS II: Test D

A. 1. C
2–5. *(Wording of answers may vary.)*
    Main idea: Various reasons explain the rapid population growth in Europe from 1800–1870.
    1. b. Curbing of cholera through sanitary reforms
    2. Less undernourishment
    3. Earlier marriages
B. 6. B
7–10. *(Wording of answers may vary.)*
    Heading: There are differences . . .

Selected from among people already in Parliament

Chooses cabinet members from outside Congress

No guaranteed majority

FACT AND OPINION: Test A

A. 1. F
    2. O
    3. O
    4. F
    5. F
    6. F
    7. O
    8. O
    9. F
    10. O
B. 11. F
    12. F+O
    13. F
    14. F+O
    15. F+O
C. 16. F+O
    17. F
    18. F
    19. F
    20. O

FACT AND OPINION: Test B

A. 1. F
    2. O
    3. O
    4. F
    5. O
    6. O
    7. F+O
    8. F
    9. F
    10. F
    11. O
    12. F+O
B. 13. F
    14. F
    15. F
    16. F+O
    17. O
C. 18. O
    19. O
    20. F

FACT AND OPINION: Test C

A. 1. F
    2. F
    3. O
    4. F+O
    5. O
    6. O
    7. F+O
    8. F
    9. F
    10. O
    11. F
    12. F+O
B. 13. O
    14. F
    15. F
    16. F+O
    17. F
    18. O
    19. F
    20. F

FACT AND OPINION: Test D

A. 1. F
    2. F+O
    3. O
    4. F
    5. O
    6. O
    7. F
    8. F+O
    9. O
    10. F
B. 11. F
    12. O
    13. F
    14. F+O
    15. O
C. 16. O
    17. O
    18. F
    19. O
    20. F

INFERENCES: Test A

A. 1. C   4. C
     2. C
     3. B
B. 1, 2, 5, 6, 8, 10

INFERENCES: Test B

A. 1. C   4. C
     2. B   5. B
     3. B
B. 2, 4, 6, 8, 10

INFERENCES: Test C

A. 3, 4, 6, 8, 10
B. 3, 4, 5, 8, 10

INFERENCES: Test D

A. 2, 4, 5, 7, 8, 9
B. 7. B   9. A
     8. C   10. B

PURPOSE AND TONE: Test A

A. 1. I   6. E
     2. E   B. 7. E
     3. P   8. C
     4. I   9. F
     5. P   10. A

PURPOSE AND TONE: Test B

A. 1. B   6. J
     2. I   7. D
     3. H   8. F
     4. C   B. 9. I
     5. A   10. P

PURPOSE AND TONE: Test C

A. 1. B   C. 5. C
     2. A   6. C
B. 3. A   D. 7. B
     4. D   8. A

PURPOSE AND TONE: Test D

A. 1. C   C. 5. C
     2. D   6. B
B. 3. B   D. 7. B
     4. C   8. A

ARGUMENT: Test A

A. 1. C   4. D
     2. C   B. 5–7. B, D, F
     3. A   8–10. A, C, F

ARGUMENT: Test B

A. 1. C   B. 4. B
     2. D   5. C
     3. C

ARGUMENT: Test C

A. 1–3. A, C, E   C. 8. B
     4–6. A, D, F   9. C
B. 7. B   10. C

ARGUMENT: Test D

A. 1–3. B, D, F   C. 8. C
     4–6. A, C, F   9. A
B. 7. C   10. D

COMBINED SKILLS: Test A

1. C   6. B
2. A   7. B
3. D   8. C
4. D   9. A
5. C   10. A

COMBINED SKILLS: Test B

1. C   6. C
2. B   7. D
3. A   8. C
4. B   9. C
5. A   10. B

COMBINED SKILLS: Test C

1. B   6. C
2. A   7. D
3. C   8. B
4. D   9. A
5. D   10. D

COMBINED SKILLS: Test D

1. A   6. D
2. A   7. A
3. F   8. C
4. C   9. B
5. A   10. A

VOCABULARY IN CONTEXT: Test 1

Use context clues to choose the word closest in meaning to each capitalized word. Then write the letter of your choice.

___ 1. The LONGEVITY of the parrot surprises many people—many parrots live eighty years or more.
A. colors   B. strength   C. long life

___ 2. "Those black boots COMPLEMENT your studded leather jacket," said Lee. "They round out your biker's outfit."
A. make complete   B. clash with   C. cover

___ 3. Ramona, who considered herself quite NAIVE, never stopped marveling at how sophisticated her friend Gail was.
A. clever   B. sophisticated   C. unsophisticated

___ 4. The directions written on the tomb door were CRYPTIC. Apparently only those who understood the puzzling code were meant to unlock the vault.
A. clear   B. mysterious   C. long

___ 5. With a quick, DEFT movement, the magician expertly produced a bird cage from a silk scarf.
A. clumsy   B. skillful   C. long

___ 6. The teenage boy seemed in such a STUPOR that I had to wonder if he had taken drugs. The boy couldn't even stand up straight or tell me his name.
A. hurry   B. concentration   C. daze

___ 7. The football coach was DOGMATIC. If a player questioned his authority, he'd respond, "My way or the highway!"
A. quiet   B. dictator-like   C. flexible

___ 8. Lena sets very STRINGENT rules for her children. Her husband, in contrast, only makes mild "suggestions" to the kids.
A. few   B. strict   C. pointless

___ 9. After a long trial, the jury EXONERATED the elderly woman of murdering her nephew. When it was announced that she was found innocent, her family burst into cheers and tears.
A. found blameless   B. questioned   C. blamed

___10. I often hear people on TV use VERBOSE phrases, such as "at this point in time" (instead of "now") and "until such time as" (instead of "until").
A. creative   B. brief   C. wordy

VOCABULARY IN CONTEXT: Test 2

Use context clues to choose the word or words closest in meaning to each capitalized word.
Then write the letter of your choice.

____ 1. When our boss makes a "request," it's TANTAMOUNT TO a demand—we'd better
   do it or else.
   A. different than   B. easier than   C. the same as

____ 2. The wolverine has an INSATIABLE appetite—the animal is always hungry.
   A. small   B. never satisfied   C. fussy

____ 3. I usually find computer manuals terribly unclear, but this one is surprisingly
   LUCID.
   A. short   B. clear   C. inexpensive

____ 4. The tax reform bill was an attempt to RECTIFY unfair parts of the law.
   A. correct   B. legalize   C. write

____ 5. The day began in an AUSPICIOUS way: the sun was shining, my bus was on time,
   and I arrived at work ahead of my boss.
   A. sunny   B. favorable   C. usual

____ 6. Many people have AMBIVALENT feelings about big-city life—they enjoy the
   excitement and variety but dislike the crowds and dangers.
   A. confident   B. totally negative   C. conflicting

____ 7. The odor of the woman's perfume was PERVASIVE—it completely filled the
   closed minivan.
   A. spreading throughout   B. lovely and fresh   C. very mild

____ 8. When I'm the boss, I'll RELEGATE to others the jobs I don't enjoy doing.
   A. assign   B. deny   C. explain

____ 9. The cat appeared to be MESMERIZED by something just outside the kitchen
   window, but when I checked I could see nothing I thought would hypnotize him so.
   A. harmed   B. frightened   C. spellbound

____10. Of course, the teacher never came out and said students should cheat. But don't you
   think that by leaving the room during a test she gave TACIT approval for cheating?
   A. hasty   B. stubborn   C. implied

MAIN IDEAS: Test 1

Each of the following groups of statements includes one main idea and two supporting details. Write the letter of each main idea.

___ *Group 1*

   A. Louis's Lunch, a Connecticut restaurant, claims to have made the very first hamburger.
   B. There are conflicting explanations of where hamburgers were invented.
   C. Some say that the hamburger got its start in 1904 at the St. Louis World's Fair.

___ *Group 2*

   A. The shape and slope of a lot influence the type of house that can be built on it.
   B. The style of a house is the result of many considerations.
   C. Building codes and deed restrictions must be observed.

___ *Group 3*

   A. Sickle-cell anemia is far more common among black people than among people of other races.
   B. Certain genetic diseases are more common within specific ethnic groups.
   C. A serious disease called Tay-Sachs affects people of Eastern European Jewish descent.

___ *Group 4*

   A. Romantic love involves a strong need for physical contact with the loved one.
   B. Realistic love is less intense, but it involves steady concern and caring.
   C. Many social scientists argue that two types of love exist.

___ *Group 5*

   A. Problems that used to be accepted as part of life are now considered matters for medical attention.
   B. Physicians now help people deal with baldness, wrinkles, small breasts, and sleeplessness.
   C. Some criminologists have defined antisocial behavior as a medical problem.

___ *Group 6*

   A. A "psychic hotline" with a 900 number puts callers on hold and charges for every minute.
   B. Some 900-number companies use unfair practices to get customers' money.
   C. One "get-rich-quick" 900-number company hangs up mid-message, forcing customers to call back and pay the higher first-minute fee again.

(Continues on next page)

___ *Group 7*

    A. At the time Alaska was bought, the purchase price of $7 million seemed enormous to most Americans.

    B. Many Americans thought that the purchase of Alaska from Russia in 1867 was foolish.

    C. The United States Civil War had recently ended, and many Americans were more concerned about healing those wounds than expanding the country.

___ *Group 8*

    A. It was once thought that only uptight perfectionists suffered from migraines.

    B. Now it is known that migraines may be triggered by such common things as food additives, red wines, and smoking.

    C. Scientists now have a better understanding of the causes of the migraine, which is a painful, recurring headache.

___ *Group 9*

    A. Some believe that Jack the Ripper was a Russian doctor named Alexander Pedachenko, who had already murdered a streetwalker in Paris.

    B. There are differing opinions on just who really was Jack the Ripper, the person who murdered prostitutes by grabbing them from behind and slitting their throats.

    C. One investigator thinks that Jack the Ripper may have been a Jill—an insane woman who roamed the streets.

___ *Group 10*

    A. At the age of 19, the Marquis de Lafayette traveled to the United States and volunteered to help the Americans in their war of independence against Britain.

    B. When he returned to France, the Marquis took along enough American soil to fill a grave, in order that he might be buried in it.

    C. The Marquis de Lafayette had a passionate affection for the United States.

MAIN IDEAS: Test 2

In the space provided, write the number of the sentence that expresses the main idea in each selection.

_____ 1. [1]Many popular snack foods were introduced as health foods. [2]The familiar Graham cracker, for example, was originally sold in the nineteenth century as a health food. [3]The so-called health benefit it was supposed to provide sounds odd to us: Dr. Graham claimed that his crackers made girls less interested in sex. [4]Later, breakfast cereals like corn flakes also began as health foods. [5]And even soft drinks like Dr. Pepper and Coca-Cola (which once contained cocaine, thought to be beneficial) were first sold as health drinks.

_____ 2. [1]Steroids are powerful hormones used by doctors to treat problems such as delayed puberty in adolescents. [2]Prolonged use of steroids by athletes in order to increase muscle growth has led to various unwanted side effects. [3]Long-term use by males may result in enlarged breasts and temporary sterility. [4]Females may experience deepened voices and increased body hair. [5]Heavy users often develop "lantern jaw," a telltale bone thickening in the face. [6]Finally, taking steroids can lead to uncontrollable aggression.

_____ 3. [1]Studies have shown that color is an important part of how people experience food. [2]In one study, people fed a beautiful red tomato sauce did not notice it had no flavor until they were nearly finished eating. [3]In another experiment, people were offered foods that were strangely colored: gray pork chops, lavender mashed potatoes, dark-blue peas, and dessert topped with gray whipped cream. [4]Not one subject would taste the strange-looking food, even though it smelled and tasted normal.

_____ 4. [1]English-speaking children everywhere are taught Mother Goose nursery rhymes. [2]They may assume that the rhymes are all about fictional people and events. [3]But some Mother Goose rhymes refer to actual historical events. [4]For instance, there is "Little Jack Horner," about the boy who pulled a plum out of his Christmas pie. [5]Little Jack was actually Thomas Horner, who was given the job of delivering a Christmas pie from a wealthy abbot to Britain's King Henry the Eighth. [6]Inside the pie were legal deeds to twelve houses—a gift from the abbot to the king. [7]As he went on his journey, Thomas Horner reached under the pie crust and helped himself to the deed to one of the houses! [8]Also, the familiar phrase "Ashes, ashes, all fall down!" from the Mother Goose rhyme "Ring Around the Rosy" refers to the numerous deaths caused by the bubonic plague of the Middle Ages.

_____ 5. [1]Preindustrial Venice was, by modern standards, a city of filth, disease and crime. [2]Rotting garbage and raw sewage were dumped into the canals, causing foul odors to permeate the city. [3]The odor was so awful that, in 1438, a Spanish visitor to Venice described how residents tried to camouflage the stench by burning sweet-smelling spices in the streets. [4]But spices did little to halt the spread of bacterial and viral infections. [5]Epidemics periodically struck. [6]And the city's narrow alleys and shadowy canals were the scene of many murders and other acts of violence.

(Continues on next page)

_____ 6. ¹A small town in Massachusetts that badly needed extra elementary-school classroom space found it in an unlikely spot. ²Educators wanted the new classroom area to offer plenty of space and also to be as close as possible to the main school. ³Most of the town's available buildings seemed unsuitable in location or size. ⁴Finally, in desperation, the civic-minded townsfolk decided on a nearby location. ⁵Some were enthusiastic, citing the excellent lunchroom and recreation facilities the building offered. ⁶Others were doubtful, trying to imagine small children in such a setting. ⁷But the plans went forward. ⁸The classroom was set up in a former saloon, complete with bar, bar stools, cocktail lounge, and pool hall.

_____ 7. ¹For thousands of years, dolphins were thought to be simply playful, friendly creatures with limited mental abilities. ²Recently it was discovered that a dolphin's brain is actually larger than a human's and may be capable of highly complicated thought processes. ³Another discovery was that, although the dolphin has no vocal cords, it does have a vocabulary of at least thirty-two distinct sounds, including clicks, whistles, squeals, and groans. ⁴What's more, each dolphin has its own distinctive 'voice' when making these sounds. ⁵Obviously, dolphins are more advanced creatures than they were once thought to be.

_____ 8. ¹Trends in popular culture and fashion are very difficult to predict. ²But observers of trends have noted one pattern: when a trend has gone as far as it can go, the next move is likely to be in just the opposite direction. ³In the 1960s, for instance, miniskirts got shorter and shorter until they were suddenly replaced by ankle-length "maxis." ⁴Also, centuries ago, the Gothic arches in buildings were built ever higher and narrower till they suddenly were replaced by a squared-off Renaissance style of architecture. ⁵Similarly, during the early decades of this century, the elaborate "gingerbread" style of architecture gave way to a clean, modern style. ⁶These sharp changes may take place because designers always want to avoid "last year's look."

_____ 9. ¹In a series of experiments, chimpanzees, orangutans, gorillas, and baboons were kept in cages with mirrors so that they could look at themselves. ²Then their faces were marked with harmless red dye. ³The chimps and orangs acted surprised and alarmed when they saw themselves in the mirrors. ⁴They could recognize themselves in the mirror and realize that something was changed in their appearance. ⁵The gorillas and baboons did not. ⁶They appear to be incapable of this display of self-recognition and self-concept. ⁷These experiments suggest that, unlike gorillas and baboons, chimps and orangutans share the human quality of self-awareness.

_____ 10. ¹Inflation started during the Vietnam War and accelerated in the early 1970s as a result of a series of crop failures and sharp rises in commodities. ²The inflation of the 1960s and 70s had many negative effects on the American economy. ³It wiped out many families' savings. ⁴It provoked labor turmoil, as teachers, sanitation workers, auto workers, and others went on strike to try to win wage settlements ahead of inflation. ⁵It encouraged speculation in tangible assets—like art, antiques, precious metals, and real estate—rather than productive investment in new factories and technology. ⁶Above all, certain organized interest groups were able to keep up with inflation, while other less powerful groups, such as welfare recipients, saw the value of their benefits decline significantly.

SUPPORTING DETAILS: Test 1

Write the letter of the number of major details in each selection. Notice that the main idea is **boldfaced** in each case.

___ 1. **Peer groups serve a variety of functions.** First, they provide an arena in which children can exercise independence from adult controls. Next, they give children experience with relationships in which they are on an equal footing with others. In the adult world, in contrast, children occupy the position of subordinates, with adults directing, guiding, and controlling their activities. Another function of peer groups is to afford a social sphere in which the position of children is not marginal. In them, youngsters can acquire status and achieve an identity in which their own activities and concerns are paramount. Finally, peer groups are agencies for the transmission of informal knowledge, sexual information, folklore, superstitions, fads, jokes, and games.

   A. three major supporting details
   B. four major supporting details
   C. six major supporting details

___ 2. **Stress can contribute to extreme behaviors.** Some people react to stress by trying to escape from their problems through drug abuse. These people mistakenly see drugs as a way to cope with problems. Aggression is another extreme behavior related to stress. A person who acts aggressively tries to control people in order to get his or her own way. This person often feels intense anger and might express that anger by physically or emotionally harming others. Too much stress often also causes depression. Depressed people often feel a deep sense of loneliness that they assume will never change or go away.

   A. three major supporting details
   B. four major supporting details
   C. five major supporting details

___ 3. **According to a recent study of forty-nine business alliances, one out of three fails for one or more reasons.** In many cases, a time frame that's too short can lead to failure. Instead of focusing on long-term rewards, both parties expect immediate payoffs. In addition, difficulties in personal relationships between managers from different corporate cultures can also cause a strategic alliance to fail. For example, while a top manager can usually end an internal dispute with a word, problems in strategic alliances often require time-consuming meetings between top managers from both companies.

   A. two major supporting details
   B. three major supporting details
   C. four major supporting details

(Continues on next page)

___ 4. **The idea that people can marry for love and without parental consent developed gradually.** In the 1500s, marriages were arranged by parents, who chose partners of similar social and economic status for their children. In the eighteenth century, marriages followed after several months of intensive courting. Still, the couple had to be from families of comparable social and economic standing, and the courtship did not take place without the prior consent of both sets of parents. It was not until the nineteenth century, when romantic novels became popular, that society accepted the possibility that young men and women could fall in love and marry without parental approval.
   A. two major supporting details
   B. three major supporting details
   C. four major supporting details

___ 5. For the 50 percent of all Americans with high cholesterol, heart disease is a constant threat. **Several hints on diet can help these Americans lower their cholesterol levels.** For one thing, it is important to substitute foods low in cholesterol for those with high amounts. This means eating poultry, fish, grains, and low-fat dairy products instead of such high-cholesterol foods as red meats, eggs, and butter. Also, adding oats in the form of oat bran or oatmeal to the diet has been shown to lower cholesterol levels. And for those who are overweight, it is a good idea to lose some weight, as losing weight is known to lower blood levels of cholesterol.
   A. two major supporting details
   B. three major supporting details
   C. four major supporting details

___ 6. The potato was introduced to northern Europe from the New World. **The advantages of potatoes were numerous.** They could be grown on almost any soil—the poorest, sandiest, or wettest of lands where nothing else could be raised. Raising potatoes even in small patches was profitable because the yield of potatoes was extraordinarily abundant. And the potato provided an inexpensive means of improving the human diet. It is rich in calories and contains many vitamins and minerals.
   A. three major supporting details
   B. four major supporting details
   C. five major supporting details

___ 7. **There are several common myths about the common cold.** The first is that a shot of whiskey will help cure a cold. The theory is that the alcohol content will "kill" the germs. Sorry, no such violence takes place. Another common myth is that colds are the result of one type of virus, but the fact is that about two hundred different viruses cause the common cold. Each one creates a technically different cold, but because all two hundred viruses cause almost identical symptoms, we experience colds as a single illness. A last myth is that getting chilled and/or damp will "give" you a cold. In experiments where volunteers were subjected to hours of extreme cold and dampness, while other volunteers spent equal time in cozy surroundings, the incidence of colds that resulted in each group was the same.

(Continues on next page)

A. two major supporting details
B. three major supporting details
C. four major supporting details

___ 8. **Efforts to prevent natural disasters can backfire, making the disasters even worse.** For instance, years of fire-fighting efforts in the western United States have had unfortunate results. When small fires are not allowed to burn the brush, it collects and becomes even dryer and more likely to burn. When it finally does catch fire, the fire is much larger, more destructive, and harder to put out. A similar problem can result from flood-control efforts. Flood-control dams and dikes prevent minor floods by holding water back. But if a major flood should break the dams, the mass of stored-up water that pours out will make the flood even worse than it would have been without the dams.
A. two major supporting details
B. four major supporting details
C. six major supporting details

___ 9. **Sociologists use different models to explain how societies operate.** The functional model regards a society as a system that brings people together to accomplish needed tasks. A functional sociologist, for example, sees our educational system as a means of providing people with the variety of skills needed to keep our society working. In contrast, the conflict model sees a society as a system in which some people take advantage of others. A conflict sociologist sees our educational system as designed to give the children of the privileged the best schooling and the most opportunities. Finally, the interactionist model in sociology looks not at society as a whole, but at how individuals and small groups deal with one another. An interactionist sociologist looks not at the whole educational system, but at how individual students cope with school.
A. three major supporting details
B. four major supporting details
C. six major supporting details

___ 10. **According to one researcher, massaging premature babies yields important benefits.** A developmental psychologist found that premature babies who were massaged for fifteen minutes three times a day gained weight about 50 percent faster than a control group of premature babies who were not massaged and were left in their incubators. The massaged babies also became more active than the control group. And they became more responsive to stimuli such as faces and rattles, suggesting that their nervous systems developed more rapidly. The children who were touched were discharged earlier from the hospital. Also, the medical costs of the massaged infants averaged three thousand dollars less than those for children in the control group. Furthermore, the effects were long-lasting: Eight months later, the massaged infants performed better on measures of mental and physical abilities than did the unmassaged babies, and they weighed more as well.
A. five major supporting details
B. six major supporting details
C. seven major supporting details

SUPPORTING DETAILS: Test 2

Read each paragraph. Then write the letter of the correct answer to each supporting detail question.

A. Conflict is an inevitable part of every person's life. Everyone deals with conflict in a more or less individual manner. At the same time, five general patterns of reacting to conflict can be identified. One such pattern is withdrawal, the physical or psychological removal from a conflict situation. Another manner of dealing with conflict is surrender, giving in immediately to another's wishes in order to avoid an argument. Aggression is a third way to deal with conflict. Those favoring aggressive behavior try to force other people to accept the aggressor's opinions. Conflict also can be dealt with through persuasion, or attempting to change the behavior or attitude of another person. A final means of dealing with conflict is discussion, or verbal problem solving, in which the pros and cons of the issue in conflict are weighed and considered.

____ 1. In general, the major details of this paragraph are
   A. examples of conflicts.
   B. patterns of reacting to conflict.
   C. causes of conflict.

____ 2. Specifically, the major details are
   A. individual ways of reacting to conflict; group ways of reacting to conflict.
   B. physical withdrawal; psychological withdrawal; removal; avoiding an argument; aggression.
   C. withdrawal; surrender; aggression; persuasion; discussion.

B. Many job applicants view the employment interview as a mysterious and painful process. Part of this dread comes from the fear of the unknown. However, nearly every job interviewer will ask about certain key areas. The employer will want to ask what expectations the applicant has for the job. This helps the interviewer to make sure the job is compatible with the applicant and that the applicant's expectations are realistic. The interviewer will also want to know the academic background and work experience of the applicant. Last, the applicant will be asked about his or her strengths and weaknesses. This final line of questioning will help interviewers to find out whether hiring the applicant will enhance the organization.

____ 3. In general, the major details are
   A. key areas usually asked about in job interviews.
   B. common fears people have of interviews.
   C. expectations of the job applicant and the interviewer.

(Continues on next page)

___ 4. Specifically, the major details are
    A. fear of the mysterious, fear of a painful process, fear of the unknown.
    B. the applicant's expectations for the job, the applicant's academic background, the applicant's work experience, the applicant's strengths and weaknesses.
    C. making sure the job is compatible with the applicant, making sure the applicant's expectations are realistic, making sure the applicant will enhance the organization.

C. In 1902, a well-known mathematician wrote an article "proving" that no airplane could ever fly. Just a year later, the Wright Brothers made their first flight. In the 1950s, Britain's Astronomer Royal said in an interview that the idea of space travel was "utter bilge." Also, famous experts claimed that automobiles would never replace the trolley car and that the electric light was an impractical gimmick. Clearly, being an expert doesn't necessarily give someone a clear vision of the future.

___ 5. In general, the major details are
    A. inaccurate predictions.
    B. inaccurate predictions by experts.
    C. inaccurate predictions by experts in transportation.

___ 6. The main idea is stated in the
    A. first sentence.
    B. second sentence.
    C. last sentence.

D. Throughout the ages, a number of different types of religious beliefs have been practiced. A belief in spirits or otherworldly beings is called animism. People have imputed spirits to animals, plants, rocks, stars, and rivers. In theism, religion is centered in a belief in a god or gods who are thought to be powerful, to have an interest in human affairs, and to merit worship. Theism includes Judaism, Christianity, and Islam, which are forms of monotheism, or a belief in one god. Other theist religions include the ancient Greek religion and Hinduism, forms of polytheism, or a belief in many gods with equal or relatively similar power. Finally, some religions focus on a set of abstract ideals. Rather than centering on the worship of a god, they are dedicated to achieving moral and spiritual excellence.

___ 7. In general, the major details are
    A. spirits people have believed in.
    B. types of religious beliefs.
    C. religions based on a belief in a god or gods.

___ 8. One of the minor supporting details of the passage is
    A. animism.
    B. monotheism.
    C. religions that focus on abstract ideals.

(Continues on next page)

E. Doctors and health-care professionals agree that the most effective and inexpensive way to ensure good health is to exercise. Recent studies show a number of ways in which regular exercise is beneficial. First of all, physical activity has been proven to play a major part in preventing cardiovascular disease. In addition, people who exercise for a half hour or more four times per week live longer than those who do not. Exercise also burns up unwanted calories and can improve one's appearance. A psychological benefit of regular activity is that it can increase one's sense of well-being and self-esteem. Regular physical exercise also significantly reduces stress and tension. Finally, regular moderate exercise builds muscles and strengthens bones, reducing a person's chances of injuries from falls or other minor accidents.

____ 9. In general, the major details of the passage are
    A. ways regular exercise is beneficial.
    B. doctors and health-care officials.
    C. ways to exercise.

____10. The main idea is stated in the
    A. first sentence.
    B. second sentence.
    C. last sentence.

IMPLIED MAIN IDEA/CENTRAL POINT: Test 1

In the space provided, write the letter of the implied main idea of each selection.

____ 1. When a group of Middle Eastern Moslem friends sit down to a meal, they begin by saying *Bismillah*, or "in the name of God." Aside from washing the hands before eating, it is considered polite to eat with the hand, using the thumb and first two fingers; to detach choice morsels and offer them to a neighbor at the table; and to continue nibbling even after one is full. If one stops eating, others may feel it is necessary to stop as well, even though they have not yet satisfied their hunger. Guests are expected to talk about pleasant subjects and be entertaining, never to introduce a sad or angry note into the conversation. They compliment the hosts with the phrase "May your table always be generous to all!" meaning they hope they will be asked to dine there again soon.

Once two people have eaten a meal together, they are expected to treat one another with friendship and honesty. If not, according to traditional belief, the food they have shared will bring a curse upon them.

A. All cultures have a complicated system of accepted rules of behavior.
B. Middle Eastern cultures have more rules of etiquette than other cultures.
C. There are traditional rules of etiquette that guide behavior at the Middle Eastern Moslem table.

____ 2. Sherry Lansing, chairman of Paramount Pictures, has produced such hits as *Saving Private Ryan*, *Titanic*, and *Clueless*. In a industry dominated by men, she is considered the most powerful person in Hollywood. When asked about her success, she told this story to *Premiere* magazine. "[My mother] escaped from Nazi Germany when she was 17 and came to this country, where she sold dresses and learned to speak perfect English. When my dad died of a heart attack, I saw my mother cry and mourn and then take over his real estate business. I remember one of her office managers saying, 'You can't do this. You don't know anything about real estate,' and Mother saying, 'No, I'll do it. Teach me. I can do it.'"

"I've never forgotten that," said Lansing. "Teach me. I'll do it."

A. Lansing's mother has served as a role model for Lansing's own successful career.
B. Lansing's mother came to this country knowing no English at the age of 17.
C. As she has worked in the movie industry, it has been an advantage for Lansing to be a woman.

____ 3. While lying in bed and resting may be relaxing, it it not a substitute for real sleep. Sleeping less than you individually require can make you feel grouchy and even unwell. Researchers have seen rats deprived of sleep become deathly ill in as little as a week. Even just disturbing one's usual pattern of sleeping and waking can have unpleasant effects. When people fly across several time zones, for instance, or take a night-shift job, and have to adjust to a new schedule of waking and sleeping, they often experience fatigue, depression, and irritability. Oddly enough, no one understands exactly why we need to sleep at all. Although it might seem that the body and mind need periods of total inactivity, that does not really describe sleep. People's brain waves are nearly as active during sleep as they are during periods of wakefulness.

A. While undisturbed sleep is a key to our well-being, we don't understand it well.
B. During sleep, our brain waves are as active as they are during wakefulness.
C. Loss of sleep or a change in sleeping schedule makes people irritable and depressed.

(Continues on next page)

_____ 4. Daphne Sheldrick runs an orphanage that she founded in 1977 at her home in Nairobi, Kenya. One of her charges was Zoe, a two-week old elephant found wandering not far from her mother's badly decomposed body. "Stressed baby elephants are very fragile," Sheldrick explains. "Often they have witnessed the death of their families at the hands of ivory poachers or irate farmers whose crops have been trampled. The baby elephants are so devastated with grief that some die of a broken heart." However, under Sheldrick's care, Zoe thrived. Each day the infant consumed six gallons of vitamin-laced formula, and after about a year in the orphanage, living only with humans, Zoe was weaned and taken to a refuge where her keepers will gradually introduce her to the ways of the wild. The hope is that after some years, she will be able to be released to a wild herd. Eleven other infant elephants have also been saved over the years by the orphanage.

A. According to Daphne Sheldrick, baby elephants have strong emotions and are devastated when parents are killed.

B. Elephants are killed by ivory seekers or farmers angry at elephants that have trampled their crops.

C. One woman runs an orphanage that saves infant orphan elephants who are later prepared to return to the wild.

_____ 5. Often, a colony of tiny yellow ants lives near a colony of larger ants. These yellow ants, "thief" ants, support themselves by raiding the larger ants' tunnels and stealing their food. Then they escape through tunnels so tiny that the big ants cannot follow them. Several other species of ants are slave-keepers. In North America, for instance, there is a type of large red ant that makes slaves of smaller black ants. The red ants raid the nests of the smaller ones and carry away their young. Although the red ants can support themselves if necessary, they prefer to make the kidnapped ants do their work. Still another type of ant, the amazon ant, has lost its ability to support itself. Instead, it captures slaves from other nests and depends upon them to work. Oddly, the "slaves" of the amazon ants begin to act much like their masters. They become aggressive, even helping the amazons conduct slave raids on their own former colony.

A. Ants have the most complicated social relationships of any insects.

B. Some ants have grown so dependent on slaves that they are unable to support themselves.

C. Some species of ants relate in aggressive ways to other types of ants.

_____ 6. Babe Ruth was the son of a saloonkeeper whose family lived over the bar. His neighbors never forgot him: he was the worst kid in town. He stole. He fought. He cut school, made more noise than three kids, and stole whiskey from his own father's saloon. His parents eventually sent him to a combination training and reform school, where he began to play baseball. His reputation as a player grew until the Baltimore Orioles signed him at age 19. Orioles fans were astonished when, after he threw a runner out to win a game, Ruth whooped with joy and hurled a baseball into the stands. Baseballs were expensive, and the gesture was unheard of. The fans loved it. As the star player with the New York Yankees, Ruth alternately delighted the fans and scandalized the public. He badmouthed umpires, ate and drank too much, and climbed into the stands to punch a heckler. Although he retired in 1935, there were to be countless stories told as well as books and movies made about the "Babe."

A. Babe Ruth's colorful personality, as well as his talent, made him a legendary player.

B. Babe Ruth's professional and personal life was often troubled because of his unusual behavior.

C. Babe Ruth began as a player with the Orioles, then moved on to be the star of the New York Yankees.

(Continues on next page)

_____ 7. At the beginning of the twentieth century, when education became compulsory in France, teachers realized they had a problem. As classrooms became more crowded, the slower students held up the progress of the quicker ones. The teachers wanted a way to separate the students in terms of ability. A French psychologist named Alfred Binet started working on the problem. He realized the task of separating the children should not be left up to the teachers, who might favor the better-behaved children over the troublemakers. He realized, too, that teachers might not recognize the difference between a student who didn't perform well because of lack of interest and one that did badly because of lack of ability. In response, Binet developed the first IQ test, a test that measures intelligence and potential ability, rather than performance in school. First published in 1905, a revised version of the test is still widely used today.

  A. In France in the early 1900s, it was difficult for teachers to manage classrooms crowded with students of differing abilities.
  B. IQ testing was developed as a way to measure the potential success of students so that they could be separated according to ability.
  C. When education became compulsory, the newly crowded classes created new problems.

_____ 8. The Roman (Western) alphabet consists of twenty-six letters, each representing a different sound. Chinese writing incorporates about thirty thousand pictograms, each representing a different word. Just as Roman letters can be combined to produce any word, Chinese pictograms can be combined to express any idea. Obviously, one advantage of the Roman system is that only a small number of symbols is required. The twenty-six letters are easy to learn. By contrast, the thirty thousand Chinese pictograms take a long time to learn. And it is difficult to use them with a keyboard. On the other hand, when the Roman alphabet is used, only people who speak a particular language can read text written in that language. By contrast, any language can be written and read in Chinese pictograms, as long as the reader has the "key" to those pictograms. In fact, speakers of many Chinese dialects who cannot understand one another's spoken language are able to communicate easily through text written in the Chinese style.

  A. Unlike the Roman alphabet, which consists of only twenty-six symbols, Chinese writing uses about thirty thousand pictograms.
  B. There are advantages and disadvantages to both the Roman alphabet and Chinese writing.
  C. While it is easy to learn the Roman alphabet, learning Chinese pictograms is difficult.

_____ 9. All human groups were once hunters and gatherers. About ten thousand to twelve thousand years ago, some hunting and gathering groups found that they could tame and breed some of the animals they hunted—primarily goats, sheep, cattle, and camels. Others discovered that they could cultivate plants. The key to understanding the first branching is the word _pasture_; pastoral societies are based on the pasturing of animals. Pastoral societies developed in arid regions, where lack of rainfall made it impractical to build life around crops. Groups that took this turn remained nomadic, for they followed their animals to fresh pasture. The key to understanding the second branching is _horticulture_, or plant cultivation. Horticultural societies are based on the cultivation of plants by the use of hand tools. No longer having to abandon an area as the food supply gave out, these groups developed permanent settlements.

  A. Societies based on the taming and breeding of animals became nomadic because of the need to follow the animals to fresh pasture.
  B. By learning to cultivate the land, people no longer have to abandon an area when the food supply gave out.
  C. A branching off of hunting and gathering societies resulted in the development of both nomadic, pastoral societies and settled, horticultural societies.

(Continues on next page)

_____10. A Vermont farmer named Wilson Bentley was not an expert photographer or any kind of scientist. But after peering at a snowflake through a microscope, he became fascinated by such fragile beauty. For forty-six brutal New England winters, Bentley stayed alone in a shack, studying snowflakes. He collected them on a chilly blackboard and photographed them quickly, before they could melt. Before Bentley's death in 1931, he had produced over six thousand photographs of individual snowflakes. Bentley's pictures, published in magazines and a book, fascinated the public. Jewelers bought the pictures and used them as patterns for their work. Teachers showed schoolchildren how to cut snowflakes out of construction paper, using Bentley's photographs for inspiration. Bentley described a snowflake as "an idea dropped from the sky, a bit of beauty incomparable, that if lost at that moment is lost forever to the world."

A. Wilson Bentley took more than six thousand photographs of snowflakes.
B. Out of fascination, a farmer took numerous photos of snowflakes, which in turn fascinated many others.
C. Bentley spent forty-six winters alone in a cold Vermont shack, collecting and photographing snowflakes.

IMPLIED MAIN IDEA/CENTRAL POINT: Test 2

In the space provided, write the number of the sentence that expresses the central point in each selection.

_____ 1. [1]Mary Mallon was an Irish-American woman born in about 1870. [2]She is better known to history as "Typhoid Mary." [3]A one-woman epidemic, she infected a documented 1400 people with the deadly typhoid bacteria. [4]Typhoid Mary would have infected many more people than she did if it weren't for the work of Dr. George Soper, who pursued Typhoid Mary relentlessly.

[5]Dr. Soper, a student of epidemic infections, became alarmed by the clusters of typhoid cases reported in the New York area. [6]As family after family was infected and many died, he began investigating. [7]He learned that the outbreaks had one thing in common: a heavy-set Irish cook, about forty years old, with steel-rimmed glasses and an unsmiling face.

[8]Finally Soper caught up with Mary, where she was cooking for yet another New York family—not surprisingly, three members of the family were already deathly ill. [9]When he asked that she be tested to see if she was a typhoid carrier, she cursed him and threatened him with a meat cleaver. [10]Soper called for assistance from the police and health department, which had Mary arrested and tested. [11]She was found to be a hotbed of typhoid. [12]She was confined to a cottage on North Brother Island in the East River, where she worked as a laundress at the neighboring hospital. [13]After she promised to never work with food again, she was released. [14]Mary promptly changed her name and went to work as a cook. [15]More typhoid infections followed. [16]Furious, Dr. Soper tracked her down again. [17]This time, Mary was confined for life to her cottage on North Brother Island. [18]She died there of pneumonia at the age of 68.

_____ 2. [1]Because teams in many sports earn a large part of their revenue from television contracts, they will sacrifice the interests of paid spectators, even compromise the games themselves, to increase their television income.

[2]A good example of this is the so-called "TV time-out." [3]In the old days, commercials occurred during natural breaks in a game, for example, during a time-out called by one of the teams, at half-time, or between innings. [4]But this meant that commercials appeared too intermittently, and infrequently led to bringing in the increasingly large fees advertisers were willing to pay. [5]This led to regular TV time-outs in sports such as football and basketball. [6]The owners of sports franchises may be maximizing their incomes from advertising, but they may have sacrificed the quality of the sports. [7]For example, the momentum of a team may be lost because of an inopportune TV time-out. [8]Thus, these time-outs do alter the nature of some sports; they may even affect the outcome of a game.

[9]Also, for the fans who watch in person, these time-outs interrupt the flow of the game. [10]The fans at home can at least watch the commercials; the spectators at the games have little to watch until the commercial ends and the game resumes. [11]But the owners consider such negative effects on the quality of the game insignificant compared with the economic gain from increased advertising.

(Continues on next page)

_____ 3. ¹When President John Adams and his wife Abigail moved into the White House in 1800, the building was still far from being completed. ²There was not even a toilet, and Mrs. Adams had to hang the family laundry to dry in the East Room. ³Trying to stay warm in the enormous building, the family had to keep thirteen fireplaces going and soon ran out of firewood.

⁴During the Abraham Lincoln presidency, the building functioned as military headquarters, with troops often staying in spare rooms. ⁵When Lincoln's mentally unstable wife, Mary, redecorated the White House, spending far more than the $20,000 allotted by Congress, the President was furious. ⁶He asked how she could spend taxpayers' money on "flub dubs for this damned old house, when the soldiers cannot have blankets?"

⁷Teddy Roosevelt and his wife brought six very lively children to live in the White House. ⁸Aged 3 to 17, the youngsters turned the house into a huge playground, galloping ponies across the lawns and scaring visitors with pet snakes.

⁹John F. Kennedy's First Lady, Jacqueline, left a lasting mark on the White House by privately raising more than $100,000 to furnish it with a beautiful collection of American antiques. ¹⁰Her famous TV tour of the White House was immensely popular and watched by millions of Americans.

¹¹As these examples show, life in the White House has varied according to the times and the interests and activities of the president and his family.

_____ 4. ¹Some helpful acts are either done to gain rewards or avoid punishment or done to relieve inner stress. ²However, there is evidence that sometimes people do focus on others' welfare, not on their own. ³One Vietnam War veteran reports the story of stray mortar rounds exploding in a village orphanage, leaving its missionary caregivers dead and an eight-year-old girl bleeding profusely. ⁴When an American Navy doctor and nurse arrived, it was immediately apparent that the little girl needed a life-saving transfusion, which neither of them had the blood match to provide. ⁵Using pidgin Vietnamese and sign language, they explained the girl's desperate need to the other children and asked if anyone would be willing to give blood.

⁶After long moments, a small hand slowly went up, and a boy named Heng was laid on a pallet, swabbed with alcohol, and given the needle. ⁷As his blood started to flow, he shuddered, sobbed, and covered his face with his free hand. ⁸"Is it hurting, Heng?" the doctor asked. ⁹The boy shook his head and with eyes tightly shut tried to stifle his crying.

¹⁰At this point a Vietnamese nurse arrived and talked with the boy, whereupon a look of great relief spread over his face. ¹¹"He misunderstood you," she explained quietly to the Americans. ¹²"He thought you had asked him to give all his blood, and his life, so the little girl could live."

¹³"But why would he be willing to do that?" asked the Navy nurse. ¹⁴The Vietnamese nurse repeated the question to Heng, who answered, "She's my friend."

¹⁵This story, told by one soldier to another as fact, cannot be verified. ¹⁶But we do know that during the Vietnam war 63 soldiers received Medals of Honor for using their bodies to shield their buddies from exploding devices. ¹⁷Most were in close-knit combat groups. ¹⁸Most threw themselves on live hand grenades. ¹⁹In doing so, 59 made the ultimate sacrifice. ²⁰Unlike other altruists, such as the 50,000 Gentiles now believed to have rescued 100,000 Jews from the Nazis, these soldiers had no time to reflect upon the shame of cowardice or the eternal rewards of self-sacrifice. ²¹Yet something drove them to act.

(Continues on next page)

_____ 5. ¹At the center of Swedish family laws is the welfare of children. ²Health care for mothers and children, for example, is free of charge. ³This includes all obstetric care and all health care during pregnancy. ⁴Maternity centers offer free health checks and courses in preparation for childbirth. ⁵Fathers are also encouraged to attend the childbirth classes.

⁶When a child is born, the parents are offered fifteen months' leave of absence with pay. ⁷The leave and compensation are available for either or both parents. ⁸Both cannot receive compensation at the same time, and the parents decide how they will split the leave between them. ⁹For the first twelve months the state pays 90 percent of gross income, and then a generous fixed rate for the remaining three months. ¹⁰The paid leave does not have to be taken all at once, but can be spread over eight years. ¹¹The parents can stay at home full time, or they can work part time for a longer period. ¹²Because most mothers take all the leave, the law now includes a "father's month," one month that cannot be transferred to the mother.

¹³The government also guarantees other benefits. ¹⁴All fathers are entitled to ten days' leave of absence with full pay when a child is born. ¹⁵When a child is sick, either parent can care for the child and receive full pay for missed work—up to sixty days a year per child. ¹⁶Moreover, by law local governments must offer childcare. ¹⁷And if a husband becomes violent or threatens his wife, the woman can have a security alarm installed in their home free of charge.

¹⁸The divorce laws also have been drawn up with a view to what is best for the child. ¹⁹Local governments are required to provide free counseling to any parent who requests it. ²⁰If both parties agree and if they have no children under the age of 16, a couple is automatically entitled to a divorce. ²¹Otherwise, the law requires a six-month cooling-off period so they can more calmly consider what is best for their children. ²²Joint custody of children is automatic, unless one of the parents opposes it. ²³The children may live only with one of the parents. ²⁴The parent who does not live with the children is required to pay child support in proportion to his or her finances. ²⁵If the parent fails to do so, the social security system makes the payments.

_____ 6. ¹A colleague of mine was in the hospital suffering from a bad back. ²He was confined to his bed and was dependent upon others to do many things for him. ³One of the few tasks he could do for himself was to open and close the curtains in his room by pressing buttons on a console beside his bed. ⁴But when he pressed the button labeled "Open," the curtain closed; pressing "Close" opened the curtains. ⁵A hospital maintenance man was called to fix the mechanism. ⁶He defined the problem as a defective motor that controlled the curtain and began to disconnect the motor when my colleague suggested, "Couldn't we look at this problem differently? ⁷The curtains will open and close properly if the labels on the buttons are switched." ⁸The maintenance man agreed, and the problem was solved quickly and inexpensively. ⁹In effect, my colleague had reframed the problem as "how to get the direction of the curtains to coincide with the labels on the buttons."

¹⁰Clearly, a fresh perspective of a problem may provide an efficient, inexpensive solution. ¹¹Here's another example. ¹²A former client worked for an engineering consulting firm that had consulted with a manager of a large office building. ¹³The manager was receiving an increasing number of complaints about the elevator service, particularly during rush hours. ¹⁴When several of the larger tenants threatened to move out unless the service improved, the manager decided to look into the problem. ¹⁵Engineers from the consulting firm were called to make recommendations about

(Continues on next page)

increasing the speed of the elevator service. [16]They made three alternative but expensive recommendations: adding new elevators, replacing existing elevators with faster ones, and adding a central computerized control system to route the elevators to congested floors. [17]Unfortunately, the earnings of the building would not support any of the possible solutions. [18]An assistant to the building manager solved the problem. [19]Instead of defining the problem as "how to speed up the elevator service," he reframed and defined the problem as "how to make people who wait for elevators less impatient." [20]He suggested that full-length mirrors be installed on the walls of the elevator lobbies. [21]This gave people something to do while waiting (e.g., looking at self or other people, fixing hair and makeup), and their impatience decreased.

_____ 7. [1]If we could predict when and where earthquakes will occur, many lives could be saved. [2]Therefore, many methods for earthquake prediction have been or are being explored. [3]Researchers have even tried to determine if there is a correlation between predictions made by psychics and the occurrence of earthquakes, although this is not generally considered a promising avenue for research. [4]Chinese scientists use unusual animal behavior to assist in earthquake prediction. [5]Animals may be able to sense underground changes associated with earthquakes and become restless or exhibit bizarre behavior. [6]It is possible that they are responding to some precursor of an earthquake such as subtle vibrations, electrical currents, small changes in the earth's magnetic field, the odor of gases forced out of fractured rocks, or sounds made by rocks under pressure.

[7]Other possible indicators are under study. [8]Earthquake prediction research in the United States has emphasized a theory based on observations that rocks under stress swell, or dilate, just before they rupture. [9]This dilation is associated with changes in physical characteristics that can be measured by geologists. [10]These include changes in the level and chemical composition of groundwater and increased electrical currents generated by rocks under pressure. [11]Earthquakes are also associated with abrupt changes in land elevation or tilt.

[12]In yet another approach, geologists monitor the number and strength of small earthquakes along a fault system. [13]Since these small quakes could relieve the stresses associated with rocks sliding past each other, the cessation of this activity could mean that stress is building up and a large earthquake is likely to occur. [14]Sometimes earthquake activity is at an unusually low level in a localized area, called a seismic gap, while it remains at a normal level in the surrounding region. [15]Seismic gaps are carefully watched because they are considered likely locations for earthquakes to originate.

_____ 8. [1]Barred from migrating to the United States by the Immigration Act of 1924, Japanese Americans comprised only a tiny portion of the population in 1941—no more than 260,000 people. [2]About 150,000 lived in Hawaii, with the remaining 110,000 concentrated on the West Coast. [3]It was the West Coast Japanese Americans who got a bitter taste of discrimination during World War II.

[4]After December 7, 1941—when Japanese forces attacked the American naval base at Pearl Harbor, Hawaii—rumors spread about Japanese troops preparing to land in California. [5]They were allegedly planning to link up with Japanese Americans and Japanese aliens poised to strike along with the invasion.

[6]On February 19, 1942, President Roosevelt authorized the Department of War to designate military areas and to exclude any or all persons from them. [7]Armed with this power, military authorities immediately moved against Japanese aliens. [8]In Hawaii, where residents of Japanese ancestry formed a large portion of the population and where the local economy depended on their labor, the military did not force Japanese Americans to

(Continues on next page)

relocate. [9]On the West Coast, however, military authorities ordered the Japanese to leave, making no distinction between aliens and citizens. [10]Forced to sell their property for pennies on the dollar, most Japanese Americans suffered severe financial losses. [11]Relocation proved next to impossible, as no other states would take them.

[12]When voluntary measures failed, Roosevelt created the War Relocation Authority. [13]It resettled 100,000 Japanese Americans in ten camps scattered across six western states and Arkansas called relocation camps. [14]Resembling minimum security prisons, these concentration camps locked American citizens who had committed no crimes behind barbed wire. [15]They were crowded into ramshackle wooden barracks where they lived one family to a room furnished with nothing but cots and bare light bulbs, forced to endure bad food, inadequate medical care, and poorly equipped schools.

_____ 9. [1]The rock cycle reveals the origin of the basic rock types and provides insight into the role of various geologic processes in transforming one rock type into another. [2]At first, or shortly after forming, the Earth's outer shell is believed to have been molten. [3]As this molten material gradually cooled and crystallized, it generated a primitive crust and consisted entirely of igneous rocks. [4]If igneous rocks are exposed at the surface, they will undergo weathering, in which the day-in-and-day-out influences of the atmosphere slowly disintegrate and decompose rocks. [5]The materials that result are often moved downslope by gravity before being picked up and transported by any of a number of erosional agents—running water, glaciers, wind, or waves. [6]Eventually the particles and dissolved substances, called sediment, are deposited in various locations.

[7]Next the sediment is converted to sedimentary rock by the weight of overlying layers or by minerals that are carried by water and fill pores. [8]If the resulting sedimentary rock is buried deep within the Earth, it may be subjected to great pressures and heat. [9]The sedimentary rock will react to the changing environment and turn into the third rock type, metamorphic rock. [10]When metamorphic rock is subjected to additional pressure or to even higher temperatures, it will melt, creating magma, which will eventually solidify as igneous rock.

_____ 10. [1]Historical research has found that the typical preindustrial family had only five or six members. [2]We know that in those days women gave birth to many children, often as many as eight or ten. [3]How, then could the normal household be so small? [4]One reason was high infant and child mortality. [5]One of every three infants died before the age of 1, and another third died before reaching adulthood.

[6]Another reason is that children typically left the household to take full-time employment at ages that seem incredibly young to us. [7]In the eighteenth century, for example, children in western France left home to work as servants, shepherds, cowherds, or apprentices at age 7 or 8! [8]By age 10, virtually all children had gone off on their own. [9]In England at this same time, children did not begin to leave home until age 10, but by 15 nearly all of them had left. [10]Keep in mind that people physically matured later in this period. [11]These were little kids who were having to go it alone.

[12]In addition, the traditional household contained fewer adults than one might expect. [13]High mortality meant that there were few elderly in the households, and many homes lacked either a father or mother. [14]In fact, female-headed households were as common in the past as they are today. [15]The primary cause of such households today is divorce, and thus the father often continues to see the children and to provide financial aid. [16]Back then, the cause was death. [17]The average married couple had only ten years together before one died.

[18]Thus high mortality and children leaving home at an early age account for the small size of the preindustrial family.

RELATIONSHIPS I: Test 1

Read each item, and then answer the question about relationships in the space provided. Write in either the transition or the pattern of organization.

1. Windmills were widely used for such purposes as grinding grain and pumping water. Now they are coming back into fashion.

   The time transition used is _____ *(write one word).*

2. Alcoholism can be attributed to two types of causes. First of all, heredity plays a definite part in alcoholism.

   The addition transition used is _____ *(write three words).*

3. A good way to begin a speech is with an interesting fact. You might also begin with a dramatic quotation.

   The addition transition used is _____ *(write one word).*

4. The lazy checkout clerk forced the six-pack of cola into the bottom of the bag, tearing it. Then she shrugged her shoulders and said, "I guess you'll have to carry the bag from the bottom."

   The time transition used is _____ *(write one word).*

5. Science-fiction writer Arthur C. Clarke correctly predicted that satellites would be used for communication. Moreover, in 1947 he correctly predicted that 1959 would be the year the first rocket to the moon was launched.

   The addition transition used is _____ *(write one word).*

6. William Penn first became a Quaker in the early 1660s while a college student at Oxford. Wanting to mold a harmonious society, he sailed to America in 1682. He landed in the area which was to become Delaware. Later, Penn journeyed upriver to lay out Philadelphia.

   The selection's main pattern of organization is _____ *(write **list** or **time**).*

7. In order to find needed workers, employers use various strategies. First, they may boost salaries and offer hiring bonuses. In addition, they may allow flexible hours and recruit the elderly.

   The selection's main pattern of organization is _____ *(write **list** or **time**).*

(Continues on next page)

8. In the movie *The Shining*, Jack Nicholson gives a vivid performance of a man sinking into madness. He suffers at first from mild hallucinations, then has a drink and a conversation in an imaginary bar. Finally, he chases his wife through a deserted hotel, waving an ax and screaming, "Honey, I'm home!"

The selection's main pattern of organization is _____
(write **list** or **time**).

9. The family fulfills some of the most fundamental human needs. One function of the family is to meet the individual members' need for love and emotional security. The family also fulfills the societal need to regulate sexual behavior and to produce new generations. The need to protect the young and disabled is served by the family as well.

The selection's main pattern of organization is _____
(write **list** or **time**).

10. The life cycle of animals begins when the sperm and egg join. Next, the two cells continue to divide into many more cells to form an embryo. Then the embryo continues to develop until it is time to be born.

The selection's main pattern of organization is _____
(write **list** or **time**).

RELATIONSHIPS I: Test 2

Read each item, and then answer the question about relationships in the space provided. Write in either the transition or the pattern of organization.

1. Writers persuade in several ways. One type of appeal to readers is ethical.

    The addition transition used is _____ (*write one word*).

2. On Thursday, October 24, 1929, a wave of sell orders shook the New York Stock Exchange. During the first three hours of trading, stock values plunged by $11 billion.

    The time transition used is _____ (*write one word*).

3. Scientists study Antarctica to learn the secrets of that icy land. They also study it hoping to learn how to solve climate problems that affect the whole world.

    The addition transition used is _____ (*write one word*).

4. When we are looking for a mate, we tend to zero in on potential partners whose ethnic, religious, economic, and educational background closely approximates our own.

    The time transition used is _____ (*write one word*).

5. Telephone interviewing allows for a large number of responses in a short time and at relatively low cost. Furthermore, the method permits interviewers to reach respondents at specific times of the day, an important consideration in the study of radio and TV listening habits.

    The addition transition used is _____ (*write one word*).

6. Consumers concerned about the hazards of noise can reduce noise pollution in a few ways. They can buy sound-reduced versions of ordinarily noisy products, such as garbage disposals and lawnmowers. They can also use sound-absorbing materials in their home. Carpeting can be installed instead of hard flooring, and cork and fabric can be used in rooms that tend to be noisy. In addition, people can become less noisy themselves. They can learn to avoid shouting, to close doors without slamming them, and to play radios, TV sets, and stereos at moderate levels.

    The selection's main pattern of organization is _____
    (*write **list** or **time***).

7. Some scientists have designed on paper a fascinating computer: a pen. If it existed, during lunch, you could write a note on a paper napkin to, say, your professor. As you wrote the message, the pen would be recording your motions in its memory. After, to switch the pen into command mode, you could push a button on the side.

    (Continues on next page)

Then you could simply write down your professor's fax number or e-mail address on the same paper napkin, and the miniature cellular phone in the pen would zap your memo to your professor's computer.

The selection's main pattern of organization is _____
*(write **list** or **time**).*

8. A growing sexual permissiveness during the 1920s evoked sharp reactions. For one thing, purity forces crusaded to discourage indecent styles of dancing, immodest dress, and impure books and films. Also, religious journals denounced popular dance styles as "impure, polluting, corrupting, debasing, destroying spirituality, [and] increasing carnality." In the Ohio legislature it was proposed that cleavage be limited to two inches and that the sale of any "garment which unduly displays or accentuates the lines of the female figure" be prohibited. Yet another reaction was the bill introduced in the Utah state legislature to fine and imprison women who wore, on the streets, skirts "higher than three inches above the ankle."

The selection's main pattern of organization is _____
*(write **list** or **time**).*

9. Many scientists believe that a star dying in a brief but enormous explosion was the first stage in the creation of our solar system. Then the shock wave from the explosion disturbed a cloud of gas and dust, compressing a portion of it. The compressed gas became more and more compact, pulling into itself by its own gravity. The process of falling in toward its center heated the gas. The next stage occurred when the mass of gas and dust grew hot enough to support thermonuclear fusion reactions. At this point, the sun was born. It was surrounded by cold gas and dust. Finally, the radiation of the young sun soon blew away most of this outer material, but a small portion of it condensed to form the Earth and other planets.

The selection's main pattern of organization is _____
*(write **list** or **time**).*

10. Most children go through several distinct stages as they develop their ability to speak. Initially, children babble; that is, make speechlike but meaningless sounds. This stage usually occurs between the ages of three months and a year. While babbling produces sounds found in all languages, it soon begins to reflect the particular language being spoken around the child. A later distinct stage in speech development is known as telegraphic speech. The average two-year-old can put together short sentences that resemble those used in telegrams in that they include only the most important words. "I show book" or "Grandma come my house" are examples of telegraphic speech. By the time children are three, they learn to make plurals by adding "s" to nouns, and to form the past tense by adding "ed" to verbs. This leads to a speech stage known as overregularization, in which children apply rules even when they lead to errors. Overregularization leads children to invent words such as "runned," "goed," and "eated."

The selection's main pattern of organization is _____
*(write **list** or **time**).*

RELATIONSHIPS II: Test 1

Read each item, and then answer the question about relationships in the space provided. Write in either the transition or the pattern of organization.

1. A water main downtown broke this morning. As a result, several businesses had no water for hours.

    The cause and effect transition used is _____ *(write three words)*.

2. Perennials are plants that continue to live for several years or more. Annuals, on the other hand, are plants that live for only one season and need to be replanted each year.

    The contrast transition used is _____ *(write four words)*.

3. Just as turtles stay in their shells when they are frightened, puppies put their tails between their legs when in unfamiliar situations.

    The comparison transition used is _____ *(write two words)*.

4. The Communist Chinese are becoming more tolerant of capitalist ideals. For example, the old New Year's greeting "May you grow rich" is being heard again in Beijing.

    The illustration transition used is _____ *(write two words)*.

5. Because of exposure to the various chemicals dumped at Love Canal, nearby residents have had an excessive number of serious illnesses, a high incidence of miscarriages, and an unusual number of children born with birth defects.

    The cause and effect transition used is _____ *(write two words)*.

6. Homogamy is marrying someone with social characteristics similar to one's own. For instance, it is common to marry someone in the same social class. People also tend to choose mates of the same religious faith and of an age close to their own.

    The selection's main pattern of organization is _____ *(write **def and example**, or **comparison**, or **contrast**, or **cause and effect**)*.

(Continues on next page)

7. While animals use only a few limited cries, human beings, on the other hand, use extremely complicated systems of sputtering, hissing, gurgling, clucking, cooing noises called *language,* with which they express and report what goes on in their nervous systems. Language is, in addition to being more complicated, immeasurably more flexible than the animal cries from which it was developed—so flexible indeed that it can be used not only to report the tremendous variety of things that go on in the human nervous system, but *to report those reports.* That is, when an animal yelps, he may cause a second animal to yelp in imitation or alarm, but the second yelp is not *about* the first yelp. However, when a man says, "I see a river," a second man can say, "He says he sees a river"—which is a statement about a statement.

The selection's main pattern of organization is _____
(write **def and example,** or **comparison,** or **contrast,** or **cause and effect**).

8. Vegetation covering the ground has beneficial effects. It protects the soil from the pelting of rain. That pelting can break up the soil, leaving a layer of fine material that blocks soil openings and reduces soil infiltration. Vegetation can increase infiltration rates up to three to seven times.

The selection's main pattern of organization is _____
(write **def and example,** or **comparison,** or **contrast,** or **cause and effect**).

9. Displaced workers are workers who have been laid off and who face never finding a job at their previous pay scale because their training and skills have now become outdated. Older workers are especially likely to be displaced because companies may not be willing to invest in retraining them. A specific example of a displaced worker is someone who has been working in the auto industry and whose job can now be done more quickly by a robot.

The selection's main pattern of organization is _____
(write **def and example,** or **comparison,** or **contrast,** or **cause and effect**).

10. Many researchers report that women are less competitive and more cooperative than men and more concerned with social relationships. As opposed to their friendships with men, both men and women report their friendships with women to be higher in intimacy, enjoyment, and caring. One study found that in 94 percent of published studies of adults smiling, females smiled more than males. More recent studies outside the laboratory confirm that women's generally greater warmth is often expressed as smiling. A study of 9000 college yearbook photos revealed that females were more likely to smile. Studies of 1100 magazine and newspaper photos and 1300 people in shopping malls, parks, and streets came to the same conclusion. In groups, men contribute more task-oriented behaviors, such as giving information. Women provide more positive social-emotional behaviors, such as giving help or showing support.

The selection's main pattern of organization is _____
(write **def and example,** or **comparison,** or **contrast,** or **cause and effect**).

RELATIONSHIPS II: Test 2

Read each item, and then answer the question about relationships in the space provided.
Write in either the transition or the pattern of organization.

1. Many people clip cents-off coupons from newspapers and magazines. They therefore save several dollars a week on groceries.

   The cause and effect transition used is _____ *(write one word)*.

2. Murder and assault rank as the top two criminal acts on television; in real life, however, the two most common crimes are burglary and larceny.

   The contrast transition used is _____ *(write three words)*.

3. Chemical reactions are represented in a concise way by chemical equations. For example, when hydrogen, H_2, burns, it reacts with oxygen, O_2, in the air to form water, H_2O.

   The illustration transition used is _____ *(write two words)*.

4. A movie's success often depends upon how it is marketed. Similarly, promotion is important in making a book a bestseller.

   The comparison transition used is _____ *(write one word)*.

5. Airline customers often make reservations they don't keep. The airlines thus often overbook passengers in order to have full flights.

   The cause and effect transition used is _____ *(write one word)*.

6. Socialization is the process by which people learn ways of thinking, feeling, and acting that are needed to get along well in a community. It can be seen as the way society passes on its values to new generations. For instance, young men in ancient Sparta were socialized to be obedient, to practice self-denial, and to show great physical bravery. Strict rules and punishment were used to make sure young males followed this value system.

   The selection's main pattern of organization is _____
   *(write **def and example**, or **comparison**, or **contrast**, or **cause and effect**)*.

(Continues on next page)

7. Lyle Rosenbaum and Steven Leventhal were identical twins who had been separated at birth. When they finally met, the identical twins learned that despite being separated since birth, their lives had been very similar. Both had done well in school, and both had prematurely gray hair. When holding a glass, each held his little finger in the air. Both loved Donna Summer records, both owned the same make of car, both had been married since their late teens, and both were nonsmokers despite having been raised in smoking households.

The selection's main pattern of organization is _____
(write **def and example**, or **comparison**, or **contrast**, or **cause and effect**).

8. Here's some good news for candy fans. Dental researchers say that sweet treats do not play as large a role in cavity-making as commonly believed. The researchers tested such candies as jellybeans and caramels against eighteen other snack foods, to see how long they stuck to teeth. The surprising result was that these sticky sweets actually dissolved quickest. The foods with the most staying power on teeth were crackers and potato chips. The reason for this, say the researchers, is that non-sweet snack foods tend to have more complex carbohydrates than candies do. Since complex carbohydrates take much longer to dissolve in the mouth than the simple sugars of most candies, they have more time to do their "dirty work": producing the plaque bacteria that cause dental cavities.

The selection's main pattern of organization is _____
(write **def and example**, or **comparison**, or **contrast**, or **cause and effect**).

9. Envy and jealousy are two different feelings. Envy is a desire to acquire something that another person possesses. Typically, this occurs in situations in which people we like or associate with have things or take actions that threaten our definition of ourselves. Someone who defines himself or herself as successful might become envious if a coworker was given a larger raise, a close friend purchased a more expensive car, or a friend received a higher grade point average. On the other hand, jealousy is a fear of losing something to which we have become attached. We are jealous when we fear losing a dating partner or spouse to another person or when we feel excluded from the company of someone we like or love.

The selection's main pattern of organization is _____
(write **def and example**, or **comparison**, or **contrast**, or **cause and effect**).

10. Have you ever wondered why, after looking away from a scene you've been staring at, you can sometimes see its "ghost image"? Here's the explanation for this trick your eyes seem to play. After steadily looking for several minutes at a scene—a painting, for example—your eyes will naturally make an adjustment to the light and dark portions. Specifically, your eyes' retinas become less sensitive to light areas, and more sensitive to dark ones, until there is a "sensitivity-reversal." Then, when you move your eyes away from the painting and stare at a plain, white surface, you'll see an after-image of the scene, but in negative form (light areas will be dark and dark areas light).

The selection's main pattern of organization is _____
(write **def and example**, or **comparison**, or **contrast**, or **cause and effect**).

FACT AND OPINION: Test 1

In each answer space, write an **F** if the sentence states a fact or an **O** if it expresses an opinion.

_____ 1. Identical twins account for one birth in two hundred and fifty.

_____ 2. People who are twins are lucky.

_____ 3. About a third of all twins born are identical.

_____ 4. As long as smoking is legal, there should be no limitations on where and how cigarettes are advertised.

_____ 5. Cigarettes should be outlawed.

_____ 6. In the mid-1800s, the workday for some Americans was as much as fifteen hours.

_____ 7. The workday should be limited to seven hours instead of eight.

_____ 8. In fact, the day will come when most people will need to work only twenty hours a week to make a living.

_____ 9. While the dog is known as "man's best friend," studies show that cats are now the most common American pet.

_____ 10. Because cats don't bark and don't have to be walked every day, they make better pets than dogs.

FACT AND OPINION: Test 2

In each answer space, write an **F** if the sentence states a fact or an **O** if it expresses an opinion.

_____ 1. Emergency-room admissions generally rise during the summer months.

_____ 2. Irresponsible parents ought to be fined for the swimming and boating accidents that injure children during the summer.

_____ 3. There is a swimming pool in Casablanca, Morocco, that is filled with salt water and covers 8.9 acres.

_____ 4. A university study shows that heavy drug use seriously affects a teenager's transition to adulthood.

_____ 5. Hard drugs, according to the study, encourage thoughts of suicide.

_____ 6. The worst problem faced by young people today is drug addiction.

_____ 7. According to historians, Harriet Beecher Stowe's novel *Uncle Tom's Cabin,* published in 1852, began a public debate on the practice of slavery.

_____ 8. The Civil War could certainly have been avoided if *Uncle Tom's Cabin* hadn't been written.

_____ 9. Homes are now being built with computer "brain centers" that can detect fires and burglars, regulate the temperature, and operate electrical appliances.

_____ 10. If people rely too much on computers, they are sure to become lazy thinkers.

INFERENCES: Test 1

In the space provided, write the letter of the inference that is most firmly based on the given facts in each selection.

____ 1. The dog snarled fiercely when it heard the door open, but when Tom walked in, it rolled onto its back to let Tom scratch its belly.

   A. The dog knew Tom.
   B. Tom was the dog's owner.
   C. The dog would have bitten anyone but Tom.

____ 2. Actress Ruth Gordon described her new role in a play to playwright George Kaufman: "There's no scenery at all. In the first scene, I'm on the left side of the stage and the audience has to imagine that I'm eating dinner in a restaurant. Then in scene two, I run over to the right side of the stage, and the audience imagines I'm in the drawing room." Kaufman responded, "And the second night, *you* have to imagine there's an audience out front."

   A. Kaufman wrote the play Gordon was describing.
   B. Gordon was a very poor actress.
   C. Kaufman thought the play sounded like a bad one.

____ 3. Overconfidence stems partly from our human tendency to seek information that supports our ideas, rather than proving them wrong. Reflecting on many experiments, one psychology researcher reports that once people have a wrong idea, they often will not budge from their illogic. Ordinary people, the researcher says, avoid the facts and become inconsistent. They defend themselves against the threat of new information that will shed light on the issue.

   A. People are usually wrong.
   B. People are often not objective.
   C. People tend to seek the truth.

____ 4. Patients under anesthesia were reassured in the operating room that their surgeries were progressing nicely. The patients were unconscious and later had no memory of the words of encouragement. Nevertheless, they were likely to experience faster, better recoveries than those patients who received no words of encouragement.

   A. Even though unconscious, patients under anesthesia understand on some level what is being said to them.
   B. Being talked to during surgery is the single most important factor affecting a patient's recovery.
   C. Words of *discouragement* to unconscious patients would not affect their recovery at all.

(Continues on next page)

___ 5. Several years ago, Father Bernard Pagano, a Roman Catholic priest, went on trial for a series of armed robberies of small shops. Newspapers labeled the gunman the "gentleman bandit" because he always was well groomed and displayed perfect manners. Seven eyewitnesses positively identified Father Pagano as the robber. Yet, at the last minute, another man, Ronald Clouser, confessed to the robberies. Clouser knew details of the crimes that only the real bandit could have known. Only then were charges against the priest dropped.

    A. Father Pagano really did commit the robberies.
    B. Father Pagano looked somewhat like Clouser.
    C. If Clouser had not confessed, he would have been caught anyway.

___ 6. In 1953, relations between America's two political parties reached a new low. A few conservative Republicans had made a startling claim. They accused the New Deal Democrats under Franklin Delano Roosevelt of stealing the gold deposits from Fort Knox! President Eisenhower was not impressed with the accusation, but under political pressure from the Daughters of the American Revolution, he had the gold counted. The final total was $30,442,415,581.70—ten dollars less than it should have been. The Democratic treasurer under the previous administration sent a check to cover the shortage.

    A. The Daughters of the American Revolution did not really believe that the New Deal Democrats may have stolen gold from Fort Knox.
    B. The New Deal Democrats in fact did steal gold from Fort Knox.
    C. The Democratic treasurer paid the $10 as a way to mock the Republicans.

___ 7. Coney Island, a strip of land on Long Island, New York, is best-known as a center of amusement parks. It was first settled by the Dutch in the mid 1600s. The word "coney" is an old-fashioned term for rabbits. Nowadays, roller coasters and hot-dog vendors are what most people think of when they hear the name Coney Island.

    A. The Dutch settlers probably settled more of New York than any other European group.
    B. The Dutch probably found many rabbits on Coney Island.
    C. It is very likely that the hot dog is a Dutch food.

___ 8. "Waving a red flag at a bull" is an expression meaning to deliberately provoke someone to anger. And bullfighters do wave red cloaks as they taunt the bull in the ring. But does the color red really anger a bull? Experiments at the University of California concluded that bulls and other cattle are pretty much colorblind. They more quickly notice bright colors than dark ones, but that's about it. Red is naturally an attractive color for bullfighters to use, both because it is the color of blood and audiences find the color exciting. But waving a cloak of any color at the bull would probably annoy it just as much as a red one.

    A. The experiments at the University of California included bullfights.
    B. Bulls are not really annoyed when they charge at a bullfighter.
    C. A bull would pay more attention to a white cloak than to a gray one.

(Continues on next page)

___ 9. Symbols can be classified in two basic ways. Referential symbols are those which denote real objects in the external world. The word *door* is a referential symbol: it refers to an object or a class of objects whose existence in the external world can be objectively proven. If someone asks you what a door is, you can simply point to a door. Expressive symbols, on the other hand, refer to things or events that cannot be established in the external world. The meanings they communicate are often emotional and highly personal. The word *god* is an expressive symbol. To some it may evoke feelings of love and brotherhood; to others it may evoke fear; to still others it may carry no particular emotional meaning.

A. The words *heaven* and *hope* are examples of referential symbols.
B. An example of an expressive symbol is *pencil.*
C. The word *door* is called a symbol because it is the name of an object, not the object itself.

___10. When you stir sugar into a glass of water, the sugar granules break up into individual molecules that disperse throughout the water. The resulting mixture is called a solution. A solution forms when the particles of one substance are dispersed into another substance to make a uniform mixture. Solutions can be mixtures of gases; mixtures of liquids; mixtures of gases and liquids; or mixtures of gases, liquids, or solids. For example, fish get the oxygen they need from the oxygen dissolved in water.

A substance that can dissolve other substances is called a solvent. The substance that dissolves in the solvent is called the solute. Water is often called the "universal solvent" because it can dissolve a great variety of substances. Most of the chemical processes of living things take place in water solutions. In fact, life on Earth would not be possible without water.

A. A solution is a mixture of any two substances.
B. In the passage, sugar is a solute.
C. In nature, water and sand form a solution.

INFERENCES: Test 2

Read each passage and then write the letter of the answer to the inference question.

___ 1. Two men—one a theologian, the other an atheist—often discussed their differing views on the nature of the universe. Eventually the two visited Germany together, where they toured a memorial on the site of a Nazi death camp where thousands of Jews, Gypsies, and others had died during the war. The men walked through the old gas chambers, saw the barracks where the prisoners had been kept, and viewed a film on the horrors of the Holocaust. As they left the memorial, the atheist burst out: "Isn't that enough to convince you? How can you see what was allowed to happen here and not ask, 'Where was God?'" The theologian shook his head. "I know that God was here," he answered. "But where was man?"

What does the passage imply about the theologian?
A. He felt that man has free will to do evil.
B. He began to change his mind about God.
C. He felt that God could protect man against his own inhumanity.

___ 2. Experimental programs in schools and workplaces often seem to work well at first, but then they may be disappointing when tried on a larger scale. The reason is that people like being singled out for special treatment. When a new program is first tested, it is usually tried out in just a few classrooms or workshops. These students and workers enjoy the escape from the standard routine. They may also get the best equipment and supplies. Their special status causes them to perform better, and the experiment looks successful. But when the new system is adopted by all classes or workshops, people no longer feel special or privileged. Thus the new system quickly becomes old hat, and performance falls back.

What does the passage imply about students and workers?
A. It's best not to inject experimental programs in schools and workplaces.
B. Students and workers are more productive when they have a standard routine.
C. Feeling special and being involved in new programs motivate students and workers.

___ 3. Children everywhere have secret places. Whether a musty attic, a grove in the woods, or the crawl space under the front porch, they need a space to call their own. Away from the adult world of rules and regulations, children are free to make-believe, role-play, or just dream. If one could eavesdrop on a typical conversation, it might run the gamut from career planning to the possibility of flying without a plane. So, parents, pay attention to the sign saying "Keep Out." It may not be the boardroom at AT&T, but a secret place can hold the road map of the future.

What does the author feel happens when children spend time making-believe, role-playing, dreaming, and talking among themselves?
A. In some cases, the children are harming themselves.
B. Such behavior weakens parental rules, so parents should be prepared to provide regulation.
C. Making-believe and role-playing provide a foundation and direction for children's future.

(Continues on next page)

___ 4. When the editors of the *Oxford English Dictionary* began work in the late nineteenth century, they appealed to "men of letters" to provide help compiling the mammoth dictionary. The most helpful respondent was Dr. W. C. Minor, an American surgeon living in the town of Crowthorne, England. Over the years, he sent in thousands of beautifully researched entries.

Professor James Murray, the supervisor of the dictionary project, grew curious about Dr. Minor. Murray often asked if Dr. Minor couldn't visit him in London to see the dictionary work in progress. Dr. Minor always made some excuse. Finally, Murray took the train to Crowthorne to personally thank Dr. Minor for his enormous contribution. He was shown to Broadmoor, an asylum for the criminally insane. At first he assumed that Dr. Minor was the medical director at Broadmoor, but he was mistaken. Dr. Minor was an inmate, having been confined to Broadmoor after he had senselessly murdered a workman that he believed was an assassin sent by imaginary enemies to kill him.

Over the next several decades, Murray visited Dr. Minor many times at the asylum, always writing ahead to make sure Dr. Minor was calm enough to have a visitor. Dr. Minor continued his excellent contributions and is thanked in the credits of the *Oxford English Dictionary.*

Which of the following ideas is suggested by the paragraph?
A. Mental illness detracts from a person's intelligence.
B. The *Oxford English Dictionary* was compiled with the assistance of scholarly amateurs.
C. The *Oxford English Dictionary* is no longer being published.

___ 5. George Forsythe of the Maryland State Police has an unusual method of crime prevention. He poses as a murder-for-hire hit man. The young officer—he's only 34—gets his "clients" from members of the underworld anxious to curry favor with the police. If someone approaches them about hiring a hit man, they call Forsythe. He then contacts the person planning a murder and arranges a series of meetings. During the meetings, he tapes the conversations until his clients have seriously incriminated themselves. At that point, his fellow police officers, who have been listening all the while, move in to make the arrest. To get an admission of murderous intent, Forsythe occasionally fakes photos of the murder scene, with the potential victim posing as the bullet-ridden corpse covered in red salad dressing that looks just like blood. According to a rare interview Forsythe gave on public radio, most of his clients are not people with criminal records. They are ordinary men and women who have decided that someone in their lives—often a spouse—has gone too far and needs to be permanently laid to rest. Equally surprising is the policeman's claim that most of the people he has duped thank him when they are taken into custody. According to Forsythe, they are grateful that someone has prevented them from committing murder. Momentarily at least, the fact that they are about to spend thirty or forty years in jail does not seem to diminish their gratitude.

What does the paragraph suggest about murders?
A. Most murderers kill strangers.
B. People usually do not regret crimes of passion.
C. Even unsuccessful attempts to kill someone are against the law.

___ 6. About 85 percent of college students agree that memory is like a storage chest. As a recent ad in *Psychology Today* magazine put it, "Science has proven the accumulated experience of a lifetime is preserved perfectly in your mind." Actually, psychological research has very nearly proven the opposite. Many memories are not copies of our past experience that

(Continues on next page)

remain on deposit in a memory bank. Rather, memories often are constructed at the time of withdrawal. Like a paleontologist inferring the appearance of a dinosaur from bone fragments, we may reconstruct our distant past from fragments of information. Thus we can easily (though unconsciously) revise our memories to suit our current knowledge. When one of my sons complained that "The June issue of *Cricket* magazine never came" and was shown where it was, he delightedly responded, "Oh good, I knew I'd gotten it."

From the paragraph, what could one conclude about the author's son?
A. He deliberately lied when he claimed his issue of *Cricket* had not arrived.
B. He reconstructed his past after seeing the magazine.
C. He accurately remembered not having received the June issue of *Cricket*.

___ 7. With a little self-reflection, it is easy to identify the presence of irrational thinking. Once its presence is recognized, the thoughts that characterize it can be successfully challenged and their influence lessened. Here are three ways to counter irrational beliefs:

1. Examine the objective facts in a situation. What would an instant replay on television bring to light? *Example:* "A replay would show my girlfriend left me, but I was not treating her very well. I can honestly admit I helped to force her out of the relationship."
2. Interpret events in a less extreme and a more balanced fashion. Seek and accept another valid way of interpreting the event that provides a more balanced perspective. *Example:* "The situation is not pleasant, but her leaving is not the end of the world. I have bounced back from such things in the past."
3. Develop plans to overcome the problem and reduce negative emotions. New ways of thinking need to be backed up with behaviors that support them. *Example:* "I guess I made some mistakes in our relationship. Maybe it's not too late for me to apologize and to try and work on the relationship. I'll call her early next week and see if she is willing to talk about how we relate to each other."

What does the author imply about irrational thinking?
A. Reducing its influence requires mental discipline.
B. Fortunately, it has little influence upon behavior.
C. It is not very common.

___ 8. About a million African Americans served in the armed forces during World War II, about half serving overseas. The armed forces were segregated, and many African American soldiers complained that they were treated like prisoners of war. Nevertheless, all-black units like the famous "Tuskegee Airmen," which flew combat missions in Europe; the 92nd Division, which suffered 3161 casualties in campaigns in Italy; and the 761st Tank Battalion, which fought at the Battle of the Bulge, played key battlefield roles.

At the same time, black leaders fought racism at home vigorously. The NAACP conducted legal campaigns against discrimination. Some African Americans, however, considered the NAACP too slow and too conciliatory. Rejecting legal action, the Congress of Racial Equality (CORE), founded in 1942, organized a series of "sit-ins." Civil disobedience produced a few victories in the North, but the South's response was brutal. In Tennessee, for example, angry whites savagely beat the civil rights leader Bayard Rustin for refusing to move to the back of the bus.

What does the passage imply about African Americans during World War II?
A. During the war, African Americans had to fight both on the battlefield and at home.
B. African American soldiers were treated just like white soldiers.
C. Civil disobedience was a key part of African-American strategy on World War II battlefields.

(Continues on next page)

_____ 9. Human beings, it is presumed, walk around with a variety of unfulfilled urges and motives swirling in the bottom half of their minds. Lusts, ambitions, tenderness, vulnerabilities—they are constantly bubbling up. These mental forces energize people, but they are too crude and irregular to be given excessive play in the real world. They must be capped with the competent, sensible behavior that permits individuals to get along well in society. However, this upper layer of mental activity, shot through with caution and rationality, is not receptive to advertising's pitches. Advertisers want to circumvent this shell of consciousness if they can and latch on to one of the subconscious drives. In effect, advertisers over the years have blindly felt their way around the underside of the American psyche, and by trial and error have discovered the softest points of entry, the places where their messages have the greatest likelihood of getting by consumers' defenses.

What does the paragraph suggest about advertisements?
A. They cause people to get along well in society.
B. Ads are based partly on the advertisers' analysis of human psychology.
C. Ads are calculated to lead people to actions they will later regret.

_____ 10. A fallacy is an error in reasoning. The slippery-slope fallacy takes its name from the image of a boulder rolling uncontrollably down a steep hill. Once the boulder gets started, it can't be stopped until it reaches the bottom. A speaker who commits the slippery-slope fallacy assumes that taking a first step will lead inevitably to a second step and so on down the slope to disaster—as in the following examples:

> If we allow the government to restrict the sale of semi-automatic weapons, before we know it, there will be a ban on ownership of handguns and even hunting rifles. And once our constitutional right to bear arms has been compromised, the right of free speech will be the next to go.

> Passing federal laws to control the amount of violence on television is the first step in a process that will result in absolute government control of the media and total censorship over all forms of artistic expression.

If a speaker claims that taking a first step will inevitably lead to a series of disastrous later steps, he or she should provide evidence or reasoning to support the claim. To assume that all the later steps will occur without proving that they will is to commit the slippery-slope fallacy.

Which of the following illustrates the slippery-slope fallacy?
A. Senator Bowman has no children—that's why he favors nuclear power. He doesn't mind our kids being born with birth defects.
B. First Victor comes over to play, and the next thing that happens is my little Petey has fallen down. Victor is just too wild to play with Petey any more.
C. Passing laws requiring people to wear seat belts will only lead to laws about every other safety problem; before long, we'll be arrested for not using a rubber mat in the shower.

Note: Selection 5 on page 182 is reprinted with permission of the author, Laraine Flemming.

PURPOSE AND TONE: Test 1

In the space provided, indicate whether the primary purpose of each sentence is to inform (**I**), to persuade (**P**), or to entertain (**E**).

_____ 1. With funerals so expensive, I can't afford to die.

_____ 2. As it grows older and larger, the anemone fish changes from male to female.

_____ 3. All cities should build bicycle lanes in busy traffic areas.

_____ 4. We must begin to teach vegetarianism because it is the way to end world hunger.

_____ 5. Hispanics are the fastest-growing segment of America's population.

_____ 6. When I asked my little nephew if he knew who the world's greatest baseball player was, he answered, "Batman?"

_____ 7. If you're not wearing Wright brand shoes, you're wearing the wrong ones.

_____ 8. Scientists have discovered evidence of a carbonated ocean beneath the miles of ice on Jupiter's moon Europa.

_____ 9. There should be stricter regulations aimed at cutting down on the high death rate among the animals at some zoos.

_____ 10. A London researcher is perfecting a vaccine that fights the bacterium which causes tooth decay.

PURPOSE AND TONE: Test 2

In the space provided, write the letter of the word that expresses the tone in each passage.

____ 1. Often you feel you've done nothing when you've actually done a lot. That's because what you did do seemed beneath notice—it was so small that it didn't "count." But it did—just as each stitch counts toward a finished dress, each brick or nail toward a house you can live in, and each mistake toward knowing how to do things right.

    A. hesitant

    B. encouraging

    C. amused

____ 2. A vaccine is a preparation of killed or weakened germs that is injected under the skin and causes the blood to produce antibodies against the disease. Effective vaccines, for instance, have been developed for smallpox, rabies, and polio.

    A. objective

    B. fearful

    C. tolerant

____ 3. We have come together this afternoon to mourn the deaths of sixteen miners—our friends and neighbors—who were trapped by fire yesterday, deep below the surface of the earth. They lived bravely and they died too soon, leaving behind grieving wives and bewildered children. We bid them a final farewell.

    A. forgiving

    B. sorrowful

    C. angry

____ 4. Each year in the middle of February, when slush is underfoot and the sky is a depressing gray, I begin dreaming of warm beaches, tropical fruits, and sunsets. If only I could save enough for a winter vacation! Maybe next year I'll win the lottery. Meanwhile, I'll read travel brochures and sigh.

    A. unsure

    B. joyous

    C. longing

____ 5. Why do these things always happen to me? First I forget an important meeting, and nobody reminds me until it's over. Then my boss dumps a big project on my desk and wants it done by yesterday. And to top everything off, I leave my wallet on the bus.

    A. objective

    B. self-pitying

    C. optimistic

(Continues on next page)

_____ 6. Our little cockapoo puppy is truly the light of our lives. She's the sweetest bundle of love ever created. When I hold her in my lap and she looks at me with her melting brown eyes, I know that she feels love and loyalty as deeply as any human being.

    A. sentimental
    B. optimistic
    C. superior

_____ 7. What's the matter with those idiots in the city council? First they pass new parking regulations saying we can't park our cars in front of our own houses without a special permit. Now they've gone and slapped another tax on gas purchases—just to widen a road that's already wide enough. Anyway, nobody enjoys the traffic delays resulting from road construction. The sooner we vote those incompetents out, the better off we'll all be.

    A. matter-of-fact
    B. angry
    C. uncertain

_____ 8. Yet another public figure has come forward to announce he has signed into an addiction-treatment center to deal with his alcohol problem. Reports say he has shown courage and honesty. Perhaps so, but what it really takes to enter a treatment center is money. What about the poor man, like my father, who may also have a drinking problem—and courage—but who doesn't happen to have $500 a day for a fancy rest home?

    A. bitter
    B. revengeful
    C. optimistic

_____ 9. My therapist asked me to write down how I'm feeling about my life right now. There isn't much to say. Every day is pretty much like the last one. I go to work, I eat, I sleep. I don't go out much, and it seems like I've lost touch with most of my friends. When I'm at home I may pick up a book and try to read, but nothing really interests me. Mostly I just turn on the TV and sit on the couch until I fall asleep.

    A. nostalgic
    B. sympathetic
    C. depressed

_____10. Botulism, a type of rare, severe food poisoning, has been reported recently in New Jersey. It is believed that the victim, who is in critical condition at a local hospital, was stricken after eating from a jar of incorrectly preserved homegrown green beans from last summer's garden. It has been ten years since the last instance of botulism poisoning was reported in the state.

    A. depressed
    B. serious
    C. impassioned

Name _____

Section _____ Date _____

SCORE: (Number correct) × 10 = _____%

ARGUMENT: Test 1

One statement in each group is the point of an argument. The other statements are support for that point. Write the letter of the statement that is the point of each argument.

____ 1. A. Lights were on all over the house.
    B. The television was blaring.
    C. It looked as though someone was home.

____ 2. A. The local school is overcrowded.
    B. Students have to eat lunch in shifts running from 10:45 until 1:45.
    C. Some classes are held in trailers parked on the athletic fields.

____ 3. A. The Vietnamese diet is based on rice, noodles, and other wholesome grain-based foods.
    B. Vietnamese food generally depends on fresh herbs and spices for its flavor.
    C. Many Vietnamese dishes are made with little or no fat.
    D. Vietnamese food is generally quite healthful.

____ 4. A. Important political and national events are covered so quickly on local news shows that little information is given.
    B. Many positive things that happen—new businesses openings, personal success stories—are rarely shown, if at all.
    C. Local news programs do a poor job of covering what is really happening.

____ 5. A. Mozart composed music for all instruments—plus mechanical clocks and musical glasses.
    B. Music is not limited to traditional musical instruments.
    C. The twentieth-century American composer John Cage once wrote a musical piece for twelve radios—the piece never sounds the same way twice!

____ 6. A. Our office has recycling bins for glass, aluminum, and scrap paper.
    B. Most of my coworkers bring their own coffee mugs to work rather than use paper cups.
    C. People in my office are concerned about the environment.
    D. Our office memos are printed on the backs of old order forms to save paper.

____ 7. A. The new playground gives neighbors something to be proud of in their neighborhood.
    B. Building a new playground was good for the neighborhood.
    C. Now kids have a place to play after school and on weekends.
    D. People coming into the neighborhood to visit the park have been spending their money in nearby stores, giving local businesses a boost.

(Continues on next page)

___ 8. A. Dust contains pollen from plants—which cause allergies in many people.
   B. Although it appears harmless, dust contains many harmful substances.
   C. Particles from tiny insects called dust mites are carried in dust and have been known to cause asthma.
   D. Bits of paint and other household products in dust can block off tiny air passages in the lungs and have been linked to many lung diseases.

___ 9. A. An hour before his death, the butler called his brother and arranged for them to have dinner together at a restaurant later that night.
   B. The gun was lying by the butler's right hand, although he was left-handed.
   C. The butler did not commit suicide, as the police had thought—he was murdered.
   D. The telephone was knocked off the hook, as though there had been a struggle in the room.

___10. A. Money allowed remote communities to trade easily with merchants, freeing them from the need to grow or make everything they needed themselves.
   B. The ability to purchase necessities freed people to specialize, instead of producing a little of everything they needed.
   C. With the freedom to specialize comes greater productivity, which provides even more goods to sell.
   D. The creation of money was crucial to the development of commerce and industry.

Name _____

Section _____ Date _____

SCORE: (Number correct) × 10 = _____%

ARGUMENT: Test 2

In the space provided, write the number of the sentence in each paragraph that does **not** support the conclusion of the argument.

_____ 1. ¹Rats are not as bad as people make them out to be. ²For example, studies of free-living rats indicate that rat societies are based on cooperation. ³Two rats have been filmed working together to haul an egg back to their colony: while one rat grasped the egg with all four feet, the other pulled the first along by the tail. ⁴If a mother rat with infants dies, other female rats in the community adopt the infants and raise them as their own. ⁵Rats often help provide care for their younger brothers and sisters. ⁶They also take care of their parents and grandparents when these older rats become too weak to find food. ⁷Finally, in rat societies, unlike human societies, violence is rare. ⁸However, rats do transmit diseases to humans.

*Which of the above sentences does **not** contribute to the author's conclusion that rats are not as bad as people make them out to be?*

_____ 2. ¹Ruth is not suited to her job of receptionist. ²Because she is shy, she seems stiff and cold when people come up to her desk. ³She can be friendly when you get to know her. ⁴But she has a hurried, clipped way of speaking that is unpleasant on the telephone. ⁵She quickly becomes impatient when a caller doesn't get straight to the point. ⁶She gives people the impression that they're bothering her just by asking her to do her job.

*Which of the above sentences does **not** contribute to the author's conclusion that Ruth is not suited to the job of receptionist?*

_____ 3. ¹My landlord is not in the least reliable. ²A classmate of mine used to live here, and she said he used to be much better. ³When I moved in here, the glass in two of my windows was cracked. ⁴He promised to have the windows fixed within one week. ⁵That was three months ago, and they're still broken. ⁶Last week the oven in the apartment stopped working. ⁷I left a message on his answering machine, but he hasn't even returned my call yet.

*Which of the above sentences does **not** contribute to the author's conclusion that his or her landlord is not in the least reliable?*

_____ 4. ¹Teresa, there are plenty of reasons you and Ron shouldn't marry at age 17. ²Although you think you'll feel this way forever, you are still growing and changing so fast that you'll be another person in six months. ³You are being unfair to yourself to cut off the opportunities of single young adulthood. ⁴And if you marry and have a child, your opportunities will be that much more limited. ⁵It's true, your mother married young too, and she had a good marriage. ⁶But teenage marriages are a mistake far more often than not.

(Continues on next page)

*Which of the above sentences does **not** contribute to the author's conclusion that Teresa and Ron should not marry at age 17?*

_____ 5. ¹Many jobs take a particular kind of physical toll on the people who do them. ²Waitresses, for instance, hurt their backs carrying heavily-laden trays. ³People who work with computers often develop pain in their wrists and forearms, not to mention eyestrain. ⁴Some overcome the problem by putting a long padded cushion in front of the keyboard to rest their arms on. ⁵And hairdressers deal with aching feet and varicose veins in their legs from constantly standing.

*Which of the above sentences does **not** contribute to the author's conclusion that many jobs take a particular kind of physical toll on those who do them?*

_____ 6. ¹Our townhouse complex is built in a way that is particularly unwelcoming to people in wheelchairs. ²All of the homes have tall, narrow winding stairs leading from the living room to the top floor. ³The doorways of most rooms are too narrow for a wheelchair to pass through, and a number of steep steps lead up to the front stoop. ⁴Moreover, the manager is very slow at responding to residents' complaints. ⁵In effect, townhouses built as ours are exclude people in wheelchairs from being either residents or visitors.

*Which of the above sentences does **not** contribute to the author's conclusion that the townhouse complex is built in a way that is unwelcoming to people in wheelchairs?*

_____ 7. ¹The student who enrolls in a self-paced algebra class may spend as much time as he or she needs to master a chapter in the textbook. ²Unlike those in a traditional class, students progress through material on their own. ³Moreover, they may finish the class several weeks before the semester ends if they are willing to spend the extra time in the lab. ⁴Because the lab is open at convenient hours—8 a.m. until 8 p.m.—students can easily work math study time into their schedule. ⁵Finally, the lab is staffed by math instructors who can answer the students' questions. ⁶Thus the self-paced algebra class is ideal for the self-directed student who finds the traditional math class goes too slowly or too quickly for him or her. ⁷For the student who benefits from more guidance and supervision, a traditional class works better.

*Which of the above sentences does **not** contribute to the author's conclusion that the self-paced algebra class is ideal for the self-directed student who finds the traditional math class goes too slowly or too quickly for him or her?*

(Continues on next page)

_____ 8. ¹The company I work for is obviously sexist. ²This is no surprise from a company that has a history of racial discrimination. ³Although many of the company's female employees have shown outstanding ability, few have risen to top positions. ⁴In general, the company's female employees receive lower pay than male employees who do the same or similar work. ⁵The company's publications use language that denies women equal consideration. ⁶For example, businesspersons as a group are always referred to as "businessmen."

Which of the above sentences does **not** contribute to the author's conclusion that his or her company is sexist?

_____ 9. ¹Americans should care about the problems people face in Third World countries. ²In addition to moral considerations, the effects of the Third World's underdevelopment are felt everywhere, even in the richest countries, because our world has become increasingly interdependent. ³Americans depend on workers in South Korea to make cars, computers, stereos, and other products that we use every day. ⁴Americans depend on the working class of the United States to make and sell fast food cheaply and to clean offices and homes. ⁵We buy copper from Zambia, oil from the Arabian peninsula, and coffee from Central America. ⁶We depend on Third World countries not just for material goods but also for cooperation in the quest for a clean environment and for world peace. ⁷In short, Americans should be concerned about citizens of the Third World because their problems are our problems.

Which of the above sentences does **not** contribute to the author's conclusion that Americans should care about the problems people face in Third World countries?

_____ 10. ¹Your pharmacist can be a helpful part of your health-care team. ²Pharmacists can advise you when and how to take your prescription medicine so as to get the greatest good from it. ³They can warn you about any unpleasant interaction your medicine might have with another medication you're taking. ⁴Having your physician call in your prescription can save you valuable time you would otherwise spend waiting at the store. ⁵Upon request, a pharmacist can put an easy-open top on your medication if you don't need a child-resistant cap. ⁶On the other hand, if you've got a fussy young patient on your hands, the pharmacist can flavor liquid medicine with bubble gum, mint, or chocolate.

Which of the above sentences does **not** contribute to the author's conclusion that a pharmacist can be a helpful part of your health-care team?

COMBINED SKILLS: Test 1

After reading the textbook passage, write the letter of the best answer to each question.

> [1]It is sometimes said that curiosity killed the cat, but nothing could be further from the truth. [2]The curiosity drive seems to aid survival for most animals. [3]Its existence might be explained by the life-and-death necessity of keeping track of sources of food, danger, and other important details of the environment. [4]However, the curiosity drives seem to go beyond such needs. [5]In an experiment, monkeys confined to a dimly lit box learned to perform a simple task in order to open a window that allowed them to view the outside world. [6]In a similar experiment, monkeys quickly learned to solve a mechanical puzzle made up of interlocking metal pins, hooks, and hinged metal fastenings. [7]In both situations, no external reward was offered. [8]The monkeys seemed to work for the sheer fun of it. [9]An interest in video games, chess, puzzles, and the like offers a human parallel. [10]Curiosity—and the drive to know—also seem to be powerful in humans. [11]Scientific investigation, intellectual curiosity, and other advanced activities may be an extension of this basic drive.

____ 1. As used in sentence 11, the word *extension* means
    A. replacement.
    B. added part.
    C. opposing part.
    D. cause.

____ 2. The relationship of the two parts of sentence 1 is
    A. time.
    B. comparison.
    C. contrast.
    D. cause and effect.

____ 3. A transition that could appropriately be used at the beginning of sentence 5 is
    A. *Furthermore.*
    B. *As a result.*
    C. *For example.*
    D. *In contrast.*

____ 4. Sentence 5 is
    A. a fact.
    B. an opinion.

____ 5. The author's purpose is to
    A. persuade readers that amusements such as video games and chess are worthwhile.
    B. entertain readers with stories about odd findings in research.
    C. predict what would happen if animals were not curious.
    D. inform readers about curiosity in humans and other animals.

(Continues on next page)

_____ 6. The tone of this passage can best be described as
   A. critical.
   B. straightforward.
   C. humorous.
   D. hesitant.

_____ 7. From the experiment in which monkeys were confined to a dimly lit box, we might conclude that
   A. the monkeys needed to open the window to get food and water.
   B. the monkeys were curious about the world outside the box.
   C. the monkeys would probably not have learned to open the window as quickly if an external reward was offered.
   D. there were other monkeys outside the box.

_____ 8. One can conclude from this paragraph that
   A. in nature, curiosity is no longer necessary for survival.
   B. the process of satisfying curiosity can be fun.
   C. animals that are not in danger no longer tend to be curious.
   D. curiosity often puts animals in danger.

_____ 9. The author mentions video games, chess, and puzzles as evidence that humans
   A. are clever too.
   B. have survival needs, like most other animals.
   C. are inclined toward scientific investigation.
   D. will also work at satisfying their curiosity just for the fun of it.

_____10. Which is an appropriate title for this passage?
   A. Curiosity Killed a Cat
   B. Curiosity: A Survival Aid and More
   C. How Monkeys Can Solve Mechanical Puzzles
   D. The Role of Curiosity in Scientific Investigation

COMBINED SKILLS: Test 2

After reading the textbook passage, write the letter of the best answer to each question.

[1]Between 1860 and 1890, more than 10 million immigrants arrived on America's shores; between 1890 and 1920, over 15 million more arrived. [2]Essentially there were two types of immigrants during the late nineteenth and early twentieth centuries—permanent immigrants and migrant workers. [3]The people in the second group, often called birds of passage, never intended to make the United States their home. [4]Unable to earn a livelihood in their home countries, they came to America, worked and saved, and then returned home. [5]Most were young men in their teens and twenties. [6]They left behind their parents, young wives, and children, indications that their absence would not be too long. [7]Before 1900, an estimated 78 percent of Italian immigrants and 95 percent of Greek immigrants were men. [8]Many traveled to America in the early spring, worked until late fall, and returned to the warmer climates of their southern European homes for the winter.

[9]In contrast to the birds of passage were the permanent immigrants, for whom America offered political and religious freedom as well as economic opportunity. [10]The promise of America was especially appealing to members of ethnic and religious minorities who were persecuted, abused, and despised in their homelands. [11]Germans from Slavic countries, Greeks from Romania, Serbs from Hungary, Turks from Bulgaria, Poles from Russia—for these men and women, home held few warm associations.

[12]Czarist Russia, for example, was a country notoriously and historically inhospitable to many minorities. [13]In 1907, 250,000 "Russians" emigrated from Russia to the United States. [14]But who were these Russians? [15]More than 115,000 were Jews, and another 73,000 were Poles. [16]Others were Finns, Germans, and Lithuanians. [17]Only a small percentage were of Russian ethnic stock.

____ 1. In sentence 17, the word *stock* means
   A. immigration.
   B. citizenship.
   C. ancestry.
   D. language.

____ 2. The birds of passage were
   A. permanent immigrants.
   B. migrant workers.
   C. both of the above.

____ 3. The migrant workers came to America for
   A. political freedom.
   B. religious freedom.
   C. economic opportunity.
   D. all of the above.

(Continues on next page)

____ 4. Between 1860 and 1920, the immigrants that arrived in America numbered around
   A. 10 million.
   B. 15 million.
   C. 20 million.
   D. 25 million.

____ 5. The relationship of sentence 11 to sentence 10 is one of
   A. addition.
   B. time.
   C. illustration.
   D. comparison.

____ 6. The passage contrasts
   A. two centuries, the nineteenth and the twentieth.
   B. young men and older men.
   C. Italian immigrants and Greek immigrants.
   D. permanent immigrants and migrant workers.

____ 7. The passage is mainly
   A. fact.
   B. opinion.

____ 8. We can conclude from the passage that birds of passage must be birds that
   A. are endangered.
   B. migrate seasonally.
   C. are unsure about where they are going.
   D. cannot fly.

____ 9. The author implies that
   A. there were plenty of good jobs in southern Europe in the late 1800s.
   B. America offered economic rewards to both types of immigrants.
   C. many Russian immigrants returned to Russia each winter.
   D. there were few minorities in Czarist Russia.

____ 10. Which sentence best expresses the main idea of the passage?
   A. Sentence 1
   B. Sentence 2
   C. Sentence 3
   D. Sentence 12

ANSWERS TO THE TESTS IN THE SECOND TEST BANK

VOCABULARY IN CONTEXT: Test 1

1. c
2. a
3. c
4. b
5. b
6. c
7. b
8. b
9. a
10. c

VOCABULARY IN CONTEXT: Test 2

1. c
2. b
3. b
4. a
5. b
6. c
7. a
8. a
9. c
10. c

MAIN IDEAS: Test 1

1. b
2. b
3. b
4. c
5. a
6. b
7. b
8. c
9. b
10. c

MAIN IDEAS: Test 2

1. 1
2. 2
3. 1
4. 3
5. 1
6. 1
7. 5
8. 2
9. 7
10. 2

SUPPORTING DETAILS: Test 1

1. b
2. a
3. a
4. b
5. b
6. a
7. b
8. a
9. a
10. c

SUPPORTING DETAILS: Test 2

1. b
2. c
3. a
4. b
5. b
6. c
7. b
8. b
9. a
10. b

IMPLIED MAIN IDEAS/CENTRAL POINT: Test 1

1. c
2. a
3. a
4. c
5. c
6. a
7. b
8. b
9. c
10. b

IMPLIED MAIN IDEAS/CENTRAL POINT: Test 2

1. 4
2. 1
3. 11
4. 2
5. 1
6. 10
7. 2
8. 3
9. 1
10. 18

RELATIONSHIPS I: Test 1

1. Now
2. First of all
3. also
4. Then
5. Moreover
6. time
7. list
8. time
9. list
10. time

RELATIONSHIPS I: Test 2

1. One
2. During
3. also
4. When
5. Furthermore
6. list
7. time
8. list
9. time
10. time

RELATIONSHIPS II: Test 1

1. As a result
2. on the other hand
3. Just as
4. For example
5. Because of
6. def and example
7. contrast
8. cause and effect
9. def and example
10. contrast

RELATIONSHIPS II: Test 2

1. therefore
2. however
3. For example
4. Similarly
5. thus
6. def and example
7. comparison
8. cause and effect
9. contrast
10. cause and effect

FACT AND OPINION: Test 1

1.	F	6.	F
2.	O	7.	O
3.	F	8.	O
4.	O	9.	F
5.	O	10.	O

FACT AND OPINION: Test 2

1.	F	6.	O
2.	O	7.	F
3.	F	8.	O
4.	F	9.	F
5.	F	10.	O

INFERENCES: Test 1

1.	a	6.	c
2.	c	7.	b
3.	b	8.	c
4.	a	9.	c
5.	b	10.	b

INFERENCES: Test 2

1.	a	6.	b
2.	c	7.	a
3.	c	8.	a
4.	b	9.	b
5.	c	10.	c

PURPOSE AND TONE: Test 1

1.	E	6.	E
2.	I	7.	P
3.	P	8.	I
4.	P	9.	P
5.	I	10.	I

PURPOSE AND TONE: Test 2

1.	b	6.	a
2.	a	7.	b
3.	b	8.	a
4.	c	9.	c
5.	b	10.	b

ARGUMENT: Test 1

1.	c	6.	c
2.	a	7.	b
3.	d	8.	b
4.	c	9.	c
5.	b	10.	d

ARGUMENT: Test 2

1.	8	6.	4
2.	3	7.	7
3.	2	8.	2
4.	5	9.	4
5.	4	10.	4

COMBINED SKILLS: Test 1

1.	b	6.	b
2.	c	7.	b
3.	c	8.	b
4.	b	9.	d
5.	d	10.	b

COMBINED SKILLS: Test 2

1.	c	6.	d
2.	b	7.	a
3.	c	8.	b
4.	d	9.	b
5.	c	10.	b

Notes

Notes

Notes

Notes

Notes

Notes